# Media Law
Its Ethics and Ethos

AF517471

# Media Law

## Its Ethics and Ethos

Devesh Kishore
Ganga Sagar Singh

HAR-ANAND
PUBLICATIONS PVT LTD

Copyright © 2010, Publishers

All rights reserved with the Publisher. No part of this publication may be reproduced, stored in a retrieval system, or transmitted in any form or by any means, electronics, mechanical, photocopying, recording or otherwise without the prior written permission of the Publisher.

**Reprint, 2019**

Published by Ashok Gosain and Ashish Gosain for:
HAR-ANAND PUBLICATIONS PVT LTD
E-49/3, Okhla Industrial Area, Phase-II, New Delhi-110020
Tel: 41603490
E-mail: info@haranandbooks.com/haranand@rediffmail.com
Shop online at: www.haranandbooks.com

Printed in India

# Preface

The book has been designed to cater to the requirements of the students of Media Education. It gives a general and comprehensive study of all laws related to media and code of ethics to be followed by journalists while discharging their duties. It is covering the oldest media law in India, the Press and Registration of Books Act, 1847 to the Right to information Act, 2005. The book also details the Web Laws which is still in full formative shape to take and is proving a challenging job for law enforcement authorities.

The form taken by the book has for the most part been determined by the syllabuses drawn up by the Universities of Northern India and Himalayan States. Media Laws are being added in India at every turn of the history and development. The latest edition is the Right to Information Act, 2005. Under the provisions of the Act information sought by an ordinary citizen can not denied which can not be denied to either House of the Parliament or State Legislature. There is also a provision of an independent Central Information Commission and State Information Commission in every State to adjudicate the matter.

India is a democratic country and in a democracy great emphasis is laid on the freedom of the press and the sanctity of its role as an independent and fearless body voicing popular feelings and opinions. But it is a basic philosophy of any freedom that no freedom can be availed as licence. The freedom of the press must be reconciled with the collective interests of the society, also known as 'public interest.'

A brief history of Media Laws enacted both during pre-Independence and post-Indepence period is under History of Media Law in India: After the enactment of the Right to Information Act, 2005, it is generally believed that the Officials Secrets Act, 1923 has become infructious. But recently a case has been filed in the court against an ex-Officer of RAW (Research and Analysis Wing) for mentioning some functioning of RAW in his book, even though authority failed to ban his book.

For the convenience of students, the relevant Sections of Indian Constitution Indian Penal Code, and criminal Procedure Code applicable to Media have been compiled and given in a separate chapter in the book.

The Code of Ethics became necessary in spite of the laws of the land being fully applicable to all journalists as there were areas in their functioning which were not covered by the laws of the land. The press Commission had to formulate Code of Ethics and were duly endorsed by representative organisations of Journalists Still the Code of Ethics for Broadcast Journalists is in a formative State, as their representative body is still to agree to a Code for them.

Efforts have been made to present an update list of Media Laws in India in the book, with comments and the Acts in its form as annexure for a comprehensive study.

DEVESH KISHORE
GANGA SAGAR SINGH

# Contents

# 1

# Importance of Media Law and Media Freedom

In a democracy great emphasis is laid on the freedom of the press and the sanctity of its role as an independent fearless body voicing popular feeling and opinions. On the role of the press, Mahatma Gandhi said, "One of the objects of the newspaper is to understand the popular feeling and give expression to it, another is to arouse among the people certain desirable sentiments. The third is fearlessly to expose popular defects."

The freedom of speech and expression refers to the right to express one's ideas and opinions freely, either by words of mouth, writing, printing, illustration or in any other way. In India this right broadly includes the freedom of the press according the decision of the Supreme Court of India in Sakal Papers (P) Ltd. Vs Union of India. The Supreme Court said, "It is a settled law that Right to Freedom of Speech and Expression in Article 19(1)(*a*) includes the liberty of the press."

Article 19(1)(*a*) of, of the Constitution secures every citizen of India, the freedom of speech and expression. This clause should be read with clause (2) of the Article, which states that the right shall not prevent the operation of making a law relating to the subject specified therein.

In **Brij Bhushan** Vs **State of Delhi** in 1950 the Supreme Court while striking down an executive order to a newspaper to submit the materials for scrutiny before publication observed, the Supreme Court. "There can be little doubt that the imposition of pre–censorship on a journal is a restriction on the liberty of the press which is an essential part of the freedom of speech and expression declared by Article 19(1)(*a*)."

In **Remesh Thapar** Vs **State of Madras** the Supreme Court observed that unless a law restricting the freedom of speech and expression was directed solely against the undermining the security of the state or its overthrow, that law could not fall within the reservation under article 19(2) of the constitution, although the restriction which it seeks to impose might have been received generally in the interests to the public order. The situation, created by a number of decisions by different High Courts after apex court's decision, was remedied by amending Article 19(2) in 1951. The state was allowed to make laws with object of imposing reasonable restrictions on the exercise of rights conferred by Article 19(1) in the interests of the security of the state, friendly relation with foreign states, public order, defamation and incitement to an offence.

Hence the freedom of the press means the right to print and publish without any interference from the state or any public authority. But this freedoms, like any other freedoms, cannot be absolute but is subject to well know exception acknowledged in the public interest, which is enumerated in Article 19 of the Constitution.

As is clear from Article 19(1)(*a*) of our Constitution, the press as an institution has no constitutional or legal privilege. What is known as the freedom of the press in nothing but the freedom of expression of every citizen (guaranteed by Article 19(1)(*a*)) which includes:

1. The right to lay what sentiments he pleases before the public or the right to impart information and ideas from others.
2. The right to receive information and ideas from others through any lawful medium.

A democratic political society of government, which rests on the consent of the people and the contribution of their ideas to public questions, can rest only on the free debate and free exchange of views amongst the people.

On the one hand, the widest dissemination of information from diverse sourcing is necessary of public educations which is the foundation of democratic society. On the other hand, it is by means of a free discussion and criticism that the government remains responsive to the will of the people and peaceful change is effected and errors of government are peacefully corrected and eliminated through a process of popular government.

The people must be allowed freedom to discuss public issues and express their judgment, if democracy means government by the people themselves.

Mere freedom of election is not enough if there is no free press to crtitcize the programmes and actions of party in power. In the words of Madison.

"A popular Government, without popular information or the means of acquiring it, is but a prologue or to face a Tragedy, or perhaps both. And a people who mean to be their own government must arm themselves with the power which knowledge gives."

In short, democracy, which is government of the people ,by the people themselves, cannot function unless the people are well informed and free to participate in discussion of public issues by having the widest choice of alternative solutions of the problems being faced by them.

Freedom of the press does not allow the state to assume the role of guardian of public mind. Authority is to be controlled by public opinion, not public opinion by authority.

The function of the press is to expose the abuse of power by and corruption of public officials and keep them responsible to the people whom they are expected to serve public criticism is essential to the working of democracy.

In one case (Express Newspaper Vs Union of India) in 1959 the Supreme Court of India, held to be applicable in the interpretation of freedom of press in India derived from Article 19(1)(*a*) of the Constitution.

(a) The freedom of the press rests on the assumption that the widest possible dissemination of information from diverse and antagonistic sources is essential to the welfare of the public.

(b) Such freedom is the foundation of free government of free people.

(c) The purpose of such a guarantee is to prevent public authorities from assuming the guardianship of public mind and:

(d) Freedom of the press involves freedom of employment or non–employment of the necessary means of exercising this right or in other words, freedom from restrictions in respect of employment in editorial force."

## REASONABLE RESTRICTIONS ON FREEDOM OF THE PRESS

It is a basic philosophy of any philosophy of any freedom that no freedom can be availed as license. Freedom of press does not mean that press is free to ruin a reputation or break a confidence or to course of justice or to do anything that is unlawful. The freedom of the press must be reconciled with the collective interests of the society, also known, as 'public Interest'. If no guarantee of individual right; can be absolute, so is the freedom of the press. In other words, the press is not entitled to any absolute immunity from action for unlawful conduct any more other individual.

Though the First Amendment to American Constitution has enunciated the Freedom of the press, the need for restriction has been explained.

"Freedom carries with it responsibility even for the press, freedom of the press is not a freedom from responsibility for its exercise....

Liberty, in an orderly society, cannot mean a license that is why no individual right, even if guaranteed by the Constitution in absolute terms, can be absolute.

Again since a pre–condition for the enforcement of individual rights is that the corresponding rights of other persons should be similarly safeguarded, the freedom of expression cannot be so exercised as to undermine the reputation of any member of public.

In India the court's role in balancing the two interests is enshrined in the Constitution's itself, by expression 'reasonable restriction' in Article 19(2)–(6). The grounds on which restriction upon the freedom of the press should be held have been enumerated in Article 19(2) and any expansion of these grounds can be legitimate only by way of interpreting these constitutionally specified grounds.

## CONSTITUTIONAL RESTRICTIONS ON THE FREEDOM OF THE PRESS IN INDIA

A balance between the two competing social interests namely, the need for the freedom of the press and the need for public order, security of the State and the like has sought to be achieved by the words 'reasonable restrictions' in Article 19(2) and (6). By this the State is empowered to impose by law restrictions on the freedom of the press on the ground of any of the social interests specified in these clauses and the judiciary is empowered to determine whether in given scale such restriction is reasonable, that is to say, whether it effects a reasonable balance between the two competing public interests. Freedom of press has no constitutional protection in India, as in American Constitution. It can be deduced from the freedom of guaranteed to all citizens under Article 19(1) (*a*)

Freedom of the press is to be derived from the freedom of expression guaranteed by Article 19 (1) (*a*) and the constitutional limitations on freedom have been under Article 19(2), as amended are :

(a) Sovereignty and integrity of India.
(b) Security of the State
(c) Friendly relations with foreign states,
(d) Public order.
(e) Decency or morality,
(f) Contempt of Court.
(g) Defamation,
(h) Incitement to an offence

Elaborating the tests of reasonableness, the Supreme Court has broadly laid down following touchstones:

1. Directive Principles of State policy.
2. Restrictions mist not be arbitrary or of an excessive nature so as to go beyond the requirement of the general public.
3. In order to judge the reasonableness of the restrictions, no abstract or general pattern a fixed principle can be laid down.

4. A just balance has to be struck between the restrictions imposed and the social control envisaged by Article 19(1) (*b*)
5. Prevailing social values as also social need, which are intended to be satisfied by the restrictions.
6. There must be direct and proximate nexus or a reasonable connection between the restrictions imposed and the object sought to be achieved.

By the Constitutional Amendment Act, 1951, Article 19 (2) of the Constitution was replaced with the following.

"Nothing in sub–clause (*a*) of clause (1) shall affect the operations of any existing law, or prevent the State from making any law, in so far as such law imposes reasonable restrictions on the exercise of the right conferred by the said such clause in the interest of the security of the state, friendly relations with foreign states, public order, decency or morality, or in relation to contempt of Court, defamation or incitement to an offence."

So the additional subjects to which restrictions could be imposed on the right of the freedom of speech and expression were (1) friendly relations with foreign states. (2) public orders. (3) incitement to an offence. The restrictions under Article 19 (2) thus become a justiciable matter as other restriction enumerated in clause (3) (4) (5) and (6) of Article 19 were justiciable.

The Supreme Court of India observed:

"It is plain that speeches or expressions on the part of an individual which incite to or encourage commission of violent crimes such as murder cannot but be matters which would undermine the security of the state and come within the ambit of law sanctioned by article 19(2)."

In Romesh Thapar V State of Madras the Supreme Court drew a clear distinction between "public order" and "security of the state":

"The constitution, in formulating the varying criteria for permissible legislation imposing restrictions on the fundamental rights enumerated in Article 19 has placed in a posing restrictions on the fundamental rights enumerated in Article 19 has placed in a distinct category those offences against public order which aim at undermining the security of the state or overthrowing it, and made their prevention the sole justification for legislative abridgment of freedom of speech and expression..."

Thus very narrow and stringent limits have been set to permissible legislative abridgement of the right of free speech and expression, and this was doubtless due to the realization that freedom of speech and of the press lay at the foundation of all democratic organizations, for without free political discussion no public education, so essential for the proper functioning the process of popular government, is possible.

(1) **Public order:** The ground "public order" is being discussed because the expression is very wide and there have been a number of judicial pronouncements on its true ambit and scope. Which deserve notice.

While considering the meaning of the expressions "law and order," "public order" and "security of state" Justice Hidayatullah posed the analogy of three concentric circles "law and order represents the largest circle within which is the next circle representing public order and the smallest circle represents the security of state. It is then easy to see that an act may affect public order but not security of the state.

In O. K Ghosh and other, the Supreme Court reaffirmed while considering the provisions of clauses (2)(4) of article 19, that expressly provided for, public order could not include the security of the State. The expression "public order" was virtually synonymous with "public peace, safety and tranquility."

(2) **Security of the State :** Any external and internal matter which affects the security of the state would attract the application of the exception contained in Article 19 "The security of the State may will be endangered by crimes of violence intended to overthrow the government, levying of war rebellion against the Government, extreme aggression or war, etc."

In the case challenging the Punjab Security of the State, the Supreme Court observed that if Section–19 of the Act and Article 19 (2) were read together the only matter impugned related to offending speech, words or other publication which tends to overthrow the state. The additional matter fell within the expression "incite to an offence prejudicial to the State contained in Section–9 of the Act and Article 19(2)

In was pointed out that anything. Which tended to overthrow the state must necessarily be prejudicial to the state. It was fully accepted that right to freedom of speech was a very valuable and cherished right. But public order and security of the state could be ignored at the peril of the country.

(3) **Friendly relation with foreign states:** When the Constitution was amended in 1951, there was considerable opposition to the introduction of the words "friendly relations with foreign State" in Article 19(2) of the Constitution. At that time the Prime Minister pointed out, that this was merely an enabling clause, which empowers the parliament to frame legislation, in case the necessity arises and gave an assurance that it was not the intention of the Governmental to promote the legislation which would prevent discussing of foreign policy of the Government. Since then no clear case has been made for depriving the parliament of the power of legislation in case of necessity, placing restriction of speech and expression in the interest of friendly relations with foreign states.

Sometimes it may be feared that the words "in the interest of friendly relations with foreign states" are of wide connotations and may conceivably relied upon for supporting any legislation which may restrict even legitimate criticism of the foreign policy of Government. The constitution at best can indicate the topics in respect to which there may be reasonable resections on the wisdom of parliament to define the precise scope of those restrictions and to the impartiality of the Supreme Court to pronounce upon the reasonableness of those restrictions.

In Kedarnath Vs. State of Bihar the constitutionality of sections 124 A and 505 of the Indian Penal Code came up for determination. Under section 124 A sedition include public disorder or disturbance of law and order or incitement to violence; it would be protected by clause (2) of Article 19. Thus a limit was put on the width of the ambit and scope of the section. The validity of Section 505 which makes the spread of rumours of reports with intent to cause meeting or offence similarly against public tranquillity, etc. was also upheld.

(4) **Incitement to an offence:** There has been considerable criticism of the clause because the word "offence "as used in Article 19 (2) has, under Article 367 of the constitution to be given the same meaning as is given to in the General Causes Act 1897.

The Supreme Court had also recognized the right of the State, in exercise of its police power, judging by "the clear and present danger" test, to restrict the freedom of speech and expression, where such "expression" is likely to incite people to commit crimes or do to disturb the public peace.

It is generally appreciated that incitement is one of the forms of abetment and if these words were removed from Article 19(2) there will be no constitutional authority for punishing any utterances, which incite persons to commit offences.

The restriction, however must "not be far fetched, hypothetical or problematical or too remote in the chain of its relating with he public order." In Superintend Central prison Vs. Ram Manohar Lohia (1960) the Supreme Court annulled the Section 3 of Uttar Pradesh Special Power Act, which punished a person, even if he incited a single person not to pay or defer the payment of Government dues. The Supreme Court held,

"We cannot accept the argument of the learned Advocate General that the instigation of single individual not to pay tax or dues is a spark which may in the long run ignite revolutionary movement, destroying public order. We can only say that fundamental rights cannot be controlled on such hypothetical and imaginary consideration."

The Supreme Court in Shailbala Devi's case has probably saved legal provisions punishing the incitement to the commission of aggravated offences such as murder on the ground that they may jeopardize the security of the State. But in absence of the words "incitement to an offence" there would be no constitutional authority for punishing abetments, by means of incitement, to commit offences involving violence in a less aggravated form or offences such as bribery, corruption, forgery, cheating criminal breach of trust, counterfeiting which involves no violence at all.

It is true that word 'offence' is very wide and that it would be possible for the Legislature to create any kind of offence, in that event the provision with regard to punishment for incitement to commit that offence would acquire constitutional validity' where the law is not void under Article 19 of the Constitution. It is a good law that must command obedience of the public in any democratic set up which proclaims and maintains the supremacy of law, and there is no reason why incitement to commit breaches of that law should not be punishable.

When a law is enacted it must be regarded as an expression of the will of the people, and if the law is disliked by certain sections of the people, the remedy lies not in disobeying the law but in persuading the public to see the iniquity of it and getting it changed by legitimate and constitutional means. Both the persons disobeying a law and a person instigating to disobey the law should be punishable. It would be wrong in principle to punish a person who breaks the law and allow instigators to escape the consequences of their acts on the plea of freedom of expression . This justifies the inclusion of "incitement to an offence" inserted in Article 19 of the Constitution.

(5) **Safeguard for the Freedom of Expression:** The provisions contained in Article 19 (2) of the Constitution are enabling provisions and the ultimate sanction behind any legislation must be the will of the people. All that the Constitution lays down is that certain fundamental principles may not be disregarded in attempting to harmonize the freedom of expression of an individual with the requirements of public good.

Apart form such safeguards as the Constitution has laid down, there are two other lines of safeguard against undue encroachment over the fundamental right of freedom of expression. One is the Legislatures itself and the other is judiciary. Although the Constitution invests the Legislatures with power to place restrictions on the freedom of speech and expression for certain purposes, the power by the Legislature on the fundamental right, we have no doubt that impartiality of the High Court and the Supreme Court will ensure that the power is not exercised by the Legislatures in an arbitrary or unrealistic manner.

# 2

# History of Media Law in India

The history of Press Law begins almost simultaneously with the publication of the first newspaper in India. The Indian Newspaper the "Bengal Gazette" was published in 1780 from Calcutta. The first attempt to control the press in India was made through Regulations issued by the Governor General in 1790. Under the Regulation, it was required to print the names of the printer, publisher, proprietor and submit all materials for precensorship by Secretary to the Government.

**Licensing of the Press :** Pre–censorship was abolished in 1818, an ordinance was issued in 1823 introducing licensing of the press under which a license was required for all matters to be printed. Similar regulations were made in Bombay in 1825 and 1827.

In 1835 Metcalf's Act was introduced and it was made applicable to the whole of the territory of East India Company. In required the printer and publisher of every newspaper to declare the location of the premises of he publication failing which a penalty of Rs. 5000 and imprisonment of two years could be imposed.

**Canning Act:** Licensing was re–introduced by Lord Canning's Act, 1857 and it applied to all kinds of publication including books in all languages. This was rightly called the gagging Act.

**Indian Penal Code:** Indian penal Code was passed in 1860, which laid down offences that writers, editor or publishers are liable to commit. These offence are those of obscenity and defamation. Later amendments to IPC introduced the offence of sedition (1870) promotion enemity between classes (1898), imputations, assertions prejudicial to national integration, out raging religious feelings (1927).

**Press and Registration of Books Act, 1867:** In 1867 the press and Registration of Books Act was passed. This was a regulatory law which enabled the Government to regulate the printing presses and newspapers by a system of registration and to preserve copies of books and other printed matters in India.

**Vernacular Press Act, 1878:** The Act was passed for punishing and suppressing seditious writings in newspapers published in Indian languages. It was repealed in 1881.

**Code of Criminal Procedure (Cr PC):** In 1898 the Indian penal Code 1860 was amended and the Criminal procedure Code, 1898 was enacted, which replaced the Criminal Procedure Code, 1882.

**The Newspaper (Incitement to Offences) Act, 1908:** The Act empowered a magistrate to seize a press if a newspaper printed by it published matter which incited murder or any other act of violence or an offence under the Explosive Substances Act.

**Indian Press Act, 1910:** The Act which was passed in 1910 was directed against offences involving violence and sedition. The Newspaper (Incitement of Offences) Act, 1908 and Indian Press Act. 1910 ware repealed in 1922 and provisions of these Acts were incorporated in the Press and Registration of Books Act, Sea Customs Act and Post Office through subsequent amendments.

**Official Secrets Act, 1923:** The Act is aimed at maintaining the security of the State against leakage of secret information, sabotage and the like.

**The Indian Press (Emergency) Powers Act, 1931:** An ordinance to this effect was promulgated to control the press which was later embodied in the Act of 1931. Originally a temporary Act was made permanent in 1935. It made it obligatory for the press to furnish security at the call of the Executive. This was replaced by the Presss (Objectionable Matter) Act, 1951

**The Newspaper (Price and Page) Act, 1956:** The Act was formed to prevent unfair competition among newspapers through price cutting. In exercise of the powers conferred by this Act, the Central Government issued the Daily Newspaper (Price and Page) Order, 1960, whereby the number of pages published by a newspaper was made to depend upon the price charged to the readers, so that a newspaper could not increase the volume of its publications without raising its price. The Supreme Court in Sakal Papers Vs Union of India, 1962, annulled the Act. The supreme Court held that the freedom of the press could be interfered with by the Government indirectly by enacting laws which did not directly impose any restriction on that freedom on the ground of the security of State or the like.

**Criminal Law Amendment Act, 1961:** Subsequent to the expiry of the press (Objectionable Matter) Act, 1951, parliament enacted the Criminal Law

Amendment Act, 1961 imposing restrictions upon the freedom of expression and of press as well as the freedom of assembly and of movement on the ground of 'Security of the State' and Public Order.

**Press Council Act, 1965:** The Press Council of India was constituted in 1966 under the Press Council Act, 1965 to preserve the freedom of the press and to maintain and improve the standard of newspapers in India. The Act was repealed with the promulgation of the publication of Objectionable Matter Ordinance, 1975. This became the Prevention of Publication of Objectionable Matter Act, 1976. The PPOM act, 1976 was repealed in 1977. The press Council Act, 1978 was enacted, re-establishing the Press Council.

**The Criminal and Election Laws Amendment Act, 1969:** The Act was passed to amend the Indian penal Code, the Code of Criminal Procedure ... and to provide against printing and publication of certain objectionable matters.

**The Indian Penal Code Amendment Act, 1969:** The Act was passed to make certain amendments in IPC to make the punishment for obscene publication more severe. The Copy Right Act, 1957.

**Prasar Bharti Act, 1990:** The Act to provide for the establishment of Broadcasting Corporation of India was known as Prasar Bharti (Broadcasting Corporation of India) Act, 1990. A public Broadcasting Corporation of India was established to organize and conduct public services to inform, educate and entertain the public and to ensure a balanced development of broadcasting on radio and television.

**The Cable Television Network Rules, 1994:** It contains the definition of certain terminology like "Cable Service," Cable Television Networks," Later on Cable Television Networks (Regulation) Act, 1995 was passed.

**Broadcasting Act, 1997:** There is a provision of "Indian Broadcasting Authority" in the second chapter of the Bill.

**Freedom of Information Act, 2002:** This is a Bill to provide to every citizen to secure access to information under control of public authorities, consistent with public interest, in order to promote openness, transparency and accountability in administration. The "freedom of information" has been defined as "the right to obtain any information from any public authority."

**Right to Information Act, 2005:** The Act provides the right to the people to seek information from public authorities and inspect the work, documents and records of public authorities. No information could be denied to the public, which cannot be denied to parliament or State Legislature.

**The Information Technology Act, 2000:** In India Cyber Laws is governed by the provisions contained in the Information Technology Act, 2000. New communication system and digital technology have made dramatic changes in the field for dissemination of information. Governance of content in digital technology for dissemination of information is of critical importance for users. The Act enlists the types of crimes committed in the content and provides for their punishment and fine.

# 3

# Media Freedom and Constitutional Provisions

"Freedom of the press" generally means the right to print and publish, broadcast without any interference from the state or any authority. Ideologically the indispensability of the freedom press and other mass media has become an institutional limb of democracy and it is also being called the Fourth Estate after Legislature, executive and judiciary.

The importance of the freedom of media led to the first amendment to the American Constitution in 1791,

"The Congress shall make no law ... abridging the freedom of the press."

"The Constitution of India guaranteed the fundamental right of freedom of expression in Article 19 (1) (a) and the supreme Court declared that the freedom of press was included in that guarantee.

In Sakal Press (P) Ltd. vs. Union of India in 1962 the Supreme Court declared that:

"It is a settled law that the right to freedom of speech and expression in Article 19 (1) (*a*) includes the liberty of the press."

In Romesh Thapar vs State of Madras, in 1950 the Supreme Court observed "Freedom of speech and of the press lay at the foundation of all democratic organization, for without free political discussion, no education, so essential for the proper functioning of the process of popular government, is possible. A freedom of such amplitude might involve risks of abuse. But the framers of the Conduction may have well reflected with Madison, who was the leading spirit in the preparation of the First Amendment of the Federal Constitution, that it is, better to leave a few of its noxious branches to their luxuriant than by pruning them away, to injure the vigor of those yielding the proper fruits."

In India the right to freedom of speech and expression broadly refers freedom of press. The role of the press as an independent body voicing popular feelings and opinions in democracy can hardly be over emphasized. Mahatma Gandhi, on the role of the press said "One of the objects of a news paper is to understand the popular feeling and give expression to it, another is to arouse among the people certain desirable sentiments; the third is fearlessly to expose popular defects.

The positive trend of American decision has influenced the decision of the Supreme Court of India in the matter of interpreting Article 19 (1) (*a*). In the Express Newspaper Vs Union of India (1959) down to Bennel Colemn. The Supreme held from time to time,

"The freedom of press rests on the assumption that widest possible dissemination of information from diverse and antagonistic sources is essential to the welfare of the public...."

As the freedom of the press is included in the freedom of speech and expression and is a fundamental right guaranteed by Article 19 (1) (*a*) of the Constitution, any person aggrieved by the infringement of the right can approach the Supreme Court under Article 32 or a High Court under Article 226 of the Constitution.

However Article 358 of the Constitution suspends the operation of Article 19 during emergency period. But laws made prior to the coming into operation of the proclamation of emergency are not protected from the challenge of unconstitutionality on the ground of contravention of Article 19. As also as soon as Emergency period is over, the laws passed during the period become inoperative to the extent, which are in contravention to the fundamental rights guaranteed under Article 19.

The fundamental right of freedom of speech and expression has been guaranteed under Article 19 the Constitution. But it is subject to certain restrictions which may be imposed by the State under clause (2) of that Article which has to be read along article 19 (1) (*a*).

"Article 19 (1) All citizens shall have the right to freedom of speech and expression. (2) Nothing in such Clause (*a*) of Clause (1) shall affect the operation of any existing laws, or prevent the State from making any laws, in so far such law imposes resasanable restrictions on the exercise of the right conferred by the said Sub–clause in the interests of the sovereignty and integrity of India, the security of the state, friendly relations with foreign states. Public order, decency or morality, or in relation to contempt of court, defamation or incitement to an offence."

The ambit to freedom of the press in comparison with the freedom of expression would be circumscribed by the interpretation put by the court on Act 19 (1) (*a*).

Since the press is not only medium of expression but also a business, the commercial activities of the press, the ambit of its rights and the limitations there to own are to be derived from the provisions in Article 19 (1) (g) and (6). No additional restrictions can be imposed on the freedom to the press under clause (6) so far as business aspect of the press are concerned.

The power of the State to impose restriction on business is derived from Article 19 (6). It authorizes the state to impose "in the interest of general public", "reasonable restriction" on the exercise of right to carry on any occupation, trade or business' which is guaranteed under Article 19 (1) (*g*). So the restrictions upon the press, as in the case of individuals, may be constitutionally valid if they are within the limits of reasonable restrictions within the meaning of Article 19(6).

**Censorship:** Pre–censorship during emergency under Article 358 of the Constitution as it stood up to the 44th Amendment Act. 1978, Article 19 remained suspended during the operation of a proclamation of emergency under Article 352. Pre–censorship was imposed under part V of Defence of India Rules, 1971.

After the revocation of emergency in March 1977, pre–censorship order was itself revoked . The article 358 was amended .The operation of Article 358 (1) has been confined to war or external aggression. Hence Article 19 can no longer be suspended by any proclamation of Emergency on any domestic ground. Even during the future emergency on the ground of war or external aggression, government will have to make a law authorizing such censorship and making a recital to impose a censorship order.

Pre-censorship in time of peace–Article 19 (2) of the Constitution of India makes no distinction between times of war and peace. It authorizes the State to impose restrictions on any of the grounds provided in Article 19 (2). The concept of reasonableness only refers to 'substantive' and 'procedural' reasonableness of the restriction imposed by the law.

Self-censorship–The guidelines issued for the press during the emergency were voluntarily followed by the press in most of the States. But the acceptance of guidelines offered by a censoring authority as an alternative to the enforcement of the censoring order cannot be said to be a voluntary acceptance of the code of conduct for the press for its own guidance. After the cessation of emergency the press Council was revived by Janta Government. So that Press Council which consists of the representatives of the press, may frame code of conduct for the press without imposition from the Government.

Preventive Measures other than Censorship–The Constitutional support for preventive measures is provided by the expression in the interest of public order in Article 19 (2). Thus the State would be justified 'in the interest of public order' not only to meet actual breach of public order, but also to impose restrictions on utterances or publication which have a tendency to cause public disorder. The

State would be justified in taking reasonable precautions to restrain certain acts by issuing prohibitory orders under Section 144 of the Criminal Procedure Code, 1973 or a ban on the entry of particular newspaper in an area in order to maintain communal harmony.

**Statutory Restrictions on publication:** In all modern countries the publication of certain materials is prohibited in the public interest.

**Objectionable Advertisements:** The publication of an 'objectionable advertisement' as defined in Sections 3-5 of the Durgs and Magic Remedies (Objectionable Advertisements) Act, 1954 is punishable under section 7 of the Act.

**Causing of class hatred:** Any publication which promotes or attempts to promote enmity, hatred or ill will between different sections of the people, thereby disturbing public tranquility, is punishable under section 153 A of Indian Penal Code.

**Conspiracy:** Conspiracy means an unlawful act done by several persons in pursuance of common object or in a pre–arranged plan. A person may be guilty of an offence of conspiracy, if the ingredients of section 34 of Indian Penal Code are satisfied.

**Contempt of Court:** Thus scandalization of a judge individually or the administration of justice, in general, is contained in Section 12 of the Contempt of Courts Act, 1971. A journalist, when attending a Court or summoned by it, may be dealt with summarily in contempt under section 345, 348–350 or the Criminal procedure Code, 1973, read with the provisions of the Indian Penal Code.

**Infringement of Copyright:** In addition to the civil remedies prescribed by section 54 the Copyright Act, 1957, it makes it an offence, punishable under Section 63 of the Act to knowingly infringe or abet the infringement of the copyright of a work or of any other right conferred by this Act.

**Defamation:** Publication of any material imputing thereby the reputation of a person, with the intention to harm him, is an offence punishable under section 499, of Indian Penal Code, unless it comes under any of the exception to that Section.

**Improper use of Emblems or names:** To use, without the permission of the central Government its emblems or names, etc. as specified in the Emblem and Names (Prevention of Improper Use) Act, 1950, for the purpose of any trade business are punishable under Section 5 of the Act.

**Essential Services and Commodities:** Incitement to interfere with essential services, or the production, supply and distribution of essential commodities are punishable under the Defence of India Rule and Internal Security Act., 1971.

**Young Person (Harmful Publication) Act, 1956:** The making, distributing or advertisement of a publications which tends to corrupt a young man by portraying stories of (*i*) the commission of offences (*ii*) Acts of cruelty, or (*iii*) incidents of repulsive or horrible nature is punishable under Section 3 of the Act.

Publications Prejudicial to Integrity (Territorial) of India : Any matter which questions the territorial integrity of India in a manner in which is prejudicial to the interests of the safety and security of India is punishable under Section 2 of the Criminal Law Amendment Act, 1961.

**Press and Registration of Books Act, 1867:** The printing or publishing of any newspaper without complying with the requirements of section 5-6 of the Act is punishable under Section 15 of the Act.

**Obscenity:** The making, circulation, advertisement or sale of any 'obscene' book, pamphlet or other writing is an offence punishable under section 292 of India Penal Code.

**Official Secrets Act, 1923:** No author, publisher or other journalist should :

(*i*) Make any sketch, plan or note which is or may be useful to an 'enemy'.

(*ii*) Obtain, collect, record or publish or communicate to any other person any secret official document or information which may be useful to any enemy or foreign agent, likely to affect the sovereignty and integrity of India, the security of the State of friendly relations with foreign States.

**Public Mischief:** To make, publish or circulate any statement rumor or report likely to cause, mutiny, inducement to a person to commit an offence against any other class or promotion to enemity or hatred between different groups, castes or communities, is punishable under section 505 of Indian Penal Code.

Under Section 3 (2) of Criminal Law Amendment Act, 1961, certain acts which is prejudicial to the interests of the safety or security of India is punishable.

**Outraging Religious Feelings:** To outrage the religious feelings or beliefs of any citizen by any publication made with such deliberate intention is an offence under section 295 A of IPC, the causing of class hatred is punishable under Section 153 A.

**Sedition:** Any publication, if its object is to subvert the Government of India by inciting public order, is punishable under Section 124 A of the Indian Penal Code.

**Privacy Versus Freedom of the Press:** The right to privacy has been declared in International Charters of Human Rights, such as Article 12 of the Universal Declaration of Human Rights, 1948 and Article 17 of the International Covenant on Civil and Political Rights, 1966. But so far no country has incorporated in any national Constitution or statute.

The Supreme Court of India has held the right of privacy has a two-fold source (*a*) Common Law, and (*b*) Constitutional Law.

(*a*) **Common Law:** The printer and publisher of a journal magazine or book may be liable, if he publishes, for advertising or non-advertising purposes, any matter concerning the private life of a citizen, without such person's consent, of course subject to some exceptions.

(*b*) **Constitutional Law:** The right to privacy is implicit in the fundamental right to life and liberty, guaranteed under Article 21 of the Constitution. However, this right is to be read together with constitutional right of the Press under Article 19 (1) (*a*) to punish any matter of public interest.

**Relief from Judiciary in Case of Infringement of the Freedom of the Press:** Freedom of the Press is a fundamental right guaranteed by Art 19 (!) (*a*) of our Constitution. In case of a person aggrieved by an infringement of this right by a law or order may apply for relief to the Supreme Court under Article 32 or a High Court (having territorial Jurisdiction) under Article 226 of the Constitution of India.

In such application under Article 32 or 226 the petitioner may also challenge the constitutional validity of the Act or the statutory rule under which the impugned order may have been issued, the implementation of which infringes the fundamental right of the petitioners.

**Freedom of the Press and Article 19 (2):** Under the Constitutional Amendment Act, 1951, Article 19 (2) of the Constitution was replaced with the following:

"Nothing in sub-clause (*a*) of clause (1) shall affect the operation of any existing laws, or prevent the State from making, any law, so far as such law, imposes reasonable restrictions on the exercise of the right conferred by the said sub-clause, in the interest of the security of the state, friendly relations with foreign States, Public order, decency or morality, or in relation to Contempt of Court, defamation or incitement to an offence."

The restrictions under Article 19 (2), thus, became a Justiciable matter, as other restrictions enumerated in clause (3) (4) (5) and (6) of article 19 were justiciable.

The grounds specified in Article 19 (2)-(6) had been held to be exhaustive.

A. **Sovereignty and integrity of India:** The ground was added by the Sixteenth Amendment Act, 1963. The object of the amendment was to confer on Parliament specific power to legislate on this subject so that the constitutionality of the acts, like the Criminal Amendment Act, 1961 or the Unlawful Activity (Prevention) Act, 1976 could not be challenged on the ground of being inconsistent with Article 19 (1) (*a*).

The publication of official Secrets, which is likely to affect the soveignity or integrity of India is also punishable under the Official Secrets Act, 1923.

B. **Security of the State:** Every state has a right to maintain its own existence; the right of self protection there are certain provision in other all India statutes which seek to protect this interest from different aspect :

(*i*) Official secrets Acts, 1923.

(*ii*) Criminal Amendment Act, 1961 sections 2-3

(*iii*) Customs Act, 1962 (section 11 (2) (*a*).

(*iv*) Indians Penal Code:

- Abutment or conspiracy to wage war against the Government of India, under section 121–121 A.
- Section, to incite disaffection against the Government established by law in India, by words which have a tendency to create public disorder; (under section 124 (A)).
- Abutting or inciting mutiny or seductions from duty of a member of the armed forces (under section 131).

(*v*) Dramatic performance Act, 1876, under section 3 and 8 of the Act empower the state Government to prohibit and seize paraphernalia required for a dramatic performance which is likely to excite feeling of disaffection against the Government in India. It is also in the same sense in case of sedition under section 124 A of Indian Penal Code.

(*vi*) Criminal Procedure Code 1973 : Provision under sections 95 (1), 108 (1) (*i*) (*a*) are auxiliary measures to prohibit the commission of the offence of 'section'.

(*vii*) The Police Incitement Disaffection, Act, 1922 under section 3 of the Act makes it an offence to do any which causes or is likely to cause "disaffection towards the Government established by law in India amongst the members of a police force or induces or attempts to induce...' any member of a police force to withhold his services or to commit breach of discipline....'

C. **Friendly relation with foreign states:** In the interest of friendly relations with foreign state are of wide connotations and may conceivably relied upon for supporting any legilsation may restrict even legitimate criticism of the foreign policy of the Government it is feared. The expression will include inducement against foreign enlistment propaganda in favour of war with a state at peace with India and the like.

D. **Public Order:** In, O. K. Ghos and other, the Supreme Court reaffirmed, while considering the provision of clauses (2) (4) of the Article 19 that so far clause (2) was concerned, security of the State having been expressly provided for, Public

Order could not include the security of the State. The expression "Public Order" was virtually synonymous with "Public Peace, safety and tranquility." Out of the three circles, 'law and order' represents the largest circle, within which is the next circle of public order and security of the state being the smallest circle. It is then easy to see that an act may affect 'Public order' but not 'the security of the state'.

Absence of 'Public Order is an aggravated from disturbance of public peace, which merely affects the general current of public life and any act which merely affects the security of the states may not constitute a breach of 'public order'

The laws on the Indian statute book relating on the freedom of speech and expression in the interest of 'Public Order' are the following:

(*i*) Indian Penal Code : To promote enimity between different classes of citizens, by words, spoken or written is an offence under section 153 A of IPC. Also, together utter words or to make visible representation with deliberate intent to wound the religious feelings or beliefs of any class of citizens is an offence.

(*ii*) The Indian Telegraph Act, 1885 and the Post Office Act, 1898.

(*iii*) The Police (Incitement to Disaffection) Act, 1922

(*iv*) The Security and Public Safety Acts of various States

(*v*) The Drug and Magic Remedies (Objectionable Advertisements) Act, 1954

(*vi*) The Customs Act, 1962

E. **Obscenity:** This is derived from the expression 'decancy' or 'morality' in Article 19 (2) of our constitution, as an offence against 'public morals' obscenity is covered by the expression 'public morals and section 292 of IPC the term "obscene."

F. **Contempt of Court:** The Contempt of Courts Act, 1971 codifies the law related to the Contempt of Court. Broadly speaking, it consists of any conduct that tends to bring the administration of justice into disrespect or to obstruct or interfere with the due course of justice. The proposition is codified in section 2 (*b*) (*iii*) of the Act. The 'Contempt of Court' comprises of two kinds of sentiment; civil and criminal under section 2 (*a*)–(*c*) of the Act of 1971. But Article 19 (2) refers to 'criminal' contempt only liability for Contempt of Court may arise both out of publishing materials in a newspaper and other printed matter like pamphlet or book.

G. **Defamation:** Defamation has been enumerated in Article 19 (2). A press would be liable for defamation, if the printed or published is defamatory to a person. Defamation is an injury to a man's reputation, which is regarded an his property.

H. **Incitement to an offence:** It is generally agreed that incitement is one of the forms of abetment and if these words were removed from Article 19 (2) there will be no constitutional authority for punishing any utterances which incite persons to commit offences.

The Supreme Court had also recognized the right of the State, in exercise of its police powers indignity by "the clear and present danger" to restrict the freedom of speech and expression, when such "expression" is likely to people to commit crime or disturb the public peace.

The restrictions however must not be, far fetched, hypothetical or problematical or too remote in the chain of it relations with the public order."

**(Relevant Provisions) The Constitution of India**

**Right to Equality**

14. **Equality before law:** The State shall not deny to any person equality before the law or the equal protection of the laws within the territory of India.

**Right to Freedom**

**19. Protection of certain rights regarding freedom of speech.** *etc* : (1) All citizens shall have the right.

(a) to freedom of speech and expression;

(b) to assemble peaceably and without arms;

(c) to form associations or unions;

(d) to move freely throughout the territory of India;

(e) to reside and settle in any part of the territory of India; and

(f) to practise any profession. or to carry on any occupation, trade or business.

(2) Nothing in sub–clause (*a*) of cause (1) shall affect the operation of any existing law. or prevent the State from making any law, insofar as such law imposes reasonable restrictions on the exercise of the right conferred by the said sub–clause in the interests of the sovereignty and integrity of India, the security of the State, friendly relations with foreign States, public order, decency or morality, or in relation to contempt of court. defamation or incitement to an offence.

(3) Nothing in sub–clause (*b*) of the said clause shall affect the operation of any existing law in so far as it imposes, or prevent the State from making any law imposing, in the terests of the sovereignty and integrity of India or public order, reasonable restrictions on the exercise of the right conferred by the said sub–clause.

(4) Nothing in sub–clause (*c*) of the said clause shall affect the operation of any existing law insofar as it imposes, or prevent the State from making any law imposing, in the interests of the sovereignty and integrity of India or public order or morality, reasonable restrictions on the exercise of the right conferred by the said sub–clause.

(5) Nothing in sub–clauses (*d*) and (*e*) of the said clause shall affect the operation of any existing law in so far as it imposes, or prevent the State from making any law imposing, reasonable restrictions on the exercise of any of the rights conferred by the said sub–clauses either in the interests of the general public or for the protection of the interests of any Scheduled Tribe.

(6) Nothing in sub–clause (*g*) of the said clause shall affect the operation of any existing law insofar as it imposes, or prevent the State from making any law imposing, in the interests of the general public, reasonable restriction on the exercise of the right conferred by the said sub–clause and in particular, nothing in the said sub–clause shall affect the operation of any existing law insofar as it relates to, or prevent the State from making any law relating to,–

(*i*) the professional or technical qualifications necessary for practising any profession or carrying on occupation, trade or business, or

(*ii*) the carrying on by the State, or a corporation owned or controlled by the State, of any trade, business, industry or service, whether to the exclusion, complete or partial, of citizens or otherwise.

129. **Supreme Court to be a court of record:** The supreme Court shall be a court of record and shall the power of such a court including the power to punish of contempt of itself.

142. **Enforcement of decrees and orders of Supreme Court and orders as to discovery, *etc*:** (1) The Supreme Court in the exercise of its jurisdiction may pass such decree or make such order as is necessary for doing complete justice in any cause or matter pending before it, and any decree so passed or order so made shall been forceable throughout the territory of India in such manner as may be prescribed by or under any law made by Parliament and, until provision in that behalf is so made, in such manner as the President may by order prescribe.

(2) Subject to the provisions of any law made in this behalf by Parliament. The Supreme Court shall, as respects the whole of the territory of India, have all and every power to make any order for the purpose of securing the attendance of any person, the discovery or production of any documents, or the investigation or punishment of any contempt of itself.

215. **High Courts to be courts of record:** Every High Court shall be a court of record and shall have all the powers of such a court including the power to punish for contempt of itself.

352. **Proclamation of Emergency:** (1) If the President is satisfied that a grave emergency exists whereby the security of India or of any part of the territory thereof is threatened, whether by war or external aggression or armed rebellion, he may, be proclamation, make a declaration to that effect in respect of the whole of India of such part of the territory thereof as may be specified in the Proclamation.

*Explanation :* A Proclamation of Emergency declaring that the security of India or any part of the territory thereof is threatened by war or by external aggression or by armed rebellion may be made before the actual occurrence of war or of any such aggression or rebellion, if the President is satisfied that there is imminent danger thereof.

(2) A Proclamation issued under clause (1) may be varied or revoked by a subsequent proclamation.

(3) The President shall not issue a Proclamation under clause (1) or a Proclamation varying such Proclamation unless the decision of the Union Cabinet (that is to say, the Council consisting of the Prime Minister and other Ministers of Cabinet rank appointed under article 75) that such a Proclamation may be issued has been communicated to him in writing.

(4) Every Proclamation issued under this article shall be laid before each House of Parliament and shall, except where it is a Proclamation revoking a previous Proclamation, case to operate at the expiration of one month unless before the expiration of that period it has been approved by resolutions of both Houses of Parliament:

Provided that if any such Proclamation (not being a Proclamation revoking a previous Proclamation) is issued at a time when the House of the People has been dissolved, or the dissolution of the House of the People takes place during the period of one month referred to in this clause, and if a resolution approving the Proclamation has been passed by the Council of States, but no resolution with respect of such Proclamation has been passed by the House of the People before the expiration of that period, the Proclamation shall cease to operate at the expiration of thirty days from the date on which the House of the People first sits after its reconstitution, unless before the expiration of the said period of thirty days a resolution approving the Proclamation has been also passed by the House of the People.

(5) A Proclamation so approved shall, unless revoked cease to operate on the expiration of a period of six months from the date of the passing of the second of the resolutions approving the Proclamation under clause (4).

Provided that if and so often as a resolution approving the continuance in force of such a Proclamation is passed by both Houses of Parliament the Proclamation shall, unless revoked, continue in force for a further period of six months from the date on which it would otherwise have ceased to operate under this clause.

Provided further that if the dissolution of the House of the People takes place during any such period of six months and a resolution approving the continuance in force of such Proclamation has been passed by the Council of States but no resolution with respect to the continuance in force of such Proclamation has been passed by the House of the People during the said period, the Proclamation shall cease to operate at the expiration of thirty days from the date on which the House of the People first sits after its reconstitution unless before the expiration of the said period of thirty days, a resolution approving the continuance in force of the Proclamation has been also passed by the House of the People.

(6) For the purpose of clauses (4) and (5), a resolution may be passed by either House of Parliament only by a majority of the total membership of that House and by a majority of not less than two–thirds of the members of that House present and voting.

(7) Notwithstanding any thing contained in the foregoing clauses, the President shall revoke a Proclamation issued under clause (1) or a Proclamation varying such Proclamation if the House of the People passed a resolution disapproving, or, as the case may be, disapproving the continuance in force of, such Proclamation.

(8) Where a notice in writing signed by not less than one–tenth of the total number of members of the House of the People has been given, of their intention to move a resolution for disapproving, or as the case may be, for disapproving the continuance in force of, a Proclamation issued under clause (1) or a Proclamation varying such Proclamation:

(a) to the Speaker, if the House is in session ; or

(b) to the President, if the House is not in session.

A special sitting of the House shall be held within fourteen days from the date on which such notice is received by the Speaker, or, as the case may be, by the President, for the purpose of considering such resolution.

(9) The power conferred on the President by this article shall include the power to issue different Proclamations on different grounds, being war or external aggression or armed rebellion or imminent danger of war or external aggression or armed rebellion, whether or not there is a Proclamation already issued by the President under clause (1) and such Proclamation is in operation.

358. **Suspension of provisions of article 19 during emergencies:** (1) While a Proclamation of Emergency declaring that the security of India or any part of the territory thereof is threatened by war or by external aggression is in operation, noting in article 19 shall restrict the power of the State as defined in Part III to make any law or to take any executive action which the State would but for the provisions contained in that Part be competent to make or to take, any law or to take any executive action which the State would but for the provisions contained

in that Part be competent to make to take, but any law so made shall, to the extent of the incompetency, cease to have effect as soon as the Proclamation ceases to operate, except as respects things done or omitted to be done before the law so ceases to have effect:

Provided that where such Proclamation of Emergency is in operation only in any part of the territory of India, any such law may be made, or any such executive action may be taken, under this article in relation to or in any State or Union territory in which or in any part of which the Proclamation of Emergency is not in operation, if and in so far as the security of India or any part of the territory thereof is threatened by activities in or in relation to the part of the territory of India in which the Proclamation of Emergency is in operation.

(2) Nothing in clause (1) shall apply

(a) to any law which does not contain a recital to the effect that such law is in relation to the Proclamation fo Emergency in operation when it is made; or

(b) to any executive action taken otherwise than under a law containing such a recital.

359. **Suspension of the enforcement of the rights conferred by Part III during emergencies:** (1) Where a Proclamation of emergency is in operation, the President may by order declare that the right to move any court for the enforcement of such of the rights conferred by Part III (except articles 20 and 21) as may be mentioned in the order and all proceedings pending in any court for the enforcement of the rights so mentioned shall remain suspended for the period during which the Proclamation is in force or for such shorter period as may be specified in the order.

(1A) While an order made under clause (I) mentioning any of the rights conferred by Part III (except article 20 and 21) is operation, nothing in that Part conferring those rights shall restrict the power of the State as defined in the said Part to make any law or to take any executive action which the State would but for the provisions containing in that Part be competent to make or to take, but any law so made shall, to the extent of the incompetency, cease to omitted to be done before the law so ceases to have effect:

Provided that where a Proclamation of Emergency is in operation only in any part of the territory of India, any such law may be made, or any such executive action may be taken, under this article in relation to or in any State or Union territory in which or in any part of which the Proclamation of Emergency is not in operation, if and is so far as the security of India or any part of the territory thereof is threatened by activities in or in relation to the part of the territory of India in which the Proclamation of Emergency is in operation.

(IB) Nothing in clause (IA) shall apply :

(a) to any law which does not contain a recital to the effect that such law is in relation to the Proclamation of Emergency in operation when it is made; or

(b) to any executive action taken otherwise than under a law containing such a recital.

(2) An order made as aforesaid may extend to the whole or any part of the territory of India.

Provided that where a Proclamation of Emergency is in operation only in a part of the territory of India, any such order shall not extent to any other part of the territory of India unless the President, being satisfied that the security of India or any part of the territory thereof is threatened by activities in or in relation to the part to the territory of India in which the Proclamation of Emergency is in operation, considers such extension to the necessary.

(3) Every order made under clause (1) shall, as may be after it is made, be laid before each House of Parliament.

361. **Protection of publication of proceedings of Parliament and State Legislatures:** (1) No person shall be liable to any proceedings, civil or criminal, in any court in respect of the publication in a newspaper of a substantially true report of any proceedings of either House of Parliament or the Legislative Assembly, or, as the case may be, either House of the Legislature, of a State, unless the publication is proved to have been made with malice:

Provided that nothing in this clause shall apply to the publication of any report of the proceedings of a secret sitting of either House of Parliament or the Legislative Assembly, or, as the case may be, either House of the Legisluture, of a State.

(2) Clause (1) shall apply in relation to reports or matters broadcast by means of wireless telegraphy as part of any programme or service provided by means of a broadcasting station as it applies in relation to reports or matters published in a newspaper.

# 4

# Defamation

Any matter, which exposes a person about whom it is published, to hatred, to ridicule or contempt, is said to be defamatory. Defamation can be either libel or slander. Defamatory matter becomes libel, if it is in writing, is printed or is in some other permanent medium. Slander has to be in spoken words or gestures.

What is defamation? Under the provision of Section 499 of India penal Code, 1860 every person has a right to maintain and defend his name fame, honour, dignity and honesty. Defamation under this law implies "if anybody makes a spoken, written or printed statement using the words intended to damage the reputation of a person, or does so by signals or pictures; and he does it deliberately with the intention of vicious slander, it attracts a defamation case against the person making such statements or actions. Such a person can be sued in the court of law under civil and criminal law, and if it is proved the accused person can be awarded, fine two years imprisonment or both."

Under Article 19 (2) of the Constitution of India defamation has been mentioned as one of the reasonable restrictions on the freedom of speech and expression guaranteed under Article 19 (1) (a).

The definition of defamation as given by Robin Calender Smith is that defamation is the publication to a third party of a statement which tends to lower a living person in the estimation of right thinking members of society generally, or which makes them shun or avoid that person, or which disparages his reputation in relation to his work.

According to Durga Das Basu "Defamation is an injury to man's reputation. The right to reputation is an absolute right.

To invoke the law of defamation, a statement must fulfill their essential conditions.

1. The statement made by anyone should have the intent of defamation;
2. The name of the plaintiff should form necessary part of speech or statement.
3. The statement should have necessarily been published by the defendant.
4. The statement should necessarily be false.

A Statement is defamatory if it has a tendency to injure a person's reputation. The test is whether the statement has a tendency to excite against the plaintiff the "adverse opinions or feelings of others" such as hatred ridicule or contempt.

In D. P. Choudhary Vs Manjula, a statement was published in local daily in Jodhpur that Manjula went out of her house in the night on the pretext of attending night classes and eloped with a boy named Kamlesh. The news was false and was published with utter irresponsibility. This brought the plaintiff to ridicule and contempt and even affected her marriage prospect. As she was a young girl. The statement being defamatory and false and defendants were held liable.

The second condition is that the name of the plaintiff should form necessary part of speech or statement. The plaintiff must be able to prove that the defendant intended to be so. A person charged with liable cannot defend himself by showing that he intended in his own breast not to defame, or that he intended not to defame the plaintiff, if in fact he did both.

The third condition for defamation is that the statement should have necessarily been published by the defendant. The communications must be made atleast, to one third person. A libelous statement if straight to the person of whom it is made in sealed envelope addressed to him will not amount to defamation.

It is the responsibility of the press to see that defamatory statements are not published. If a libel appears in a newspaper, all those involved with the process of publications the proprietor, the editor, the printer and the publisher, can be jointly and severally sued, if it had an intention to defame the plaintiff.

The fourth condition for a matter to be defamatory is that it should be necessarily false. There can be no civil action for the publication of defamatory statement which is true The burden of proof lies on the defendant to prove that the statement is true.

**Elements of Defamation Crime:** The following elements could constitute a defamation crime.

1. Attribution and publication of blame somebody through: (*i*) words (*ii*) signals or (*iii*) Display though the medium
2. Blaming through acting or through pictures
3. Casting aspersions with an intent to cause somebody suffer and damage his reputation.

**Civil Law of Defamation:** Whereas the criminal law on defamation is codified in India, the civil law on defamation has not yet been codified and is still based on the British laws on the subject.

The Criminal law on defamation has been explicitly under section 499 of the IPC. No new exception, which is not contained with in the ten exceptions under section 499 of the IPC can, therefore, be imported on the basis of general rules of the British law

**Exception to the Law of Defamation:** The are conditions under which a Journalist can effectively defend himself against the charges of defamation. But the journalist should be able to substantiate the facts reported by him with appropriate proof of his report. The news publications of which is in the interest or well being of the public which are free from any selfish motive or pre–juice or prompted by revenge, may be published.

**First exception:** Any factual matter based on truth can be published. It is not defamation to publish anything which is true, if it is to be for public good that should be published.

**Second exception:** Any comments on the character or public deeds of public servant, not intended to humiliate such person nor prompted by prejudice.

**Third exception:** Any comments on the conduct or the apparent character of people answerable to public or of any person touching any pubic question do not attract a case of defamation.

**Fourth exception:** Truthful and factual report on the proceeding of the court expressed/published in good faith is not defamation.

**Fifth exception:** Honest comments, without any intention on the court decrees, conduct of any person as part, witness or agent, as far as his character appears in that conduct is not defamation.

**Sixth exception:** Any comment in good faith, any opinion respecting the merits of any; performance respecting the character of the author, as it appears in such performance is not defamation.

**Seventh exception:** If any person has legal right, either conferred by law or arising out of a contract made with the other, it is not defamation to pass, in good faith to pass any censure on the conduct of his subordinate or to criticize him.

**Eighth exception:** Any accusation made on any person in good faith or with out any ill will or prejudice, is not defamation if the person making accusations has lawful authority over that person with a subject matter of accusation.

**Ninth exception:** Any accusation made in good faith in self-decency or for the protection of self-interest or in the public interest on any other person is not defamation against another is not defamation.

**Tenth exception:** Any words covering caution, in good faith to one person against another is not defamation.

In an action for defamation. A defendant can take up three general defences,

(a) justification;

(b) Fair comment; and

(c) Privilege.

According to Durga Das Basu, possible defences to an action for defamation in India, can be:

(*i*) That the alleged statement was not published.

(*ii*) That the statement did not refer to the plaintiff.

(*iii*) That words complained of did not bear any defamatory meaning.

(*iv*) That the statement was true in substance and in fact.

(*v*) That the statements absolutely privileged

(*vi*) That the statement was published in good faith and without malice towards the plaintiff on a matter of public interest.

(*vii*) That the publication was made by authority or with the consent of the plaintiff.

(*viii*) That the plaintiff has agreed to forgo the claim or has given a written release from liability.

(*ix*) That the person defamed has died.

(*x*) That the suit is barred by limitation.

(*xi*) That suit is barred by resjudicata.

A. **Justification:** The truth of defamatory statement is the plea of justification where by a defendant justifies his statement.

B. **Fair comment:** No statement can be said to be defamatory if it is a fair comment on the matter of public interest. The statement in question must be only a comment and not a statement of fact.

C. **Privileges:** There are certain privileges under law which allow to make defamatory statement. These privileges are of two types:

(*i*) Complete privileges and

(*ii*) Qualified (relative) privileges

(*i*) **Complete Privileges:** Complete privileges arise in matter of public policy, where a man is allowed to express freely without any of its consequences; under the following three situations.

(*a*) **During the parliament session:** During the debate in the parliament, every member has the privilege of free expression even if it is defamatory for someone. Publication of any statement in the house and its propagation have been granted as privilege under Article 105(2) and 194 (2) of the Constitution of India.

(*b*) **During Court proceedings:** Any statement made by a judge, lawyer, witness or party before a court of law during the court proceedings cannot be termed as a defecation.

(*c*) **Official Correspondence:** In accordance with the public office, any exchange of correspondence between, two officials does come under the purview of defamation.

(*ii*) **Qualified (relative) privileges:** Qualified privilege is recognized in cases where the defendant had some lawful interest or duty in making the statement. Under certain circumstances, some statement, which may by termed as wrong, do not attract any defamations.

However, absence of malice or improper motive has to be proved.

(*a*) **Statement made during the discharge of duty:** If a defendant has the legal, moral or social responsibility to say something against the plaintiff and the plaintiff is required to listen to that statement, in such cases no utterances by the defendant would be termed defamatory. Replying to the questions asked by someone for throwing light on any matter is a social duty.

(*b*) **Statement made in self-defence:** Any complaint made by any officer against somebody to some authorized person under certain conditions, would be termed defamatory. The right to receive such complaint is reserved for the elected representatives of the people.

In Adam vs. Word, it was held that the basis of qualified privilege is that the person making the statement "has an interest or duty legal, social or moral, to make it to the person to whom it is made, and the person of whom it is so made, has a corresponding interest to duty to receive it. The reciprocity is essential."

**Punitive action for Defamation:** The punitive action for defamation has been specified under certain sections of the Indian penal Code.

**Section 500:** A person found guilty of defamation can be awarded a fine, or imprisonment for two years, or both under section 500 of the Indian penal Code.

**Section 501:** if any person publishes a defamatory material fully knowing that it is a wrong act, which could be a subject of defamation, he could be awarded a fine or could be sentenced for two years imprisonment, or both under section 501 of the Indian penal Code.

**Section 502:** If any person deliberately sells off any defamatory printed material, directly or indirectly, he can be awarded fine or two years imprisonment, or both under section 502 of the Indian penal Code.

# 5

# Press and Registration of Books Act, 1867

Among the various Acts affecting the Press, the Press and Registration of Books Act, 1867 is the oldest serving Act. According to the Preamble of the Act, it is an Act for the regulation of Printing Presses and of newspaper, for the preservation of copies of every book and newspaper in India, and for the registration of such books and newspaper. The Bill was passed by the legislatures and it came on the statute book as Press and Registration of Books Act, 1867 (C25 of 1867). Since then a number of amending acts and adaptation orders have been included in the original Act. Some of the Acts, the provisions of which have inserted major changes, are the following:

1. The Press and Registration of Books Act (1867) Amendment Act, 1890 (10 of 1890)
2. The Government of India (Adaptation of Indian Laws) Order, 1937
3. The Adaptation of Laws Order, 1950
4. The Press and Registration of Books (Amendment) Act, 1955
5. The Press and Registration of Books (Amendment) Act, 1960
6. The Press and Registration of Books (Amendment) Act, 1968

But the Act of 1867 remained the fundamental law governing the rules for the regulation of the publication of newspaper and printing presses.

According to the provisions of the Act, a declaration, made in the prescribed manner, before the District, Presidency or Sub-divisional Magistrate and authenticated by him is necessary before the newspaper is published.

In respect of printing press, the Act requires that the name of the printer, the place of printing and the name of the publisher and place of publication must be legibly printed on every book or newspaper printed/published within India.

For having a press to print books or newspaper a declaration must be made before the District, a presiding or Sub–divisional Magistrate giving its location and address.

Every time a press is shifted to a new place, a fresh declaration is necessary. But if the change of the place is for a period less than 60 days and keeper of the press is the same no fresh declaration need be made. In that case, the intimation regarding change of place is to be sent within 24 hours.

The conditions necessary to be fulfilled for publishing a newspaper are; (1) the name of the editor must be clearly printed on every copy of the newspaper (2) a declaration must be made before the District, Presidency or Sub– divisional Magistrate within shoes jurisdiction the place of the publication of the newspaper falls. The declaration should state the following fact.

(*a*) Name of the printer and the publisher

(*b*) Premises where printing and publishing is done.

(*c*) The title, language and periodicity of the newspaper.

The publication can be started only after the concerned magistrate authenticates the declaration made by the printer and publishers, either in person or in paper specifying the name of the owner.

In case any change in the title, language or periodicity a fresh declaration is required to be made. Similarly a new declaration is necessary as and when the ownership or the place of printing or publication of the newspaper is changed . If the printer or publisher leaves India for on a period exceeding 90 days, then a fresh declaration is required to be made Before the authentication the magistrate must make an enquiry from the Registrar of Newspapers in India, about the existence of any such newspaper . And , if the declaration is made according to the provision of law an if no other paper having the same similar title is already in existence in the same language or the same state, the Magistrate cannot refuse to authenticate declaration.

After authentication, the paper must be started within a specific period. In case of newspaper published once a week or more (weekly/daily) the publication must commence within six weeks of the authentications. In case of a fortnightly, a monthly or a quarterly must start publishing within three months after authentication.

If over any period of three months, a daily, a tri-weekly a bi-weekly or fortnightly newspaper publishes less than half the number of issues, which it should have published in accordance with the declaration, the newspaper shall cease to publish. In case of any other newspaper the maximum period of non–publication is 12 months for keeping the declaration alive. In cases where a publication has ceased to publish a fresh declaration must be filed before starting it again Two Copies of each issue of a newspaper and upto three copies of each book must be delivered, in a prescribed manner, to the Government free of expenses.

The declaration can be cancelled by the concerned Magistrate, after giving opportunity to show cause to the person concerned for violation of any provisions of the law. The magistrate's decision can be challenged in appeal before the Press and the Registration Appellate Board comprising a Chairman and another Member nominated by the Press Council of India.

**Registration of Newspaper:** The Central Government may appoint a Registrar of Newspaper for whole India. The Press Registrar shall maintain in the prescribed manner a register of newspapers. The register, shall contain the following particulars about every newspaper published in India, namely:

(*a*) The title of the newspaper.

(*b*) The language in which the newspaper is published;

(*c*) Periodicity of the publication of the newspaper:

(*d*) The name of the editor, printer and publisher of the newspaper;

(*e*) The place of printing an publication;

(*f*) The average number of pages per week;

(*g*) The number of days of publication in the year;

(*h*) The average number of copies printed, the average number of copies sold to the public and the average number of copies distributed free to the public, the average being calculated with reference to such period as may be prescribed;

(*i*) Retail selling price per copy.

(*j*) The name and address of the owners of the newspaper and such other particulars to ownership as may be prescribed.

(*k*) Any other particulars which may be prescribed.

The Press Registrar also issues a certificate of registration to the publisher on receipt of a copy of declaration authenticated by the concerned Magistrate.

It shall be the duty of the publisher of every newspaper to furnish to the Press Register an annual statement of the above particulars about his newspaper as may be specified by the Press Registrar. The name, address, nationality one percent or more shares in the newspaper, are to be published in the first issue after the last day of February each year.

The newspaper has also to furnish returns from time to time Non-compliance may attract fine. The press Registrar of his authorized representative has access to any record or document relating to the newspaper for the collection of any in formation about it.

**Penalties:** Printer and publisher of any book or newspaper otherwise than in conformity with the rule contained in section 3 of the Act shall on conviction be punished by fine not exceeding rupees two thousand or by simple imprisonment for a term not exceeding six months or both. The same punishment could be awarded for keeping a press in contravention of the provision contained in section–4 of the Act, or making for printing or publishing any newspaper without conforming to the rules laid down in the Act. Failure to make a declaration under section 8 of the Act may attract a fine not exceeding rupees two hundred.

Failure to supply copies of newspaper to the Government is punishable by a fine up to rupees fifty of every default. The punishment could be awarded for failure to deliver copies of the newspaper to press Register.

The Office of the Registrar of Newspapers for India (RNI) came into existence on 1 July 1956, on the recommendation of the First Press Commission in 1953 and by amending the Press and Registration of Books Act, 1867. The Registrar of Newspapers for India, commonly known as the Press Registrar, is required, inter alia to submit an Annual Report to the Government by 31 December every year on the status of newspapers. The period for which the annual statements were to be furnished, was changed from the calendar to financial year in 2002. Earlier the Annual Report was compiled on financial year basis. The total number of registered Newspapers/Periodcal was 62,550 as on 31 March 2006. These were 6,800 dailies, 369 tri/bi–weeklies, 21,453 weeklies, 8,227 fortnightlies, 18,545 monthlies 4,340 quarterlies 584 annuals, and 2,232 of the other periodicity. (The figures have been updated only for the registered newspapers for the year 2005–06).

According to the report submitted by the Press Registrar for the year 2004–05, Newspapers were registered in 123 languages and dialects. Apart from English and 22 other principal languages listed in the Eighth Schedule of the Constitution, newspapers were registered in 100 other languages and dialects mostly Indian but also in a few foreign languages too. Orissa had the distinction of publishing newspapers in 18 out of 22 principal languages. Maharashtra came next with publication in 17 languages followed by Delhi with publications in 16 principal languages.

Of the 60,413 newspapers registered as on 31 March 2005, only 7,225 submitted Annual Statement during 2004–05. The total circulation of these 7,225 newspapers was 15,67,19,209. The largest number of newspapers and periodicals registered in any Indian language is in Hindi (24017). The second largest number of newspapers and periodicals registered in any language isin English (8,768). The state with the largest number of registered newspapers is Uttar Pradesh (9,757). The state with the second largest number of registered newspapers is Delhi (8,194).

| No. | Dailies | Tri/ Biweeklies | Weeklies | Fortnightlies | Monthlies | Quarterlies | Annuals | Others | Total |
|---|---|---|---|---|---|---|---|---|---|
| Total Nos. of Reg. News Papers as on 31 March 2005 | 6530 | 364 | 20831 | 7959 | 17813 | 4227 | 556 | 2133 | 60413 |
| Total Nos. of Reg. News Papers from 1.04.2005 to 31.03.2006 | 270 | 5 | 622 | 268 | 732 | 113 | 28 | 99 | 2137 |
| Total Nos. of Reg. News Papers As on 31 March 2006 | 6800 | 369 | 21543 | 8227 | 18545 | 4350 | 584 | 2232 | 62550 |

## THE PRESS AND REGISTRATION OF BOOKS ACT, 1867

### INTRODUCTION

During the rein of the British Government in India writing of books and other informatory material took a concrete shape and with the advent of printing presses various books on all most all the subjects and periodicals touching every aspect of life started appearing. Thrust on education gave an impetus to this with the result that lot of printed material became available. Those in the field of writing, publishing and printing and printing gave a thought to organise a system for keeping a record of the publications. The then East India Company was urged to keep a record of the publications. An attempt was made by the authorities to make a collection of the books and other publications emanating from the various printing presses throughout India. Board of Directors of East India Company issued an instruction that copies of every important and interesting work published in India should be despatched to England to be deposited in the library of India House. Such an instruction had a slow impact. Again the Royal Asiatic Society in London urged the then Secretary of State for India to repeat the instruction of the late Board of Directors of East India Company and also desired that catalogues of all the works published in India should be sent to England. A system of voluntary registrations of publications was evolved but it failed. It was found necessary to establish a system of compulsory sale to Government, of three copies of each work in India. To achieve this purpose a Bill was introduced in the Legislature for the regulation of printing presses and newspaper for the preservation of copies of books and periodicals containing news printed in the whole of India and for the registration of such books and periodicals containing news.

## STATEMENT OF OBJECTS AND REASONS

It has for many years been the endeavour of the authorities to make a collection of the books and other publications emanating from the various printing presses at work throughout the country.

It was an instruction of the late Court of Directors of the East India Company, that copies of every important and interesting work published should be despatched to England to be deposited in the library at the India House.

And again, on the urgent requisition of the Royal Asiatic Society in London, the Secretary of State for India repeated the instructions of the late Court of Directors, and desired also that catalogues of all works published in India should be sent to England.

The above instructions had special reference to the province of Lower Bengal, and the local authorities of this province were set in motion, and on a plan suggested by Mr. Talboys Wheeler of the Home Office, and matured by Mr. Robinson, Bengalee Translator to the Government of Bengal, a system of registration of books on terms advantageous to publishers was notified, and a catalogue of books published in the province of Lower Bengal was prepared.

But this catalogue had necessarily to be prepared by its editor, not with the books before him, but from such imperfect and scattered notices and advertisements of such books as he could collect from newspapers and other such sources, and was found therefore to be to a great extent, and essentially, incorrect, and the registration system completely broke down, there having been but three applications for registration in the course of some nine months.

To send to England catalogues essentially and to a considerable extent incorrect, of only such books as can be routed out by private and perfunctory enquiries, is manifestly of no sort of use.

Yet the catalogue prepared in 1862, imperfect as it was, showed a list of some one thousand and five hundred books of more or less interest and importance, all published within the last ten or fifteen years, and it is notorious that, in the province of Lower Bengal at least, there has been of late years very great activity in the literary world, and every year shows no inconsiderable increase in the number of works, original or re–printed, published, and in the number of printing presses established.

The literature of a country is no doubt an index of the opinions and condition of the people, and such an index people, it is essential to good government that the rulers of a country should possess.

In the interest, too, of history and of the scholars of Europe, it is undoubtedly wise to provide that a complete collection of the publications of the press of this country should be made as well in this country as in England.

It cannot, too, but be of benefit to authors and publishers that catalogues of their works, and to a very limited extent copies of the works themselves, should be accessible to the public at certain well-known places.

Systems of voluntary registration of publications have been found to fail, and it is therefore proposed by this Bill to establish a system of compulsory sale to Government of three copies of each book or similar work printed in India.

One copy of the work will be sent to England, and the two others, after the book may registered, will be kept in this country, to be deposited in places—the proposed new Museum for instance—where they will be carefully preserved.

A list of works registered will be published each quarter in the Official Gazette.

It is not quite clear that the provisions of the proposed Bill are as yet required in any province other than that of Lower Bengal, but in as much as the said provisions are reasons and simple, and in as much as it is certain that with the spread of education there will arise the other provinces of the Empire, as there has arisen in Bengal, a corresponding activity literature, it is provided that the Bill may be extended by notification to any part of t Empire.

## ACT 25 OF 1867

The Bill was passed by the Legislature and it came on the statute book as the Press and Registration of Books Act, 1867 (25 of 1867). The nomenclature of the Act has been given by the Indian Short Titles Act, 1897 (14 of 1897).

## LIST OF AMENDING ACTS AND ADAPTATION ORDERS

1. The Repealing Act, 1870 (14 of 1870).
2. The Press and Registration of Books Act (1867) Amendment Act, 1890 (10 of 1890).
3. The Amending Act, 1891 (12 of 1891).
4. The Indian Short Titles Act. 1897 (14 of 1897).
5. The Indian Copyright Act, 1914 (3 of 1914).
6. The Repealing and Amending Act, 1914 (10 of 1914).
7. The Repealing and Amending Act, 1915 (II of 1915).
8. The Devolution Act, 1920 (38 of, 1920).
9. The Press Law Repeal and Amendment Act, 1922 (14 of 1922).
10. The Repealing and Amending Act, 1923 (11 of 1923).
11. The Government of India (Adaptation of Indian Laws) Order, 1937.

12. The Indian Independence (Adaptation of Central Acts and Ordinances) Order, 1948.
13. The Adaptation of Laws Order, 1950.
14. The Repealing and Amending Act, 1950 (35 of 1950).
15. The Part B States (Laws) Act, 1951 (3 of 1951).
16. The Press (Objectionable Matter) Act, 1951 (56 of 1951).
17. The Press and Registration of Books (Amendment) Act, 1955 (55 of 1955).
18. The Press and Registration of Books (Amendment) Act, 1960 (26 of 1960).
19. The Press and Registration of Books (Amendment) Act, 1965 (16 of 1965).
20. The Press and Registration of Books (Amendment) Act, 1968 (30 of 1968).
21. The Press Council Act, 1978 (37 of 1978).
22. The Delegated Legislation Provisions (Amendment) Act, 1983 (20 of 1983).

**Preamble:** WHEREAS it is expedient to provide for the regulation of printing-presses and of '[newspapers], for the preservation of copies of [every book and newspaper printed in India and for the registration of such books and newspapers].

It is hereby enacted as follows:

## PART I

## PRELIMINARY

**1. Interpretation-clause:** [(1)] In this Act, unless there shall be something repugnant in the subject or context,

"Book" includes every volume, part or division of a volume, and pamphlet, in any language, and every sheet of music, map, chart or plan separately printed.

"editor" means the person who controls the selection of the matter that is published in a newspaper;

"Magistrate" means any person exercising the full powers of a' Magistrate, and includes a' "Magistrate of police";

"newspaper" means any printed periodical work containing public news or comments on public news

"paper" means any document, including a newspaper, other than a book;

"prescribed" means prescribed by rules made by the Central Government under section 20A;

"Press Registrar" means the Registrar of newspapers for India appointed by the Central Government under section 19A and includes any other person appointed by the Central Government to perform all or any of the functions of the Press Registrar;

"printing" includes cyclostyling and printing by lithography;

"Register" means the Register of newspapers maintained under section 9B.l

'[(2) Any reference in this Act to any law which is not in force in the State of Jammu and Kashmir shall, in relation to that State, be construed as a reference to the corresponding law in force in that State.]

## COMMENTS

(*i*) Where a person does not fulfil the conditions of 'Editor' as provided in section 1 and does **not** perform the functions of an editor whatever may be his description or designation, the provisions to the Act would have no application; *Haji C.H. Mohammad Koya* v. *T.K. S.M.A. Muthukoya,* AIR 1979 SC 154.

(*ii*) Pamphlets giving predictions of lucky figures, numbers or dates and only stray news items cannot be considered as a newspaper; *Commissioner of Sales Tax v. Express Printing Press,* AIR 1983 Bom 190: 1983 Tax LR 2871 (FB).

**2. Repeal of Act 11 of 1835:** [*Rep. by the Repealing Act, 1870 (14 of 1870), sec. I and Sch., Pt. II.]*

## PART II

## OF PRINTING PRESSES AND NEWSPAPERS

**3. Particulars to be printed on books and papers:** Every book or paper printed within [2][India] shall have printed legibly on it the name of the printer and the place of printing, and (if the book or paper be published) [the name] of the publisher, and the place of publication.

**4. Keeper of printing** press to **make declaration:** [(1)] No person shall within [2][India], keep in his possession any press for the printing of books or papers, who shall not have made and subscribed the following declaration before "[the District, Presidency or Sub-divisional Magistrate] within whose local jurisdiction such press may be:

"1, A. B., declare that I have a press for printing at –".

And this last blank shall be filled up with a true and precise description of the place where such press may be situate.

"[(2)] As often as the place where a press is kept is changed, a new declaration shall be necessary.

Provided that where the change is for a period not exceeding sixty days and the place where the press is kept after the change is within the local jurisdiction of the Magistrate referred to in sub-section (1), no new declaration shall be necessary if.

(*a*) a statement relating to the change is furnished to the said Magistrate within twenty-four hours thereof; and

(*b*) the keeper of the press continues to be the same.]

5. **Rules as to publication of newspapers:** No '[newspaper] shall be published in India], except in conformity with the rules hereinafter laid down:

[(I) Without prejudice to the provisions of section 3, every copy of every such newspaper shall contain the names of the owner and editor thereof printed clearly on such copy and also the date of its publication.]

[(2)] The printer and the publisher of every such '[newspaper] shall appear '[in person or by agent authorised in this behalf in accordance with rules made under section 20, before a District, Presidency or Sub-divisional Magistrate within whose local jurisdiction such newspaper shall be printed or published and shall make and subscribe, in duplicate, the following declaration:

"1 A.B., declare that 1 am the printer *(or* publisher, *or* printer and publisher) of the '[newspaper] entitled—"[and to be printed or published, or to be printed and published], as *the case may be* at".

And the last blank in this form of declaration shall be filled up with a true and precise account of the premises where the printing or publication is conducted.

[(2A) Every declaration under rule (2) shall specify the title of the newspaper, the language in which it is to be published and the periodicity of its publication and shall contain such other particulars as may be prescribed.]

[(2B) Where the printer or publisher of a newspaper making a declaration under rule (2) is not the owner thereof, the declaration shall specify the name of the owner and shall also be accompanied by an authority in writing from the owner authorising such person to make and subscribe such declaration.

(2C) A declaration in respect of a newspaper made under rule (2) and authenticated under section 6 shall be necessary before the newspaper can be published.

(2D) Where the title of any newspaper or its language or the periodicity of its publication is changed, the declaration shall cease to have effect and a new declaration shall be necessary before the publication of the newspaper can be continued.

(2E) As often as the ownership of a newspaper is changed, a new declaration shall be necessary.]

[(3)] As often as the place of printing or publication is changed, a new declaration shall be necessary:

[Provided that where the change is for a period not exceeding thirty days and the place of printing or publication after the change is within the local jurisdiction of the Magistrate referred to in rule (2), no new declaration shall be necessary if.

(*a*) a statement relating to the change is furnished to the said Magistrate within twenty-four hours thereof; and

(*b*) the printer or publisher or the printer and publisher of the newspaper continues to be the same.]

[(4)] As often as the printer or the publisher who shall have made such declaration as is aforesaid shall leave India for a period exceeding ninety days or where such printer or publisher is by infirmity or otherwise rendered incapable of carrying out his duties for a period exceeding ninety days in circumstances not involving the vacation of his appointment, a new declaration shall be necessary.]

[(5) Every declaration made in respect of a newspaper shall be void, where the newspaper .does not commence publication

(*a*) within six weeks "[of the authentication of the declaration under section 6], in the case of a newspaper to be published once a week or oftener; and

(*b*) within three months "[of the authentication of the declaration under section 6], in the case of any other newspaper, and in every such case, a new declaration shall be necessary before the newspaper can be published.

(6) Where, in any period of three months, any daily, in-weekly, bi-weekly, weekly or fortnightly newspaper publishes issues the number of which is less than half of what should have been published in accordance with the declaration made in respect thereof, the declaration shall cease to have effect and a new declaration shall be necessary before the publication of the newspaper can be continued.

(7) Where any other newspaper has ceased publication for a period, exceeding twelve months, every declaration made in respect thereof shall cease to have effect, and a new declaration shall be necessary before the newspaper can be re-published.

(8) Every existing .declaration in respect of a newspaper shall be cancelled by the "Magistrate before whom a new declaration is made and subscribed in respect of the same:]

[Provided that no person "(who does not ordinarily reside in India, or] who has not attained majority in accordance with the provisions of the Indian Majority Act, 1875 (9 of 1875). or of the taw to which he is subject in respect of the attainment of" majority, shall be permitted to make the declaration prescribed by this section, nor shall any such person edit a newspaper.]

[5A. **Keepers of printing presses and printers** and publishers of **newspapers in Jammu and Kashmir to make and subscribe fresh declarations within specified period:** (1) No person who has made and subscribed a declaration in respect of any press under section 4 of the Jammu and Kashmir State Press and Publications Act, S. 1989 (Jammu and Kashmir Act, No. lot S. 1989) shall keep the press in his possession for the printing of books or papers [after the 31 st day of December, 1968, un less before the expiry of that date) lie makes and subscribes a fresh declaration in respect of that press under section 4 of this Act.

(2) Every person who has subscribed to any declaration in respect of a newspaper under section 5 of the Jammu and Kashmir State Press and Publications Act, S. 1989 (Jammu and Kashmir Act, No. 1 of S. 1989) shall cease to be the editor, printer or publisher of the newspaper mentioned in such declaration "[after the 31st day of December, 1968 unless before the expiry of that date] he makes and subscribes a fresh declaration in respect of that newspaper under rule (2) of the rules laid down in section 5 of this Act.]

6. **Authentication of declaration:** Each of the two originals of every declaration so made and subscribed as is aforesaid, shall be authenticated by the signature and official seal of the Magistrate before whom the said declaration shall have been made:

[Provided that where any declaration is made and subscribed under section 5 in respect of a newspaper, the declaration shall not, save in the case of newspapers owned by the same person, be so authenticated unless the Magistrate '[is, on inquiry from the Press Registrar, satisfied] that the newspaper proposed to be published does not bear a title which is the same as, or similar to, that of any other newspaper published either in the same language or in the same State.]

**Deposit:** One of the said originals shall be deposited among the records of the office of the Magistrate, and the other shall be deposited among the records of the High Court of Judicature, or '[other principal Civil Court of original jurisdiction for the place where] the said declaration shall have been made.

**Inspection and supply of copies:** The Officer-in -charge of each original shall allow any person to inspect that original on payment of a fee of one rupee, and shall give to any person applying a copy of the said declaration, attested by the seal of the Court which has the custody of the original, on payment of a fee of two rupees.

[A copy of the declaration attested by the official seal of the Magistrate, or a copy or the order refusing to authenticate the declaration, shall be forwarded as soon as possible to the person making and subscribing the declaration and also to the Press Registrar.]

7. **Office copy of declaration to be prima *facie, evidence*** : In any legal proceeding whatever, as well civil as criminal, the production of a copy of such declaration as is aforesaid, attested by the seal of some Court empowered by this Act to have the custody of such declarations, '[or, in the case of the editor, a copy of the newspaper containing his name printed on it as that of the editor] shall be held

(unless the contrary be proved) to be sufficient evidence, as against the person whose name shall be subscribed to such declaration, '[or printed on such newspaper, as the case may be] that the said person was printer or publisher, or printer and publisher (according as the words of the said declaration may be) of every portion of every '[newspaper] whereof the title shall correspond with the title of the '[newspaper] mentioned in the declaration, '[or the editor of every portion of that issue of the newspaper of which a copy is produced].

**8. New declaration by persons who have signed a declaration and subsequently ceased to be printers or publishers:** If any person has subscribed to any declaration in respect of a newspaper under section 5 and the declaration has been authenticated by a Magistrate under section 6 and subsequently that person ceases to be the printer or publisher of the newspaper mentioned in such declaration, he shall appear before any District, Presidency or Sub-divisional Magistrate, and make and subscribe in duplicate the following declaration:

"I, A. B., declare that I have ceased to be the printer or publisher or printer and publisher of the newspaper entitled".]

**Authentication and filing:** Each original of the latter declaration shall be authenticated by the signature and seal of the Magistrate before whom the said latter declaration shall have been made, and one original of the said latter declaration shall be filed along with each original of the former declaration.

**Inspection and supply of copies:** The Officer-in-charge of each original of the latter allow any person applying to inspect that original on payment of a fee of one rupee, and shall give to any person applying a copy of the said latter declaration, attested by the seal of the Court having custody of the original, on payment of a fee of two rupees.

**Putting copy in evidence:** In all trials in which a copy, attested as is aforesaid, of the former declaration shall have been put in evidence, it shall be lawful to put in evidence a copy, attested as is aforesaid, of the latter declaration, and the former declaration shall not be taken to be evidence that the declarant was, at any period subsequent to the date of the latter declaration, printer or publisher of the '[newspaper] therein mentioned.

[A copy of the latter declaration attested by the official seal of the Magistrate shall be forwarded to the Press Registrar.]

**[8A. Person whose name has been incorrectly published as editor may make a declaration before a Magistrate:** If any person, whose name has appeared as editor on a copy of a newspaper, claims that he was not the editor of the issue on which his name has so appeared, he may, within two weeks of his becoming aware that his name has been so published, appear before a District, Presidency or Sub-

Divisional Magistrate and make a declaration that his name was incorrectly published in that issue as that of the editor thereof, and if the Magistrate after making such inquiry or causing such inquiry to be made as he may consider necessary is satisfied that such declaration is true, he shall certify accordingly, and on that certificate being given the provisions of section 7 shall not apply to that person in respect of that issue of the newspaper.

The Magistrate may extend the period allowed by this section in any case where he is satisfied that such person was prevented by sufficient cause from appearing and making the declaration within that period.]

## COMMENTS

When a person's name is printed in the newspaper as its editor, then rebuttable presumption under section 7 can be drawn only against such editor, but when a person is not shown in the paper to be its editor no presumption under section 7 can be drawn and it must be held that he has no concern with the publishing; *Haji C.H. Mohammad Koya v. T.K.S.M.A. Muthukoya,* AIR 1979 SC 154.

[**8B. Cancellation of declaration:** If, on an application made to him by the Press Registrar or any other person or otherwise, the Magistrate empowered to authenticate a declaration under this Act, is of opinion that any declaration made in respect of a newspaper should be cancelled, he may, after giving the person concerned an opportunity of showing cause against the action proposed to be taken, hold an inquiry into the matter and if, after considering the cause, if any, shown by such person and after giving him an opportunity of being heard, he is satisfied that:

(*i*) the newspaper, in respect of which the declaration has been made is being published in contravention of the provisions of this Act or rules made thereunder; or

(*ii*) the newspaper mentioned in the declaration bears a title which is the same as, or similar to, that of any other newspaper published either in the same language or in the same State; or

(*iii*) the printer or publisher has ceased to be the printer or publisher of the newspaper mentioned in such declaration; or

(*iv*) the declaration was made on false representation or on the concealment of any material fact or in respect of a periodical work which is not a newspaper;

the Magistrate may, by order, cancel the declaration and shall forward as soon as possible a copy of the order to the person making or subscribing the declaration and also to the Press Registrar.

**8C. Appeal:** (1) Any person aggrieved by an order of a Magistrate refusing to authenticate a declaration under section 6 or cancelling a declaration under section 8B may, within sixty days from the date on which such order is communicated to him, prefer an appeal to the Appellate Board to be called the Press and Registration Appellate Board [consisting of a Chairman and another member to be nominated by the Press Council of India, established under section 4 of the Press Council Act, 1978 (37 of 1978), from among its members];

Provided that the Appellate Board may entertain an appeal after the expiry of the said period, if it is satisfied that the appellant was prevented by sufficient cause from preferring the appeal in time.

(2) On receipt of an appeal under this section, the Appellate Board may, after calling for the records from the Magistrate and after making such further inquiries as it thinks fit, confirm, modify or set aside the order appealed against.

(3) Subject to the provisions contained in sub-section (2), the Appellate Board may, by order, regulate its practice and procedure.

(4) The decision of the Appellate Board shall be final.]

## PART III

## DELIVERY OF BOOKS

**9. Copies of books printed after commencement of Act to be delivered gratis to Government:** Printed copies of the whole of every book which shall be printed in India after this Act shall come into force, together with all maps, prints or other engravings belonging thereto, finished and coloured in the same manner as the best copies of the same, shall, notwithstanding any agreement (if the book be published) between the printer and publisher thereof, be delivered by the printer at such place and to such officer as the State Government shall, by notification in the Official Gazette, from time to time direct, and free of expense to the Government, as follows, that is to say:

(*a*) in any case, within one calender month after the day on which any such book shall first be delivered out of the press, one such copy, and

(*b*) if within one calender year from such day the State Government shall require the printer to deliver other such copies not exceeding two in number, then within one calender month after the day on which any such requisition shall be made by the State Government on the printer, another such copy, or two other such copies, as the State Government may direct, the copies so delivered being bound, sewed or stitched together and upon the best paper on which any copies of the book shall be printed.

The publisher or other person employing the printer shall, a; a reasonable time before the expiration of the said month, supply him with all maps, prints and engravings finished and coloured as aforesaid, which may be necessary to enable him to comply with the requirements aforesaid.

Nothing in the former part of this section shall apply to:

(*i*) any second or subsequent edition of a book in which edition no additions or alterations either in the letter-press or in the maps, prints or other engravings belonging to the book have been made, and a copy of the first or some preceding edition of which book has been delivered under this Act, or

(*ii*) any '[newspaper] published in conformity with the rules laid down in section 5 of this Act.

**10. Receipt for copies delivered under section 9:** The officer to whom a copy of a book is delivered under the last foregoing section shall give to the printer a receipt in writing therefor.

**11. Disposal of copies delivered under section 9:** The copy delivered pursuant to clause (a) of the first paragraph of section 9 of this Act shall be disposed of as the State Government shall from time to time determine.

Any copy or copies delivered pursuant to clause (b) of the said paragraph shall be [transmitted to the Central Government].

[**11A. Copies of newspapers printed in India to be delivered *gratis* to Government:** The printer of every newspaper in '[India] shall deliver at such place and to such officer as the State Government may, by notification in the Official Gazette, direct, and free of expense to the Government, two copies of each issue of such newspaper as soon as it is published.]

[**11B. Copies of newspapers to be delivered to Press Registrar:** Subject to any rules that may be made under this Act, the publisher of every newspaper in India shall deliver free of expense to the Press Registrar one copy of each issue of such newspaper as soon as it is published.]

## PART IV

## PENALTIES

**12. Penalty for printing contrary to rule in section 3:** Whoever shall print or publish any book or paper otherwise than in conformity with the rule contained in Section 3 of this Act, shall, on conviction before a Magistrate, be punished by fine not exceeding [1][two thousand] rupees, or by simple imprisonment for a term not exceeding [2][six months], or by both.

**13. Penalty for keeping press without making declaration required by section 4:** Whoever shall keep in his possession any such press as aforesaid. In contravention of any of the provisions contained in section 4 of this Act], shall, on conviction before a Magistrate, be punished by fine not exceeding '[two thousand] rupees, or by simple imprisonment for a term not exceeding '[six months], or by both.

**14. Punishment for making false statement:** Any person who shall, in making any declaration or other statement] under the authority of this Act, make a statement which is false, and which he either knows or believes to be false, or does not believe to be true, shall, on conviction before a Magistrate, be punished by fine not exceeding '[two thousand] rupees, and imprisonment for a term not exceeding [2][six months].

**15. Penalty for printing or publishing newspaper without conforming to rules:** [(1)] Whoever shall [edit], print or publish any [newspaper], without conforming to the rules hereinbefore laid down, or whoever shall [edit], print or publish, or shall cause to be [edited], printed or published, any [newspaper], knowing that the said rules have not been observed with respect to [that newspaper], shall, on conviction before a Magistrate, be punished with fine not exceeding [two thousand] rupees, or imprisonment for a term not exceeding [2][six months] or both.

[(2) Where an offence is committed in relation to a newspaper under sub-section (1), the Magistrate may, in addition to the punishment imposed under the said sub-section, also cancel the declaration in respect of the newspaper.]

[**15A. Penalty for failure to make a declaration under section 8:** If any person who has ceased to be a printer or publisher of any newspaper fails or neglects to make a declaration in compliance with section 8, he shall, on conviction before a Magistrate, be punishable by fine not exceeding two hundred rupees.]

[**16. Penalty for not delivering books or not supplying printer with maps:** If any printer of any such book as is referred to in section 9 of this Act shall neglect to deliver copies of the same pursuant to that section, he shall for every such default forfeit to the Government such sum not exceeding fifty rupees as a Magistrate having jurisdiction in the place where the book was printed may, on the application of the officer to whom the copies should have been delivered or of any person authorised by that officer in this behalf, determine to be in the circumstances a reasonable penalty for the default, and, in addition to such sum, such further sum as the Magistrate may determine to be the value of the copies which the printer ought to have delivered.

1f any publisher or other person employing any such primer shall neglect to supply him, in the matter prescribed in the second paragraph of section 9 of this

Act with the maps, prints or engravings which may be necessary to enable him to comply with the provisions of that section, such publisher or other person shall for every such default forfeit to the Government such sum not exceeding fifty rupees as such a Magistrate as aforesaid may, on such an application as aforesaid, determine to be in the circumstances a reasonable penalty for the default, and, in addition to such sum, such further sum as the Magistrate may determine to be the value of the maps, prints or engravings which such publisher or other person ought to have supplied.]

[16A. **Penalty for failure to supply copies of newspapers *gratis* to Government:** If any printer of any newspaper published in ^India] neglects to deliver copies of the same in compliance with section 11A, he shall, on the complaint of the officer to whom copies should have been delivered or of any person authorised by that officer in this behalf, be punishable, on conviction by a Magistrate having jurisdiction in the place where the newspaper was printed, with fine which may extend to fifty rupees for every default.]

[16B. **Penalty for failure to supply copies of newspapers to Press Registrar:** If any publisher of any newspaper published in India neglects to deliver copies of the same in compliance with section 11B, he shall, on the complaint of the Press Registrar, be punishable, on conviction by a Magistrate having jurisdiction in the place where the newspaper was printed, by fine which may extend to fifty rupees for every default.]

17. **Recovery of forfeitures and disposal thereof and of fines:** Any sum forfeited to the Government under '[section 16] may be recovered, under the warrant of the Magistrate determining the sum, or of his successor in office, in the manner authorised by the '[Code of Criminal Procedure (10 of 1882) for the time being in force, and within the period prescribed by the Indian Penal Code (45 of 1860), for the levy of a fine.

## PART I

## REGISTRATION OF BOOKS

**18. Registration of memoranda of books** : There shall be kept at such office, and by such officer as the State .Government shall appoint in this behalf, a book 10 be called a Catalogue of Books printed in [India], wherein shall be registered a memorandum of every book which shall have been delivered [pursuant to clause (a) of the first paragraph of section 9] of this Act. Such memorandum shall (so far as may be practicable) contain the following particulars (that is to say):

1. the title of the book and the contents of the title-page, with a translation

into English of such title and contents, when the same are not in the English language:

2. the language in which the book is written;
3. the name of the author, translator, or editor of the book or any part thereof:
4. the subject;
5. the place of printing and the place of publication;
6. the name of firm of the printer and the name of firm of the publisher;
7. the date of issue from the press or of the publication;
8. the number of sheets, leaves or pages;
9. the size;
10. the first, second or other number of the edition;
11. the number of copies of which the edition consists;
12. whether the book is printed, [cyclostyled or lithographed];
13. the price at which the book is sold to the public; and
14. the name and residence of the proprietor of the copyright or of any portion of such copyright.

Such memorandum shall be made and registered in the case of each book as soon as practicable after the delivery of the [copy thereof pursuant to clause (a) of the first paragraph of section 9]

**19. Publication of memoranda registered:** The memoranda registered during each quarter in the said Catalogue shall be published in the Official Gazette, as soon as may be after the end of such quarter, and a copy of the memoranda so published shall be sent to the Central Government.

## PART VA

## REGISTRATION OF NEWSPAPERS

**19A. Appointment of Press Registrar and other officers:** The Central Government may appoint a Registrar of newspapers for India and such other officers under the general suprintendence and control of the Press Registrar as may be necessary for the purpose of performing the functions assigned to them by or under this Act, and may, by general or special order, provide for the distribution or allocation of functions to be performed by them under this Act.

**19B. Register of newspapers:** (1) The Press Registrar shall maintain in the prescribed manner a Register of newspapers.

(2) The Register shall, as far as may be practicable, contain the following-particulars about every newspaper published in India, namely :

(*a*) the title of the newspaper;

(*b*) the language in which the newspaper is published;
(*c*) periodicity of the publication of the newspaper;
(*d*) the name of the editor, printer and publisher of the newspaper;
(*e*) the place of printing and publication;
(*f*) the average number of pages per week;
(*g*) the number of days of publication in the year;
(*h*) the average number of copies printed, the average number of copies sold to the public and the average number of copies distributed free to the public, the average being calculated with reference to such period as may be prescribed;
(*i*) retail selling price per copy;
(*j*) the names and addresses of the owners of the newspaper and such other particulars relating to ownership as may be prescribed;
(*k*) any other particulars which may be prescribed.

(3) On receiving information from time to time about the aforesaid particulars, the Press Registrar shall cause relevant entries to be made in the Register and may make such necessary alterations or corrections therein as may be required for keeping the Register up-to-date.

**19C. Certificates of registration:** On receiving from the Magistrate under section .6 a copy of the declaration in respect of a newspaper [2][and on the publication of such newspaper, the Press Registrar shall], as soon as practicable thereafter, issue a certificate of registration in respect of that newspaper to the publisher thereof.

**19D. Annual statement, *etc.*, to be furnished by newspapers:** It shall be the duty of the publisher of every newspaper :

(*a*) To furnish to the Press Registrar an annual statement in respect of the newspaper at such time and containing such of the. particulars referred to in sub-section (2) of section 19B as may be prescribed;
(*b*) to publish in the newspaper at such times and such of the particulars relating to the newspaper referred to in sub-section (2) of section 19B as may be specified in this behalf by the Press Registrar. The clause has been omitted by Act 26 of 1960.

**19E. Returns and reports to be furnished by newspapers:** The publisher of every newspaper shall furnish to the Press Registrar such returns, statistics and other information with respect to any of the particulars referred to in sub-section / Registrar may from time to time require.

**19F. Right of access to records and documents:** The Press Registrar or any gazetted officer authorised by him in writing in this behalf shall, for the purpose of the collection of any information relating to a newspaper under this Act, have access to any relevant record or document relating to the newspaper in the possession of the publisher thereof, and may enter at any reasonable time any premises where he believes such record or document to be and may inspect or take copies of the relevant records or documents or ask any question necessary for obtaining any information required to be furnished under this Act.

**19G. Annual report:** The Press Registrar shall prepare, in such form and at such time each year as may be prescribed, an annual report containing a summary of the information obtained by him during the previous year in respect of the newspapers in India and giving an account of the working of such newspapers, and copies thereof shall be forwarded to the Central Government.

**19H. Furnishing of copies of extracts from Register:** On the application of any person for the supply of the copy of any extract from the Register and on payment of such fee as may be prescribed, the Press Registrar shall furnish such copy to the applicant in such form and manner as may be prescribed.

**19I. Delegation of powers:** Subject to the provisions of this Act and regulations made thereunder, the Press Registrar may delegate all or any of his powers under this Act to any officer subordinate to him.

**19J. Press Registrar and other officers to be public servants:** The Press Registrar and all officers appointed under this Act shall be deemed to be public servants within the meaning of section 21 of the Indian Penal Code (45 of 1860).

**19K. Penalty for contravention of section 19D or section 19E, *etc*:** If the publisher of any newspaper:

(*a*) refuses or neglects to comply with the provisions of section 19D or section 19E; or

(*c*) publishers in the newspaper in pursuance of clause (*b*) of section 19D any particulars relating to the newspaper which he has reason to believe to be false, he shall be punishable with fine which may extend to five hundred rupees.

**19L. Penalty for improper disclosure of information:** If any person engaged in connection with the collection of information under this Act wilfully discloses any information or the contents of any return given or furnished under this Act otherwise than in the execution of his duties under this Act or for the purposes of the prosecution of an offence under this Act or under the Indian Penal Code (45 of 1860), he shall be punishable with imprisonment for a term which may extend to six months, or with fine which may extend to one thousand rupees, or with both.]

## PART VI

## MISCELLANEOUS

**20. Power of State Government to make rules:** (1) The State Government may. by notification in The Official Gazette, make such rules (not inconsistent with the rules made by the Central Government under section 20A) as may be necessary or desirable for carrying out the objects of this Act.

(2) Every rule made by the State Government under this section shall be laid, as soon as may be after it is made, before the State Legislature.]

**20A. Power of Central Government to make rules:** (1) The Central Government may, by notification in the Official Gazette, make rules :

(*a*) prescribing the particulars which a declaration made and subscribed under section 5 may contain; and the form and manner in which the names of the printer, publisher, owner and editor of a newspaper and the place of its printing and publication may be printed on every copy of such newspaper];

(b) prescribing the manner in which copies of any declaration attested by the official seal of a Magistrate or copies of any order refusing to authenticate any declaration may be forwarded to the person making and subscribing the declaration and to the Press Registrar;

(c) prescribing the manner in which copies of any newspaper may be sent to the Press Registrar under section 11B;

(*d*) prescribing the manner in which a Register may be maintained under section 19B and the particulars which it may contain;

(*e*) prescribing the particulars in which an annual statement to be furnished by the publisher of a newspaper to the Press Registrar may contain;

(*f*) prescribing the form and manner in which an annual statement under clause (a) of section 19D, or any returns, statistics or other information under section 19E, may be furnished to the Press Registrar;

(*g*) prescribing the fees for furnishing copies of extracts from the Register and the manner in which such copies may be furnished;

(*h*) prescribing the manner in which a certificate of registration may be issued in respect of a newspaper;

(*i*) prescribing the form in which, and the time within which, annual reports may be prepared by the Press Registrar and forwarded to the Central Government.

[(2) Every rule made under this section shall be laid as soon as maybe alter it is made, before each House of Parliament, while it is in session, for a tola! period of thirty days which may be comprised in one session or in two or more successive sessions and if, before (lie expiry of the session immediately following the session or the successive sessions aforesaid] both houses agree in making any modification in the rule or both Houses agree that the rule should not be made, the rule shall thereafter have effect only in such modified form or of no effect, as the case may be so however, that any such inodification or annulment shall be without prejudice to the validity of any thing previously done under that rule,]

**2OB. Rules made umler this Act may provide that contravention there of shall be punishable:** Any rule made under any provision of this Act may provide that any contravention thereof shall be punishable with fine which may extend to one hundred rupees.]

**21. Power to exclude any class of books from operation of Act:** [The State Government may, by notification in the Official Gazette], exclude any class of books 'for papers] from the operation of the whole or any part or parts of this Act:

[Provided that no such notification in respect of any class of newspapers shall be issued without consulting the Central Government.]

[**22. Extent :** This Act extends to the whole of India.]

**23. Commencement of Act:** *[Rep. by the Repealing Act, 1870(14 of 1870). sec. I and Sch., Pt. II] [2nd April, 1923.*

# 6

# Official Secrets Act, 1923

The Official Secrets Act, 1923 is a comprehensive Act aimed against leakage of secret information, sabotage and like, it has broadly two parts, one relating to spying for the enemy, and the other to unauthorized communication of any other secret official code or passwords, or any sketch, plan, model, note, document or information.

The provision of Section 5 of the Act are more important from the stand point of the freedom of the press. The section contains 'wrongful communication, etc of information'.

"If any person having the possession or control of any secret official code or pass–word or any sketch, plan model article, note, document of information, which relates to or is used in a prohibited place or relates to anything in such a place, which is likely to assist directly or indirectly, an enemy of which relates to matter the disclosure of which, is likely to affect the sovereignty or integrity of India, the security of the State, or friendly relation with foreign state... (he) shall be guilty of an offence under this section."

If any other above document received, is communicated in contravention of this Act he shall be guilty of an offence under this section.

If any person having in his possession any of these documents communicates it to any foreign power, he shall be guilty of an offence under this Section.

A person guilty of an offence under this section shall be punishable with imprisonment for a term, which may extend to three year, or with fine, or with both.

The provisions of section 5 are more important for media persons. The Government has an internal system of dividing its documents into 'classified' and 'non–classified' categories. The classified documents are then marked as "Top–Secret", "Secret" and "Confidential," Not only the classified documents related to areas like defence and security of her country, but the publication or communication of any information, which may be directly or indirectly, useful to enemy, is also prohibited under the provisions of the Official Secrets Act.

In the case of the New York Times Vs United States of America in 1971, the US Supreme Court refused to issue an injunction for restraining publication of the pentagon papers relating to the US foreign policy on the Vietnam war. The Supreme Court held that the court can issue an injunction only when the publication of a matter will inevitably directly and immediately, imperil the safety of the nation. The Court decided that no injunction could be imposed upon press freedom on the basis of surmises or conjectures that word untoward consequences might result.

In India the Act prohibits free reporting and that too without defining the term 'official secret'. So any official information which has been deemed by the authorities as secret can be published only at the peril of punishment. It prescribes a punishment with imprisonment extending to five years or fine or both for a person who receives or communicates any official secret.

The law does not provide any primacy to public interest over authorities' discretion and opinion. No such information can be published in public interest which, in the opinion of the authorities should not be revealed. So the provision of law cast a chilling effect on the mind of media person while reporting about a official information. However, under this Act, not many prosecutions have been launched against newsmen and newspapers.

It has been widely demanded at various forums that section 5 of he Official Secrets Act, which inhibits free reporting, should be done away with. The Second press Commission had recommended a bill providing right to information to the people in 1990. The press Council of India prepared a draft of the bill for "the Right to Information and submitted to the Government in 1996. The Right to Information Bill was placed before the parliament in 2000 and was passed on December 16,2002. The Council had asked for he repeal of the Official Secrets Act, 1923 in toto; Exception or permissible restriction to the freedom of the press may be specified in the proposed the Right of Information Act".

In order to remove and keeping in view the shortcomings of previous Acts, the Government passed the Right to Information Act, 2005. The most distinctive feature of the Act, is that there is provision of an independent, quasi judicial and multi member body to adjudicate any dispute arising out of non supply of information by Government and public authorities, asked for by any people. There is also provision to penalize Government authority ink case of undue or non–supply of information to the people . The other distinctive provisions in the Act is that no such information which cannot be denied to parliament or State Assemblies, can be denied to the people .

After coming into effect, the Right to Information Act, 2005, much of the objectionable provisions of the Official Secrets Act, 1923 have gone and the Act of 1923 has virtually become obsolete.

## THE OFFICIAL SECRETS ACTS, 1923

### (19 of 1923)

[*2nd April, 1923*]

*An Act to consolidate and amend the law relating to official secrets.*

Whereas it is expedient that the law relating to official secrets should be consolidated and amended;

It is hereby enacted as follows :

**1. Short title, extent and application:** (1) This Act may be called the Official Secrets Act, 1923.

(2) It extends to the whole of India and applies also to servants of the Government and to citizens of India outside India.

**2. Definitions:** In this Act unless there is anything repugnant in the subject on context,

(1) any reference to a place belonging to Government includes a place occupied by any department of the Government, whether the place is or is not actually vested in Government;

(2) expressions referring to communicating or receiving include any communicating or receiving, whether in whole or in part, and whether the sketch, plan, model, article, note, document, or information itself, or the substance, effect or description thereof only be communicated or received; expressions referring to obtaining or retaining any sketch, plan, model, article, note or document, include the copying or causing to be copied of the whole or any part of any sketch, plan, model, article, note or document; and expressions referring to the communication of any sketch, plan, model, article, note or document include the transfer or transmission of the sketch, plan, model article, note or document;

(3) "document" includes part of a document;

(4) "model" includes design, pattern and specimen:

(5) "munitions of war" includes the whole or any part of any ship, submarine, aircraft. tank or similar engine, arms and ammunition, torpedo, or mine intended or adopted for use in war, and any other article, material or device, whether actual or proposed, intended for such use;

(6) "Office under Government" includes any office or employment in or under any department of the Government;

(7) "photograph" include an undeveloped film or plate;

(8) "prohibited place" means:

(*a*) any work of defence, arsenal, naval, military or air force establishment or station, mine, minefield, camp, ship or aircraft belonging to, or occupied by or on behalf of Government, any military telegraph or telephone so belonging or occupied, any wireless or signal station or office so belonging occupied and any factory, dockyard or other place so belonging or occupied and used for the purpose of building, repairing, making or storing any munitions of war, or any sketches, plants, models or documents relating there to, or for the purpose of getting any metals, oil or minerals of use in time of war;

(*b*) any place not belonging to Government where any munitions of war or any sketches, models, plans or documents relating thereto, are being made, repaired, gotten or stored under contract with, or with any person on behalf, of Government, or otherwise on behalf of Government;

(*c*) any place belonging to or used for the purpose of Government which is for the time being declared by the Central Government, by notification in the Official Gazette, to be a prohibited place for the purposes of this Act on the ground that information with respect thereto, or damage thereto, would be useful to an enemy, and to which a copy of .the notification in respect thereof has been affixed in English and in the vernacular of the locality;

(*d*) any railway, road, way or channel, or other means of communication by land or water (including any works or structures being part thereof or connected therewith) or any place used for gas, water or electricity works or other works for purposes of a public character, or any place where any munitions of war or any sketches, models, plans or documents relating thereto, are being made, repaired, or stored otherwise than on behalf of Government, which is for the time being declared by the Central Government, by notification in the Official Gazette, to be a prohibited place for the purposes of this Act on the ground that information with respect thereto, or the destruction or obstruction thereof, or interference therewith, would be useful to an enemy, and to which a copy of the notification in respect thereof has been affixed in English and in the vernacular of the locality;

(9) "sketch" includes any photograph or other mode of representing any place or thing; and

(10) "Superintendent of Police" includes any police officer of a like or superior rank, and any person upon whom the powers of a Superintendent of Police are for the purposes of this Act conferred by the Central Government.

**3. Penalties for spying:** (1) If any person for any purpose prejudicial to the safety or interests of the State:

(*a*) approaches, inspects, passes over or is in the vicinity of, or enters, any prohibited place; or

(*b*) makes any sketch, plan, model, or note which is calculated to be or might be or is intended to be, directly or indirectly, useful to an enemy; or

(*c*) obtains, collects, records or publishes or communicates to any other person any secret official code or pass word, or any sketch, plan, model, article or note or other document or information which in calculated to be or might be or is intended to be, directly or indirectly, useful to enemy or which relates to a matter the disclosure of which is likely to affect the sovereignty and integrity of India, the security of the State or friendly relations with foreign States,

he shall be punishable with imprisonment for a term which may extend, where the offence is committed in relation to any work of defence, arsenal, naval, military or air force establishment or station, mine, minefield, factory, dockyard, camp, ship or aircraft or otherwise in relation to the naval, military or air force affair of Government or in relation to any secret official code, to fourteen years and in other cases to three years.

(2) On a prosecution for an offence punishable under this section [...] it shall not be necessary to show that the accused person was guilty of any particular act tending to show a purpose prejudicial to the safety or interests of the State, and, notwithstanding that no such act is proved against him, he may be convicted if, from the circumstances of the case or his , conduct or his known character as proved, it appears that his purpose was a purpose prejudicial to the safety or interests of the State; and if any sketch, plan, model, article, note, document, or information relating to or used in any prohibited place, or relating to anything in such a place, or any secret official code or pass word is made, obtained, collected, recorded; published or communicated by any person other than a person acting under lawful authority and from the circumstances of the case or his conduct or his known character as proved it appears that his purpose was a purpose prejudicial to the safety or interests of the State, such sketch, plan, model, article, note, document, information, code or pass word shall be presumed to have been made, obtained, collected, recorded, published or communicated for a purpose prejudicial to the safety or interests of the State.

**4. Communications with foreign agents to be evidence of commission of certain offences:** (1) In any proceedings against a person for an offence under section 3, the fact that he has been in communication with, or attempted to communicate with, a foreign agent. whether within or without [India] shall be relevant for the purpose of proving that he has, for a purpose prejudicial to the safety or interests of the State, obtained or attempted to obtain information which is calculated to be or might be, or is intended to be, directly or indirectly, useful to an enemy.

(2) For the purpose of this section, but without prejudice to the generality of the foregoing provisions :

(*a*) a person may be presumed to havebeen in communication with a foreign agent if:

(*i*) he has, either within or without India visited the address of a foreign agent or consorted or associated with a foreign agent, : or

(*ii*) either within or without India, the name or address of, or any other information regarding, a foreign agent has been found in his possession, or has been obtained by him from any other person;

(*b*) the expression "foreign agent" includes any person who is or has been or in respect of whom it appears that there are reasonable grounds for suspecting him of being or having been employed by a foreign power, either directly or indirectly, for the purpose of committing an act, either within or without India, prejudicial to the safety or interests of the State, or who has or is reasonably suspected of having, either within or without India, committed, or attempted to commit such an act in the interests of a foreign power;

(c) any address, whether within or without India, in respect of which it appears that there are reasonable grounds for suspecting it of being an address used for the receipt of communications intended for a foreign agent, or any address at which a foreign agent resides, or to which he resorts for the purpose of giving or receiving communications, or at which he carries on any business, may be presumed to be the address of a foreign agent, and communications addressed to such an address to be communications with a foreign agent.

5. **Wrongful communication, *etc.*, of information:** (I) If any person having in his possession or control any secret official code or pass word or any sketch, plan, model, article, note document' information which relates to or is used in a prohibited place or relates to anything in such a place, or which is likely to assist, directly or indirectly, an enemy or which relates to a matter the disclosure of which is likely to affect the sovereignty and integrity of India, the security of the State or friendly relations with foreign States or which has been made or obtained in contravention of this Act, or which has been entrusted in confidence to him by any person holding office under Government, or which he has obtained or to which he has had access owing to his position as a person who holds or has held office under Government, or as a person who holds or has held a contract made on

behalf of Government, or as a person who is or has been, employed under a person who holds or has held such an office or contract:

(*a*) wilfully communicates the code or password, sketch, plan. model, article, note. document or information to any person other than a person to whom lie is authorised to communicate it or a court of Justice or a person to whom it is. in the interest of the State, his. duty to communicate it; or

(*b*) uses the information in his possession for the benefit of any foreign power or in any other manner prejudicial to the safety of the State; or

(*c*) retains the sketch, plan, model, article, note or document in his possession or control when he has no right to retain it. or when it is contrary to his duty to retain it, or wilfully fails **to** comply with all directions issued by lawful authority with regard to the return or disposal thereof: or

(*d*) fails to take reasonable care of, or so conducts himself as to endanger the safety of the sketch, plan, model, article, note, document, secret official code or pass word' or information,

He shall be guilty of an offence under this section.

(2) If any person voluntarily receives any secret official code or pass word or any sketch, plan, model, article, note, document or information knowing or having reasonable ground to believe, at the time when he receives it, that the code, pass word, sketch, plan, model, article, note, document or information is communicated in contravention of this Act, he shall be guilty of an offence under this section.

(3) If any person having in his possession or control any sketch, plan, model, article, note, document or information, which relates to munitions of war, communicates it, directly or indirectly, to any foreign power or in any other manner prejudicial to the safety or interests of the State, he shall be guilty of an offence under this section.

(4) A person guilty of an offence under this section shall be punishable with imprisonment for a term which may extend to three years, or with fine, or with both.

**6. Unauthorised use of uniforms, falsification of reports, forgery, personation and, false documents:** (1) If any person for the purpose of gaining admission or of assisting any other person to gain admission to a prohibited place or for any other purpose prejudicial fo the safety of the State:

(*a*) uses or wears, without lawful authority, any naval, military, air force, police or other official uniform, or any uniform so nearly resembling the same as to be calculated to deceive, or falsely represents himself to be a person who is or has been entitled to use or wear any such uniform; or (*b*) orally, or in writing in any declaration or application, or in any document signed by him or on his behalf, knowingly makes or connives at the making of any false statement or any omission; or

(*c*) forges, alters, or tampers with any passport or any naval, military, air force, police, or official pass, permit, certificate, licence, or other document of a similar character (hereinafter in this section referred to as an official document) or knowingly uses or has in his possession any such forged, altered, or irregular official document; or

(*d*) personates, or falsely represents himself to be, a person holding, or in the employment of a person holding, office under Government, or to be or not to be a person to whom an official document or secret official code or pass word has been duly issued or communicated, or with intent to obtain an official document, secret official code or pass word, whether for himself or any other person, knowingly makes any false statement; or

(*e*) uses, or has in his possession or under his control, without the authority of the department of the Government or the authority concerned, any die, seal or stamp of or belonging to, or used, made or provided by any department of the Government, or by any diplomatic, naval, military, or air force authority appointed by or acting under the authority of Government, or any die, seal or stamp so nearly resembling any such die seal or stamp as to be calculated to deceive, or counterfeits any such die, seal or stamp, or knowingly uses, or has in his possession or under his control, any such counterfeited die, seal or stamp, he shall be guilty of an offence this section.

(2) If any person for any purpose prejudicial to the safety of the State:

(*a*) retains any official document, whether or not completed or issued for use, when he has no right to retain it, or when it is contrary to his duty to retain it, or wilfully fails : to comply with any directions issued by any department of the Government or any person authorised by such department with regard to the return or disposal thereof; or

(*b*) allows any other person to have possession of any official document issued for his use alone, or communicates any secret official code or pass word so issued, for, without lawful authority or excuse, has in his possession any official document or secret official code or pass word issued for the use of some person other than himself, or, on obtaining possession of any official document by finding or otherwise, wilfully fails to restore it to the person or authority by whom or for whose use it was issued, or to a police officer; or

(*c*) without lawful authority or excuse, manufactures or sells, or has in his possession for sale, any such die, seal or stamp as aforesaid, he shall be guilty of an offence under this section.

(3) A person guilty of an offence under this section shall be punishable with imprisonment for a term which may extend to three years, or with fine, or with both.

(4) The provisions of sub-section (2) of section 3 shall apply, for the purpose of proving a purpose prejudicial to the safety of the State, to any prosecution for an offence under this section relating to the naval, military or air force affairs of Government, or to any secret official code in like manner as they apply, for the purpose of proving a purpose prejudicial to the safety or interests of the State, to prosecutions for offences punishable under that section.

**7. Interfering with officers of the police or members of the Armed Forces of the Union:** (1) No person in the vicinity of any prohibited place shall obstruct, knowingly mislead or otherwise interfere with or impede, any police officer, or any member of the Armed Forces of the Union engaged on guard, sentry, patrol or other similar duty in relation to the prohibited place.

(2) If any person acts in contravention of the provisions of this section, he shall be punishable with imprisonment which may extend to three years, or with fine. or with both.

**8. Duty of giving information as to commission of offences:** (1) It shall be the duty of every person to give on demand to a Superintendent of Police, or the police officer not below the rank of inspector, empowered by an Inspector-General or Commissioner of Police in this behalf, or to any member of the Armed Forces of the Union engaged on guard, sentry, patrol or other similar duty, any information in his power relating to an offence or suspected offence, under section 3 or under section 3 read with section 9 and, if so required, and upon tender of his reasonable expenses, to at such reasonable time 'and place as may be specified for the purpose of furnishing such information.

(2) If any person fails to give any such information or to attend as aforesaid, he shall be punishable with imprisonment which may extend to three years or with fine, or with both.

**9. Attempts, incitements, *etc.*:** Any person who attempts to commit or abets the commission of an offence under this Act shall be punishable with the same punishment, and be liable to be proceeded against in the same manner as if he had committed such offence.

**10. Penalty for harbouring spies:** (1) If any person knowingly harbours any person who he knows or has reasonable grounds for supposing to be a person who is about to commit or who has committed an offence under section 3 or under section 3 read with section 9 knowingly permits to meet or assemble in any premises in his occupation or under his control any such persons, he shall be guilty of an offence under this section.

(2) It shall be the duty of every person having harboured any such person as aforesaid, or permitted to meet or assemble in any premises in his occupation or under his control any such persons as aforesaid, to give on demand to a Superintendent of Police or other police officer not below the rank of Inspector empowered by an Inspector-General or Commissioner of Police in this behalf, any information in his power relating to any such person or persons, and if any person fails to give any such information, he shall be guilty of an offence under this section.

(3) A person guilty of an offence under this section shall be punishable with imprisonment for a term which may extend to three years, or with fine, or with both.

**11. Search-warrants:** (1) If a Presidency Magistrate, Magistrate of the first class or Sub-divisional Magistrate is satisfied by information on oath that there is reasonable ground for suspecting that an offence under this Act has been or is about to be committed, he may grant a search-warrant authorising any police officer named therein, not being below the rank of an officer in charge of a police station, to enter at any time any premises or place named in the warrant, if necessary, by force, and to search the premises or place and every person found therein, and to seize any sketch, plan, model, article, note or document or anything of a like nature, or anything which is evidence of an offence under this Act having been or being about to be committed which he may find on the premises or place or any such person, and with regard to or in connection with which he has reasonable ground for suspecting that an offence under this Act has been or is about to be committed.

(2) Where it appears to a police officer, not being below the rank of Superintendent, that the case is one of great emergency, and that in the interests of the State immediate action is necessary, he may by a written order under his hand give to any police officer the like authority as may be given by the warrant of a Magistrate under this section.

(3) Where action has been taken by a police officer under sub-section (2) he shall, as soon as may be, report such action, in a presidency town to the Chief Presidency Magistrate, and outside such town to the District or Sub-divisional Magistrate.

**12. Provisions of section 337 of Act 5 of 1898 to apply to offences under sections 3, Sand** 7: The provisions of section 337 of the Code of Criminal Procedure, 1898 shall apply in relation to an offence punishable under section 3 or under section 5 or under section 7 or under any of the said sections 3, 5 and 7 read with section 9, as they apply in relation to an offence punishable with imprisonment for a term which may extend to seven years.

**13. Restriction on trial of offences:** (1) No court (other than that of a Magistrate of the first class specially empowered in this behalf by the Appropriate Government) which *is* inferior to that of a District or Presidency Magistrate, shall try any offence under this Act.

(2) If any person under trial before a Magistrate for an offence under this Act at any time before a charge is framed, claims to be tried by the Court of Session, the Magistrate shall, if he does not discharge the accused, commit the case for trial by that court, notwithstanding that it is not a case exclusively triable by that court.

(3) No court shall take cognizance of any offence under this Act unless upon complaint made by order of, or under authority from, the Appropriate Government [***] or some officer empowered by the Appropriate Government in this behalf:

[***]

(4) For the purposes of the trial of a person for an offence under this Act, the offence may be deemed to have been committed either at the place in which the same actually was committed or at any place in India in which the offender may be found.

(5) In this section, the appropriate Government means.

(*a*) in relation to any offences under section 5 not connected with a prohibited place or with a foreign power, the State Government; and

(*b*) in relation to any other offence, the Central Government.

COMMENTS

Court of Sessions Judge is competent to try the offence under the Official Secrets Act, 1923; *Sama Rayab Saheb v. Stale of Gujaral.* (1994) I CCR 93 (Guj.).

**14. Exclusion of public from proceedings:** In addition and without prejudice to any powers which a court may possess to order the exclusion of the public from any proceedings if in the course of proceedings before a court against any person for an offence under this Act or the proceedings on appeal, or in the course of the trial of a person under this Act, application is made by the prosecution, on the ground that the publication of any evidence to be given or of any statement to be made in the course of the proceedings would be prejudicial to the safety of the State, that all or any portion of the public shall be excluded during any part of the hearing, the court may make an order to that effect, but the passing of sentence shall in any case take place in public.

**15. Offences** by **companies:** (1) If the person committing an offence under this Act is a company, every person who, at the time the offence was committed, was in charge of, and was responsible to. the company for the conduct of business of the company, as well as the company, shall be deemed to be guilty of the offence and shall be liable to be proceeded against and punished accordingly:

Provided that nothing contained in this sub-section shall render any such person liable to such punishment provided in this Act i the proves that the offence was committed without his knowledge or that he exercised all due diligence to prevent the commission of such offence.

(2) Notwithstanding anything contained in sub-section (1), where an offence under this Act has been committed by a company and it is proved that the offence has been committed with the consent or connivance of, or is attributable to any negligence on the part of, any director, manager, secretary or other officer of the company such director, manager, secretary or other officer shall also be deemed to be guilty of that offence and shall he liable to be proceeded against and punished accordingly.

*Explanation*: For the purposes of this section :

(*a*) "Company" means body corporate and includes a firm or other association of individuals; and

(*b*) "Director", in relation to a firm, means a partner in the firm.

**16. Repeals.**— *[Rep. by the Repealing Act, 1927 (12 of 1927), sec. 2 and Sch.]*

# 7

# Contempt of Court Act, 1971

There is a unified system of judiciary in India, unlike USA. The Supreme Court of India is the highest Court of the land and under heirarical system there are separate High Courts for every State or one High Court for two States. Then there are District Court under the High Court which are called subordinate courts in our Constitution.

There are three pillars of any democratic set-up, Legislature, Executive and Judiciary. For the successful functioning of democratic setup, it is desirable that Judiciary should be allowed to perform its function independently and without any interference from any outside agency.

In Ramesh Thapar Vs the State of Madras, 1950 the Supreme Court observed 'the freedom of speech and of the press does not confer an absolute right to speaker or publish, without responsibility, whatever one may choose or an unrestricted or unbridled license that gives immunity for every possible use of language and prevents punishments for those who abuse this freedom.

In our original Constitution there was no mention of 'the contempt of court' For the first time in 1952, the words 'the Contempt of Court' has been mentioned through an Act.

Under the constitutional Amendment Act, 1951 Article 19(2) of the Constitution was replaced with the following:

"Nothing in sub–clause (*a*) shall affect the operation of any existing law, or prevent the state from making, any law, so far as such law, imposes reasonable restrictions, on the exercise of the right conferred by the said sub–clause, in the interest of the security of the State, friendly relations with foreign States, public order, decent or morality, or in relation to contempt of Court, defamation or incitement to an offence."

So, the words, "Contempt of Court" was mentioned for the first time in this Amendment, but the terminology was still not defined.

Clause (2) of Article 19 specifically enables the Legislature to impose reasonable restrictions on the freedom of the Press in cases of "Contempt of

Court." The expression 'Contempt of Court ' was defined in section 2 of the Contempt of Courts Acts, 1971.

(A) 'Contempt of Court' means civil contempt or criminal contempt.

(B) 'Civil contempt, means willful disobedience to any judgment, decree, direction, order, writ, or other process of court or willful breach of an undertaking given in a Court.

(C) 'Criminal contempt' means the publication (whether by words, spoken or written , or by sings, or by visible representation or otherwise) of any matter or the doing of any other act whatsoever which:

  (*i*) Scandalizes or tends to scandalize, or lowers or tends to lower the authority of any court, or

  (*ii*) Prejudices or interferes or tends to interfere with the due course of any judicial proceedings, or

  (*iii*) Interferes or tends to interfere with, or obstructs or tends to obstruct, the administration of justice in any other manner.

Under Article 129 and Article 215 of the Constitution of India the Supreme Court and High Courts, respectively, shall be courts of record.

In Ashwani Kumar Ghose Vs Arbinda Bose, 1952, The Supreme Court observed that a court of record is one where of the acts and judicial proceedings are enrolled for perpetual memory and testimony and which has authority to fine and imprison the contempt of itself.

**Article 129 reads**

"Supreme Court to be Court of record"

"The Supreme Court shall be a court of record shall have all the powers of such a court including the power to punish for contempt of itself.

**Article 215 reads**

"Every High Court shall be a Court of record and shall have all the powers of such a court including the power to punish for the contempt of itself."

In Delhi Judicial Service Association Vs State of Gujarat, 1989, it was held that the Supreme Court could impose punishment even in cases where there was a contempt of subordinate courts. The constitutional power of the court cannot be curtailed or taken away by any legislation such as the Contempt of Court Act, 1971, nor can be denied because similar power can be found with the High Court in Article 215.

In RL Kapoor Vs State of Madras, 1972, the Supreme Court held that the

High Court's Jurisdiction to try and punish of Contempt of Court includes all necessary and incidental powers to effectuate that jurisdiction

Article 142 (2) of the Constitution of India confers additional power on the Supreme Court for "the investigation and punishment of any contempt of itself." Article 225 deals with the rule making power of the High Court.

The Contempt of Court Act, 1971 defines the power of the High Court to punish the contempt of its subordinate Courts, Section 10 of the Act reads:

"Every High Court shall have and exercise the same Jurisdiction, powers and punish, in accordance with the same procedure and practice, in respect of Contempt of Courts subordinate to it as it has and exercise in respect of Contempt of itself."

"Provided that no High Court shall take cognizance of a contempt alleged to have been committed in respect of a "Courts subordinate to it" where such contempt is an offence punishable under the Indian penal Code."

The expression 'Courts subordinate to it has been interpreted to include not only civil courts and the criminal courts referred to in Section 6 of the Criminal Procedure Code, 1973 whether exercising judicial to quasi–judicial power for the time being, but also quasi judicial tribunals which are under the supervisory jurisdiction of the High Court . (under Article 277 of Constitution) and possess the attributes of finality and authoritativeness.

How the High Court shall have cognizance of contempt committed against a court subordinate to it;

Sub–section (2) of section 15 of the Act, 1971 says that the High Court may take action as regards contempt of subordinate Court on a reference by such subordinate Court or on a motion by the Advocate General does not debar High Court from proceeding suo–motu in such a case under sub–section (1) which confers comprehensive power on it to deal with all cases of criminal contempt in presence of the Supreme Court or he High Court.

**Contempt not punishable in certain cases according to certain provisions the Contempt of Court Act, 1971:** According to section 13 of the Act 'Notwithstanding anything contained in any law for the time being in force, no court shall impose, a sentence under this Act, for a contempt of court unless it is satisfied that the contempt is of such a nature that it substantially interferes, or tends substantially to interfere with the due course of justice.

This Section embodies the salutary principles that even where an interference with the administration of justice of a tendency thereof is established, the Court will not award a punishment of fine or imprisonment (as prescribed by section (12)) unless it is further established that such interference is substantial.

But this Section has been held to be in applicable in cases;

(*i*) Where a disgruntled party makes deliberate allegations against the judge such as bribery, and expresses no repentance the last stage of the contempt proceedings when he finds he has a little chance.

(*ii*) Where the Advocate of a defeated party made vituperative attack on a judgment, before the period of appeal against that judgment expired and alleged that the judge was biased against his client, had prejudged the issue and took a sudden turn in his conclusion, actuated by such motive.

**Punishment for Contempt of Court:** The punishment in a Contempt of Court case may be with simple imprisonment for a term extendable up to six months or with fine extendable upto rupees two thousand or both. As mentioned in Section 12 (1) of the Act of 1971:

"Save as otherwise expressly provided in this Act, or in any other law, a Contempt of Court may be punished with imprisonment for a term which may extend to six months, or with fine which may extend to two thousand rupees."

Provided that the accused may be discharged or the punishment awarded may be remitted on apology being made to the satisfaction of the court.

Some points to be remembered in punishment for Contempt of Court:

(1) It is clear that an Indian Court shall have no jurisdiction to award any other punishment (except mentioned in 12 (1) of the Act) under common law or otherwise. Thus contempt is not punishable with any order to pay cost.

(2) It is clear from Sections 11-12 that court cannot punish a person for Contempt of Court in the absence of a clear finding that he is guilty of 'Contempt of Court' merely holding that the conduct of the alleged contemner was 'Contemptuous would not be enough.

(3) Contempt proceeding is often described as equal quasi criminal proceeding and cannot be equated with prosecution of criminal by the State.

(4) Contempt Jurisdiction being special Jurisdiction : It is to be used cautiously and exercised sparingly to uphold dignity of Court and majesty to law.

**Punishment for a Civil Contempt:** Where a person is found guilty of Civil Contempt and if a fine is considered to be not sufficient to meet the end of justice and that a sentence of imprisonment is necessary, the person be detained in a civil prison' instead of simple imprisonment, for a period not exceeding six months.

**Procedure in Contempt in the presence of the Supreme Court or a High Court:** When a person has been guilty of contempt committed in the presence or hearing of the Supreme Court or the High Court , the Court may cause such person to be detained in custody, and at any time before the rising of the Court, on the same day or as early as possible thereafter, shall:

(*a*) Cause him to be informed in writing of the contempt with which he is charged.
(*b*) Afford him an opportunity to make his defence to the charge.
(*c*) After taking such evidence as may be necessary or as may be offered by such person and after hearing proceed, either forthwith or after adjournment, to determine the charge and;
(*d*) Make such order for the punishment or discharge of such person as may be just.

Pending the determination of the charge, the Court may direct that a person charged with Contempt under Suction 14 of the Act shall be detained in such custody as it may specify. The Court may if it thinks fit, instead of taking bail from such person, discharge him on his executing a bond without sureties for his attendance.

## COGNIZANCE OF CRIMINAL CONTEMPT

(1) Criminal Contempt of the Supreme Court or High Court; in other cases (where it not ex–face)
    (*a*) Suo motu by such Court or,
    (*b*) On a motion by Attorney General or Advocate General
    (*c*) On a motion of any other with the consent in writing of the Advocate General according to procedure under Section 14 of the Act.
(2) Criminal Contempt of Court Subordinate to High Court According to the procedure under section 345 of criminal procedure Code, 1973:
    (*a*) On a motion by the Advocate General or
    (*b*) Suo motu

The Supreme Court or the High Court can take cognizance of a criminal Contempt other than one committed in its presence, is on the motion of the Court itself for instance;

'Serious allegation by party of bribery, against the judge of Subordinate Court, which is found, on administrative inquiry, to be false.

## A BRIEF HISTORY OF CONTEMPT OF COURT IN INDIA

There was no codified law of Contempt of Court in India before 1926. The Contempt of Court Act 1926 was passed to remove the controversy of Courts Act the power of a High to punish for contempt of a subordinate court. It provided that High Court.

"Have and exercise the same jurisdiction, power and authority in accordance with the same procedure and practice in respect of Contempt of Court subordinate to them, as they have and exercise in respect of themselves."

The Act, 1926 codified the Contempts of Court law for the first in India.

The Contempt of Court Act , 1926 and several other state enactments in existence in various Indian States were replaced by the Contempt of Court Act, 1952.

After a few years, the working of the 1952 Act was also found unsatisfactory and needed changes. In April 1960, the Government brought out a Bill on the subject But after examining, it was found that a further study of the subject was necessary, A special committee with the object in view, was set up, with A.N, Sanyal, the then Solicitor General of India as it Chairman, herein referred to as the Sanyal Committee. The Committee submitted its report on February 28, 1963, with a draft Contempt of Court Bill, 1963. The objective of the Bill was to harmonise as far as possible the interest of the individual in the freedom of expression and interest of the administration of justice within the framework of the Constitution of India. The Bill was finally passed as the Contempt of Court Act, 1971. The preamble of the Act says "to define and limit the powers of certain courts in punishing Contempt of Court" and to replace the Act of 1952, which is repealed by section 24.

This Act of 1971, has codified the law laid down in many judicial decisions and has become more elaborate and exhaustive than the Act of 1952. The Act of 1971 was amended in 1976.

The decisions of the Court have shown mixed development in interpretation of the law of contempt in India.

In case of Bathina Ramkrishna Reddy Vs the State of Madras in 1952, the Supreme Court held that if defamation of a subordinate court amounts to Contempt of Court, proceedings can be taken under the Contempt of Court Act, besides taking recourse to the remedy available to the aggrieved party, under section 499 of the Indian Penal Code, 1860. Holding that the article in question was a scurrilous attack on the integrity of a judicial officer, the Court observed "Specific instances have been given where the officers is alleged to have taken bribes, or behaved with impropriety to the litigants who did not satisfy his dishonest demands. If the allegations were true, obviously it would be to the benefit of the public or bring these matters into light. But if they were false, they cannot but undermine the confidence of the public in the administration of justice and bring the judiciary into disrepute."

But in the case of Perspective Publication Vs the State of Maharashtra in 1971, the Supreme Court held that "it may be truthfulness of factual correctness is a good defence in an action for libel, but in the law of contempt there are hardly any English or Indian cases in which such defence has been recognized"

However fair and accurate report of judicial proceedings or a fair criticism of a judicial act is not contempt.

In a happening Justice I. M. Quidishi J., a siting judge of the Allahabad High Court conducted a Court on the New Delhi railway station to try a railway employee for Contempt of court for not allotting him a berth on train on March 8, 2000. This was published in the Times of India (March 13, 2000). According to Arvind Nigam, a Supreme Court lawyer, if a person is a complaint or a witness to an offence, he cannot be a prosecutor or a judge in the same case. More over Justice Quidishi J. lacked jurisdiction and it was not Contempt of any of his orders. Another layer said, Denial of railway berth to a judge is not a contempt of the Court.'

Soli J. Sorabjee in his article "Media and Law of Contempt" made the following observation."

"In ancient Greek drama tragedy frequently results, not from the conflict between right and wrong but from the conflict of two rights, both equally moral and important, but apparently irreconcilable. Atypical example of this painful dilemma is the tension between the media and the courts in the field of the Contempt of Courts. The media invokes the invaluable right of free speech, the courts rest their authority and power upon the right to independent justice."

## THE CONTEMPT OF COURTS ACT, 1971

### INTRODUCTION

The origin of the law of Contempt of Courts in India can be traced from the English law. In England Superior Courts of record have from early times, exercised the power to commit for contempt persons who scandalised (the Court or the Judges. The right of the Indian High Courts to punish for contempt, was in the first instance recognised by the Judicial Committee of the Privy Council which observed that the offence of the contempt of court and the powers of the High Courts to punish it are the same in such courts as in the Supreme Court in England. It also observed that the three chartered High Courts of Calcutta, Bombay and Madras had inherent power to punish for contempt. Almost all the High Courts in India, apart from the chartered High Courts have exercised the jurisdiction and where its authority had been challenged each has held that it is a jurisdiction inherent in a court of record from the very nature of the court itself. It had been judicially accepted throughout India that the jurisdiction was a special one inherent in the very nature of the court.

The first Indian statute on the law of contempt *i.e.* the Contempt of Courts Act was passed in 1926. It was enacted to define and limit the powers of certain courts in punishing contempt of courts. When the Contempt of Courts Act, 1926 (XII of 1926) was in existence in British India, various Indian States also had their corresponding enactments. These States were Hyderabad, Madhya Bharat, Mysore, Pepsu, Rajasthan, Travaincore-Cochin and Saurashtra. State enactments of the Indian States and the Contempt of Courts Act, 1926 were replaced by the Contempt of Courts Act, 1952.(32 of 1952).

An attempt was made in April, 1960 to introduce in the Lok Sabha a Bill to consolidate and amend the law relating to Contempt of Courts. On an examination of the Bill, government appears to have felt that the law relating to Contempt of Courts is uncertain, undefined and unsatisfactory and that in the light of the constitutional changes which have taken place in the country, it would be advisable to have the entire law on the subject scrutinised by a Special Committee set up for the purpose. In pursuance to that decision a Committee was set up for the purpose.In pursuance to that decision a Committee was set up on 29th July, 1961.and it submitted its report on 28th February, 1963 with the Contempt of Courts Bill, 1963 to define and limit the powers of certain courts in punishing contempt of courts and to regulate their procedure in relation thereto.

Joint Select Committee of Parliament on Contempt of Courts went in detail and a new Bill, The Contempt of Courts Bill, 1968, was prepared by the Joint Select Committee.

## STATEMENT OF OBJECTS AND REASONS

It is generally felt that the existing law relating to contempt of Courts is somewhat uncertain, undefined and unsatisfactory. The jurisdiction to punish for contempt touches upon two important fundamental rights of the citizen namely, the right to personal liberty and the right to freedom of expression. It was, therefore, considered advisable to have the entire law on the subject scruitinised by a special committee. In pursuance of this, a Committee was set up in 1961 under the Chairmanship of the late Shri H.N. Sanyal the then Additional Solicitor General. The Committee made a comprehensive examination of the law and problems relating to contempt of Court in the light of the position obtaining in our own country and various foreign countries. The recommendations which the Committee made took note of the importance given to freedom of speech in the Constitution and of the need for safeguarding the status and dignity of Courts and interests of administration of justice.

The recommendations of the Committee have been generally accepted by Government after considering the views expressed on those recommendations by the State Governments, Union 'Territory Administrations, the Supreme Conn. the High Courts and the Judicial Commissioners. The Bill seeks to give effect to the accepted recommendations of the Sanyal Committee.

## ACT 70 OF 1971

The Contempt of Courts Act, 1971 (70 of 1971) was passed by the Parliament in December, 1971 and it came into force w.e.f. 24th December, 1971.

## LIST OF AMENDING ACT

The Contempt of Courts (Amendment) Act, 1976 (45 of 1976).

The contempt of Court Act 1971.

## (70 of 1971)

*[2th December, 1971]*

An Act to define and limit the powers of certain courts in punishing contempts of courts and to regulate their procedure in relation thereto.

Be it enacted by Parliament in the Twenty-second Year of the Republic of India as follows:

**1. Short title and extent:** (1) This Act may be called the Contempt of Courts Act, 1971.

(2) It extends to the whole of India:

Provided that it shall not apply to the State of Jammu and Kashmir except to the extent to which the provisions of this Act relate to contempt of the Supreme Court.

**2. Definitions:** In this Act, unless the context otherwise requires:

(*a*) "contempt of court" means civil contempt or criminal contempt;

(*b*) "civil contempt" means wilful disobedience to any judgment, decree, direction, order, writ or other process of a court or wilful breach of an undertaking given to a court;

(*c*) "criminal contempt" means the publication (whether by words, spoken or written or by signs, or by visible representation, or otherwise)'of any matter or the doing of any other act whatsoever which :

  (*i*) scandalises or tends to scandalise, or lowers or tends to lower **the** authority of, any court; or

  (*ii*) prejudices, or interferes or tends to interfere with, the due course of any judicial proceeding; or (*iii*) interferes or tends to interfere with, or obstructs or tends **to** obstruct, the administration of justice in any other manner;

(*d*) "High Court" means the High Court for a State or a Union territory, and includes the court of the Judicial Commissioner in any Union territory.

**3. Innocent publication and distribution of matter not contempt:** (1) A person shall not be guilty of contempt of court on the ground that he has published (whether by words, spoken or written, or by signs, or by visible representations, or otherwise) any matter which interferes or tends to interfere with, or obstructs or tends to obstruct, the course of justice in connection with any civil or criminal proceeding pending at that time of publication, if at that time he had no reasonable grounds for believing that the proceeding was pending,

(2) Notwithstanding anything to the contrary contained in this Act or any other law for the time being in force, the publication of any such matter as is mentioned in sub-section (1) in connection with any civil or criminal proceeding which is not pending at the time of publication shall not be deemed to constitute contempt of court.

(3) A person shall not be guilty of contempt of court on the ground that he has distributed a publication containing any such matter as is mentioned in sub-section (1), if at the time of distribution he had no reasonable grounds for believing that it contained was likely to contain any such matter as aforesaid:

Provided that this sub-section shall not apply in respect of the distribution of:

(*i*) any publication which is a book or paper printed or published otherwise than in conformity with the rules contained in section 3 of the Press and Registration of Books Act,1867 (25 of 1867);

(*ii*) any publication which is a newspaper published otherwise than in conformity with the rules contained in section 5 of the said Act.

**Explanation:** For the purposes of this section, a judicial proceeding:

(*a*) is said to be pending

(A) in the case of a civil proceeding, when it is instituted by the filing of a plaint or otherwise,

(B) in the case of a criminal proceeding under the Code of Criminal Procedure, 1898 (5 of 1898), or any other law :

(*i*) where it relates to the commission of an offence, when the charge sheet or challan is filed, or when the court issues summons or warrant, as the case may be, against the accused, and

(*ii*) in any other case, when the court takes cognizance of the matter to which the proceeding relates, and in the case of a civil or criminal proceeding, shall be deemed to continue to be pending until it is heard and finally decided, that is to say, in a case where an appeal or revision of competent, until the appeal or revision is heard and finally decided or, where no appeal or revision is preferred, until the period of limitation prescribed for such appeal or revision has expired;

(*b*) which has been heard and finally decided shall **not** be deemed to be pending merely

4. **Fair and accurate report of judicial proceeding not contempt:** Subject to the 'provisions contained in section 7, a person shall not be guilty of contempt of court for publishing a fair and accurate report of a judicial proceeding or any stage thereof.

5. **Fair criticism of judicial act not contempt:** A person shall not be guilty of contempt of court for publishing any fair comment on the merits of any case which has been heard and finally decided.

6. **Complaint against presiding officers of subordinate courts when not contempt:** A person shall not be guilty of contempt of court in respect of any statement made by him in good faith concerning the presiding officer of any subordinate court to:

(*a*) any other subordinate court, or

(*b*) the High Court, to which it is subordinate.

**Explanation:** In this section, "subordinate court" means any court subordinate to a High Court.

7. **Publication of information relating to proceeding in chambers or in *camerra* not contempt except in certain cases:** (1) Notwithstanding anything contained in this Act, a person shall not be guilty of contempt of court for publishing a fair and accurate report of a judicial proceeding before any court sitting in chambers or in camera except in the following cases, that is say:

(*a*) where publication is contrary to the provisions of any enactment for the time being in force;

(*b*) where the court, on grounds of public policy or in exercise of any power vested in it, expressly prohibits the publication of all information relating to the proceeding or of information of the description which is published;

(*d*) where the in formation relates to a secret process, discovery or invention which is an issue in the proceedings.

(2) Without prejudice to the provisions contained in sub-section (1), a person shall not be guilty of contempt of court for publishing the text or a fair and accurate summary of the whole, or any part, of an order made by a court sitting in chambers or in *camera,* unless the court has expressly prohibited the publication thereof on grounds of pubic policy, or for reasons connected with public order or

the security of the State, or the ground that it contains information relating to a secret process, discovery or invention, or in exercise of any power vested in it.

**8. Other defences not affected:** Nothing contained in this Act shall be construed as implying that any other defence which would have been a valid defense in any proceedings for contempt of court has ceased to be available merely by reason of the provisions of this Act.

**9. Act not to imply enlargement of scope of contempt:** Nothing contained in this Act shall be construed as implying that any disobedience, breach, publication or other act is punishable as contempt of court which would not be so punishable apart from this Act.

**10. Power of High Court to punish contempts of subordinate courts:** Every High Court shall have and exercise the same jurisdiction, powers and authority, in accordance with the same procedure and practice, in respect of contempts of courts subordinate to it as it has and exercises in respect of contempts of itself:

Provided that no High Court shall take cognizance of a contempt alleged to have been committed in respect of a court subordinate to it where such contempt is an offence punishable under the Indian Penal Code (45 of 1860).

**11. Power of High Court to try offences committed or offenders found outside jurisdiction:** A High Court shall have jurisdiction to inquire into or try a contempt of itself or of any court subordinate to it, whether the contempt is alleged to have been committed within or outside the local limits of its jurisdiction, and whether the person alleged to be guilty of contempt is within or outside such limits.

**12. Punishment for contempt of court:** (1) Save as otherwise expressly provided in this Act or in any other law, a contempt of court may be punished with simple imprisonment for a term which may extend to six months, or with fine which may extend to two thousand rupees, or with both:

Provided that the accused may be, discharged or the punishment awarded may be remitted on apology being made to the satisfaction of the court.

*Explanation:* An apology shall not be rejected merely on the ground that it is qualified or conditional if the accused makes it bona fide genuine.

(2) Notwithstanding anything contained in any law for the time being in force, no court shall impose a sentence in excess of that specified in sub-section (1) for any contempt either in respect of itself or of a court subordinate to it.

(3) Notwithstanding anything contained in this section, where a person is found guilty of a civil contempt, the court, if it considers that a fine will not meet the ends of justice and that a sentence of imprisonment is necessary shall, instead of sentencing him to simple imprisonment, direct that he be detained in a civil prison for such period not exceeding six months as it may think fit.

(4) Where the person found guilty of contempt of court in respect of any undertaking given to a court is a company, every person who, at the time the contempt was committed, was in charge of, and was responsible to, the company for the conduct of business of the company, as well as the company, shall be deemed to be guilty of the contempt and the punishment may be enforced, with the leave of the court, by the detention in civil prison of each such person:

Provided that nothing contained in this sub-section shall render any such person liable to such punishment if he proves that the contempt was committed without his knowledge or that he exercised all due diligence to prevent its commission.

(5) Notwithstanding anything contained in sub-section *(4)*, where the contempt of court referred to therein has been committed by a company and it is proved that the contempt has been committed with the consent or connivance of, or is attributable to any neglect on the part of, any director, manager, secretary or other officer of *the* company, such director, manager, secretary or other officer shall also be deemed to be guilty of the contempt and the such director, manager, secretary or other officer.

*Explanation* : For the purpose of sub–sections (4) and (5):

(*a*) "company" means any body corporate and includes a firm or other association of individuals, and

(*b*) "director", in relation to a firm, means a partner in the firm.

**13. Contempts not punishable in certain cases:** Notwithstanding anything contained in any law for the time being in force, no court shall impose a sentence under this Act for a contempt of court unless it is satisfied that the contempt is of such a nature that it substantially interferes, or tends substantially to interfere with the due course of justice.

**14. Procedure where contempt is in the face of the Supreme Court or a High Court:** (1) When it is alleged, or appears to the Supreme Court or the High Courtpen its own view, that a person has been guilty of contempt committed in its presence or hearing, of the court, on the same day, or as early as possible thereafter shall:

(*a*) cause him to be informed in writing of the contempt with which he is charged;

(*b*) afford him an opportunity to make his defence to the charge;

(*c*) after taking such evidence as may be necessary or as may be offered by such person and after hearing him. proceed, either forthwith or after adjournment, to determine the matter of the charge: and (*d*) make such order for the punishment or discharge of such person as may be just.

(2) Notwithstanding anything contained in sub-section (I), where a person charged with contempt under that subjection applies, whether orally or in writing, to have the charge against him tried by some. Judge other than the Judge or Judges in whose presence or hearing the offence is alleged to have been committed, and the court is of opinion that it is practicable to do so and that in the interests of proper administration of justice the application should be allowed, it shall cause the matter to be placed, together with a statement of the facts of the case, before the Chief Justice for such directions as he may think fit to issue as respects the trial thereof

(3) Notwithstanding anything contained in any other law, in any trial of a person charged with contempt under sub-section (1) which is held. in pursuance of a direction given under sub-section (2). by a Judge other than the Judge or Judges in whose presence or hearing the offence is alleaed to have been committed, it shall not be necessary for the Judge or Judges in whose presence or hearing the offence is alleged to have been committed to appear as a witness and the statement placed before the Chief Justice under sub-section (2) shall be treated as evidence in the case.

(4) Pending he determination of the charge, the court may direct that a person charged with contempt under this section shall be detained in such custody as it may specify:

Provided that he shall be released on bail, if a bond for such sum of money as the court thinks sufficient is executed with or without sureties conditioned that the person charged shall attend at the time and place mentioned in the bond and shall continue to so attend until otherwise directed by the court:

Provided further that the court may, if it thinks fit, instead of taking bail from such person, discharge him on his executing a bond without sureties for his attendance as aforesaid.

**15. Cognizance of criminal contempt in other cases:** (1) In the case of a criminal contempt, other than a contempt referred to in section 14, the Supreme Court or the High Court may take action on its own motion or on a motion made by:

(*a*) the Advocate–General, or

(*b*)

(*c*) information to the High Court for the union territory of Delhi, such Law officer as the Central Government may, by notification in the Official Gazette, specify in this behalf or any other person, with the consent in writing of such Law Officer.

(2) In the case of any criminal contempt of a subordinate court, the High Court may take action on a reference made to it by the subordinate court or on a motion made by the Advocate-General or, in relation to a Union territory, by such Law Officer as the Central Government may. by notification in the Official Gazette, specify in this behalf.

(3) Every motion or reference made under this section shall specify the contempt of which the person charged is alleged to be guilty.

*Explanation:* In this section, the expression "Advocate-General" means :

(*a*) in relation to the Supreme Court, the Attorney-General or the Solicitor-General;

(*b*) in relation to the High Court, the Advocate-General of the State or any of the Slates for which the High Court has been established;

(*c*) in relation to the court of a Judicial Commissioner, such Law Officer as the Cenrra I Government may, by notification in the Official Gazette, specify in this behalf.

16. Contempt by judge, magistrate or other person acting judicially. (1) Subject to the provisions of any law for the time being in force, a judge, magistrate or other person acting judicially shall also be liable for contempt of his own court or of any other court in the same manner as any other individual is liable and the provisions of this Act shall, so far as may be, apply accordingly of the subordinate court.

**17. Procedure after cognizance:** (1) Notice of every proceeding under section 15 shall be served personally on the person charged, unless the court for reasons to be recorded directs otherwise.

(2) The notice shall be accompanied :

(*a*) in the case of proceedings commenced on a motion, by a copy of the motion as also copies of the affidavits, if any, on which such motion is founded; and

(*b*) in case of proceedings commenced on a reference by a subordinate court, by a copy of the reference.

(3) The Court may, if it is satisfied that a person charged under section 15 is likely to abscond or keep out of the way to avoid service of the notice, order the attachment of his property of such value or amount as it may deem reasonable.

(4) Every attachment under sub-section (3) shall be effected in the manner provided in the Code of Civil Procedure, 1908(5 of 1908)', for the attachment of property in execution of a decree for payment of money, and if, after such attachment, the person charged appears and shows to the satisfaction of the court that he did not abscond or keep out of the way to avoid service of the notice, the court shall order the release of his property from attachment upon such terms as to costs or otherwise as it may think fit.

(5) Any person charged with contempt under section 15 may file an affidavit in support of his defence, and the court may determine the matter of the charge either on the affidavits filed or after taking such further evidence as may be necessary, and pass such order as the justice of the case requires.

# 8

# Parliamentary Privileges

Legislature is one of the three pillars of any democratic set up. It consists of the elected representatives of the people who are the real master in democracy. The main responsibility of the Legislature is to enact laws for public welfare and raise the points of public interest. It is in the interest of the public that the representatives of the people perform their responsibilities without any fear, hindrance or disturbance from any other agency. In order to facilitate them to work freely the members of Parliament and State Assemblies have been provided certain privileges. These privileges have been provided to the House, their members and their committees.

## PARLIAMENTARY PRIVILEGES

Under Article 105 of the Constitution of India certain privileges to Parliament and under Article 194 of the Constitution, to State Assemblies have been provided. Two privileges mentioned in the above-mentioned Articles are more important. No proceeding in any court can be drawn against any member of the House for their speeches in their house, or for casting their votes in their respective house. But so far the privileges have not been codified and they are unlimited. Parliament under Article 105 (3) and State Assemblies under Article 194 (3) are empowered to enact laws in respect of powers and privileges to the members and will also continue to the same which was to 'the House of Commons' before January 26, 1950, till such time the Parliament or State Assemblies frame any law in this regard.

Under the 44th Amendment to the constitution, the constitutional position of these Parliamentary privileges has been defined. Among other things, the powers, privileges and immunities enjoyed by each house of the Parliament and their members and Committees, will be that these will be reviewed and redefined by the Parliament from time to time. The Constitutional (44th Amendment) Act, 1978 has not made any difference in the constitutional position of the Parliamentary privileges. It has merely deleted the House of Commons words.

Otherwise these Parliamentary privileges are similar to the privileges, which were enjoyed by the members of British 'House of Commons' before the adoption of the Constitution of India on January 26, 1950.

## FREEDOM OF SPEECH IN PARLIAMENT

According to the provisions contained in Article 105 (1) and (2) no judicial proceeding can be started on the basis of any discussion during the parliamentary sessions or the voting on any mater. There is no restriction whatsoever for the Members of Parliament or the Members of Legislative Assembly to speak in the Parliament or State Legislative Assembly to speak in the parliament or State Assembly. Only the chairperson of the concerned House of the Parliament or the State Legislative Assembly is empowered to stop any member from speaking, expunge any remarks or the words of un parliamentary language, if any, used by any member. If the chairperson so desires, he can resort to voting by the members of the House for the expulsion of a member from the House for disrupting the proceedings of the House.

In respect of the publication of a substantially true report of any proceeding of either House of Parliament no person shall be liable to any proceedings Civil or Criminal in any court. According to the provision contained in section 3 (1) of the parliamentary Proceeding (Protection of Publication) Act, 1977;

"Save as otherwise provided in sub-section (2) no person shall be liable to any proceedings, civil or criminal, in any Court in respect of the publication in a newspaper or a substantially true report of any proceedings of either House of the Parliament unless the publication is proved to have been made with malice."

This Act will also apply to reports broadcast on Television or Radio.

The Act provides a legal shield to newspapers and broadcasting agencies, who may publish or broadcast "as substantially true report of the proceeding of either House of Parliament" unless the publication was made with malice, and was not for public good.

## CODIFICATION OF PARLIAMENTARY PRIVILEGES

The Parliamentary privileges in India have not so far been codified. The form and structure of these privileges are yet not clear and defined. These privileges are the same privileges enjoyed by British House of commons" before the adoption of the Constitution of India on January 26, 1950. As British has no written Constitution, privileges for British 'House of Commons' are not codified or defined.

On the other hand, the Parliament under Article 105 (3) and State Assembly under Article 194 (3) have been empowered to enact law (and define) for the powers, immunities and privileges for their Members and Committees.

No person shall be liable for prosecution in any court for publication of a true report on the proceedings of any House. Article 361 A as inserted in the Constitution (44th Amendment) Act, 1978 says;

"No person, shall be liable to any proceedings, civil or criminal, in any court in respect of the publication in a newspaper, of a substantially true report of any proceedings of either House of Parliament or State Assembly, or as the case may be, either House of the Legislature of a State, unless the publication is proved to have been made with malice."

Some constitutional problems have also arisen at times, due to non-codification and lack of clarity in parliamentary privileges. It is the sole discretion of the House to decide which act is a violation of Parliamentary Privileges and which not. The episodes of Keshav Singh in Uttar Pradesh and In administration of Andhra Pradesh Assembly are some of the examples, In 1987, Mr. As. Balasuramaniuam, the editor of 'Anand Vikatan' a periodical published from Tamil Nadu was sentenced to three years imprisonment for publication of a cartoon, which in eyes of the Tamil Nadu Assembly, was contempt of Parliamentary privileges. Such situations have created conflicts between Judiciary and Legislative Assemblies. Journalists also remain apprehensive in reporting about proceedings of State Legislature due to lack of clarity of parliamentary privileges.

Some of the other Parliamentary Privileges are as hereunder:

**1. Freedom from Arrest:** No Member of Parliament can be arrested within the premises of the Parliament without the prior permission of the Chairperson. The Parliament premises include the Parliament House, assembly Hall, Central Hall, Galleries, Street, Waiting rooms for the Members, Canteen, Library, rooms or offices of parliamentary committees, offices of Lokh Sabha and Rajya Sabha, the Parliament House estate, street or path connecting these offices and pathways.

In case of the arrest of any Member, the Chairperson of the House is to be informed within 24 hours of the arrest by the police officer. Any delay in informing the same may invite contempt of Parliamentary Privileges. Any Member arrested by the police has the privilege to write and send letters to the chairperson of the Parliamentary Committee of which he is a member. Any restriction imposed or obstructions created in sending such letters could be considered the contempt of Parliamentary Privileges.

**2. Expulsion of a Stranger from the House:** Under Article 105 (3), of the

Constitution of India, every House has the Privileges to expel any stranger out of the House and maintain the secrecy of the conduct of it business.

Any stranger found loitering in the premises of the House in any unauthorized way or if any such tranger refuses to go out when he or she is asked to leave the premises of the House, person could be not only forced to go out of the premises but could also be arrested by the security officers.

**3. Right to punish:** After the adoption of the constitution of India, the Parliament/State Assemblies have been given the powers to order the arrest of an accused person, sending him to jail and sue him in a court of law. It was important privilege granted to the Parliament and State Assemblies. Earlier the area of the Parliamentary privileges were made more extensive under the Government of India Act, 1935. Prior to that there was no provision to punish the persons found guilty of the contempt to the Parliamentary Privileges.

## PARLIAMENTARY PRIVILEGES AND MEDIA PERSONS

As discussed earlier also the scope of Parliamentary privileges are unlimited. It is the discretion of the House to decide whether any publication comes under the contempt of Parliamentary privileges or not. Under the circumstances the journalists and media person are required to keep in mind certain related Parliamentary privileges, which are mentioned hereunder:

(1) Any Comments against Parliamentary proceedings or against the Parliament, to level charges against any Parliamentary committee or pass adverse remarks, any remarks passed against any Parliamentary privileges, can be treated as contempt of Parliamentary privileges.

(2) To publish any report of any Parliamentary Committee before it is put on the table of the House, to publish any report of any Parliamentary Committee after it is distorted and misinterpreted form, come under the contempt of Parliamentary Privileges.

(3) Media persons should avoid publishing the proceedings of the secret session of the House and also the portion of the speech by any Member or any part of the proceedings expunged by the Chairperson, or unauthorized publication of any portion of the report of Parliamentary Privileges.

In the publication of such reports media persons are always in two minds. On the one hand the fear of contempt of Parliamentary Privileges is lurking in their mind and on the other hand to publish these reports as scoop are tempting them. The safest way is to publish the bare facts without any distortions or misinterpretation.

In India Parliamentary Privileges are unlimited. But the following actions are normally taken as contempt of Parliament :

1. To challenge the impartiality of the Speaker or the Chairman of Rajya Sabha.
2. Any contrary Comments against the dignity of the Parliament.
3. Any adverse comments against privileges and rights of the Parliament.
4. Allegations against/in respect of any Committee or any of the members of the Committee of the Parliament.
5. Any comments or remarks against the dignity of any House of the Parliament or any of its Members.
6. Publication of any report of any Committee of the Parliament, before the same is put on the table of the House.
7. Any incorrect or distorted publication of any report of any committee.
8. Publication of the proceedings of a secret session of any House of the Parliament.
9. Publication of the expunged portions of the proceeding by the Chairperson.

### PUNISHMENT FOR THE CONTEMPT OF PARLIAMENTARY PRIVILEGES

Any person found guilty of the contempt of Parliamentary Privileges, can be awarded the following punishment by the House:

1. Reprimand the guilty person
2. Condemn the guilty person
3. Send the guilty person to Jail for a specific period

For less serious offences, the guilty, person is called to the 'Bar' of the House and is reprimanded for his offence. If the punishment to end him jail is awarded it is upto rising of the House on the day or maximum upto to the last day of the current session of the House. Normally the guilty person is automatically set free on the conclusion of the current session of the House.

## THE PARLIAMENTARY PROCEEDINGS (PROTECTION OF PUBLICATION) ACT, 1977

**(15 of 1977)**

*[18th Apr. 9, 1977]*

*An Act to protect the publication of reports of proceedings of Parliament.*

Be it enacted by Parliament in the Twenty-eighth Year of the Republic of India as follows :

**1.** (1) This Act may be called The Parliamentary Proceedings (Protection of Publication) Act. 1977.

(2) It extends to the whole of India except the State of Jammu and Kashmir.

(3) It shall be deemed to have come into force on the 25th day of March, 1977.

**2. In this Act. "newspaper" means any printed periodical work containing public news or comments on public news, and includes a news–agency supplying material for publication in a newspaper.**

**3.** (1) Save as otherwise provided in sub–section

(2) no person shall be liable to any proceedings, civil or criminal, in any Court in respect of the publication in a newspaper of a substantially true report of any proceedings of either House of Parliament unless the publication is proved to have been made with malice.

(3) Nothing in sub-section (1) shall be construed as protecting the publication of any matter, the publication of which is not for the public good.

**4. This Act shall apply in relation to reports or matter broadcast by means of wireless telegraphy as part of any programme or service provided by means of a broadcasting station situate within the territories this Act extends as it applies in relation to reports or matters published in a newspaper.**

*In exercise of the powers under Section 23 of the Contempt of Courts Act, 1971 read with Articles 145 of the Constitution of India and all other powers enabling it in this behalf, the Supreme Court hereby makes, with the approval of the President, the following rules:*

**1.** (1) These Rules many be called the Rules to Regulate Proceedings for Contempt of the Supreme Count, 1975.

(2) They shall come into force on the date of their publication in the Official Gazette.

## PART I

**2.** (1) Where contempt is : committed in view or presence or hearing of the Court, the contemner may be p-nished by the Court before which it is committed either forthwith or on such date as may be appointed by the Court in that behalf.

(2) Pending the determination of the charge, the Court may direct that the contemner shall be detained in such custody as it may specify:

*Provided* that the conemmer may be released on bail on such terms as the court may direct.

## PART II

**3.** In case of centempt other than the contempt referred to in Rule 2. the Court may take action:

(*a*) *Suo Motu, or*

(*b*) on a petition made by Attorney—General, or Solicitor—General, or

(*c*) on a petition made by any person, and in the case of a criminal contempt with the consent in writing of the Attomey—General or the solicitor—General.

4. (*a*) Ever petition order Rule 3 (b) or (c) shall contain

(*i*) the name, description and place of residence of the petitioner or petitioners and of the persons charged.

(*ii*) nature of the contempt alleged, and such material facts, including the date or dates of commission of the alleged contempt, as may be necessary for the proper determination of the case ;

(*iii*) if a petition has previously been made by him on the same facts, the petitioner shall give the details of the petition previously made and shall also indicate the result thereof

(*b*) The petition shall be supported by an affidavit.

(*c*) Whether the petitioner relies upon a document or documents in his possession or power, he shall file such document or documents or true copies thereof with the petition.

(*d*) No Court fee shall be payable on the petition, and on any documents filed in the proceedings.

5. Every petition under Rule 3(b) and (c). shall be posted before the Court for preliminary hearing and for orders as to issue of notice. Upon such hearing, the Court, if satisfied that no prima facie case has been made out for issue of notice, may dismiss the petition, and, if not so satisfied direct that notice of the petition be issued to the contemner.

6. (1) Notice to the person charged shall be in Form I. The person charged shall, unless otherwise ordered, appear in person before the Court as directed on the date fixed for hearing of the proceeding, and shall continue to remain present during hearing till the proceeding is finally disposed of by order of the Court.

(2) When action is instituted on petition, a copy of the petition along with the annexure and affidavits shall be served upon the person charged.

7. The person charged may file his reply duly supported by an affidavit or affidavits.

8. No further affidavit or document shall be filed except with the leave of the Court.

9. Unless otherwise ordered by the Court, seven copies of the Paper Book shall be prepared in the Registry, one for the petitioner, one the opposite party and the remaining for the use of the Court. The paper Book in the case shall be

prepared at the expense of the Central Government and shall consist of the following documents:

(*i*) Petition and affidavits filed by the petitioner;

(*ii*) A copy of. or a statement relating to, the objectionable matter constituting the alleged contempt ;

(*iii*) Reply and affidavits of the opposite party;

(*iv*) Documents filed by the parties ;

(*v*) Any other document which the Registrar may deem fit to include.

**10. The Court may direct the Attomey–General or Soticitor–General to appear and assist the Court.**

**11.** (1) The Court may, if it has reason to believe, that the person charged is absconding or is otherwise evading service of notice, or if he fails to appear in person or to continue to remain present in person in pursuance of the notice, direct a warrant bailable or non-bailable for his arrest, addressed to one or more police officers or may order attachment of property. The warrant shall be issued under the signature of the Registrar. The warrant shall be Form II and shall be executed, as far as may be in the manner provided for execution of warrants under Code of Criminal Procedure.

(2) The warrant shall be executed by the officer to whom it is directed, and may also be executed by any other police officer whose, name is endorsed upon the warrant by the officer to whom it is directed or endorsed.

(3) Where a warrant is to be executed outside the Union Territory of Delhi, the Court may instead of directing such warrant to police officer, forward it to the Magistrate of the district or the Superintendent of Police or Commissioner of Police of the district within which the person charged is believed to be residing. The Magistrate or the police officer to whom the warrant is forwarded shall endorse his name thereon, and cause it to be executed.

(4) Every person who is arrested and detained shall *be* produced before the nearest Magistrate within a period of twenty-four hours of *sack* arrest excluding the time necessary for the journey from the place of arrest to the Ctourt of the Magistrate, and no such person shall be detained in custody beyond the said period without the authority of a Magistrate.

**12.** The Court may, either suo motu or on motion made for that purpose, order the attendance for cross-examination, of a person whose affidavit has been filed in the matter.

**13.** The Court may make orders for the purpose of secuning the attendance of any person to be examined as a witness and for discovery of production of any document.

**14.** The Court may pass such orders as it thinks fit including orders as to costs which may be recovered as if the order were a decree of the Court.

**15.** Save as otherwise provided by the rules contained herein, the provisions of the Supreme Court Rules, 1966, shall, so far as may be, apply to proceedings in relation to proceedings in contempt under this Part.

PART III

**16.** Where a person charged with contempt is adjudged guilty and is sentenced to suffer imprisonment, a warrant of commitment and detention shall be made out in Form IV under the signature of the Registrar. Every such 'warrant shall remain in force until it is cancelled by order of the Court or until it is executed. The Superintendent of the Jail shall in pursuance of the order receive the person so adjudged and detain him in custody for the period specified therein, or until further orders.

# 9

# The Copyright Act, 1957

**Meaning of Copyright:** Copyright is the right which a person acquires in a work which is the result of his intellectual labour. The primary function of the law of copyright is to protect from annexation by other people of the fruits of a man's work, labour, skill or test.

**History of the law of Copyright in India:** Indian Copyright Act, 1847 was the earliest Indian enactment. Prior to this the law of copyright in India was governed by English Common Law.

The Act of 1847 was replaced by the English copyright Act, 1911, which came into force in India on October 31, 1912. The Indian Copyright Act, 1914 was passed by Indian Legislature, incorporating, the English Copyright Act, 1911, with some modifications and additions to some provisions in their application in India.

The English Copyright Act, 1911 was replaced by the English Copyright Act, 1956. Consequently, the present the Copyright Act, 1957 was made. The Act was passed in 1957 and came into effect from January 21, 1958.

By The Copyright Act, 1983, extensive amendments have been made to the Act of 1957. By the Copyright Act, 1994, which came into effect from May 10, 1995 some minor changes like omittion of some words in the Act of 1957 have been made.

**Copyright Act, 1957:** The Copyright Act, 1957 is an Act to amend and consolidate the law relating to Copyright. The primary functions of Copyright law is to protect the fruits of a man's work, labour, skill and protect from annexation by other people of the fruits of man's labour. In the case of a literary work, the Copyright is vested with the author of the work and in case of musical work, the composer is the owner of Copyright.

Copyright is "intellectual property". The object of the Copyright law is to protect the exclusive right of the author of the Copyright from an unlawful reproduction of exploitation of his works by others.

Under Section 14 of the Act, "Copyright" means the exclusive right of a person in respect of a literary, dramatic or musical work, not being a computer programme. This exclusive right of Copyright owner is :

(*i*) To reproduce the work in any material form including the storing of it in any medium by electronic means.

(*ii*) To issue copies of the work to the public not being copies in circulation.

(*iii*) To perform the work in public, or communicate it to the public.

(*iv*) To make any cinematograph film or sound recording in respect of the work.

(*v*) To make translation of the work.

(*vi*) To make adaptation of the work.

(*vii*) To do, in relation to translation or adaptation of the work in relations to works specified in (*i*) to (*vi*)

**Reproduction:** To reproduce means to copy and it includes the copyright of a substantial part of the work. It can be done in any way viz. adaptation of any literary work for filmsiation or recording or converting a play into a dance drama style. For Copyright it is necessary that it should be completely original. The reproduction could be the mixture of the original work and the new author's own wisdom.

Reproduction of substantial part thereof under the provisions of sub-section 2 of section 14 of the Act, the author would be entitled to reproduce, adapt or translate not only the whole of his original work, but also a substantial part there of which would be entitled to protection.

**Reproduction of selected passage from original work:** A compilation which reprints selected passage from an original work may itself constitute an original work if sufficient knowledge, labour, judgement or literary state have been put in to give it some quality or character which differentiates it from the original work. So it would not be correct to suppose that the law of Copyright absolutely debars a person from using any materials from any original work.

**Publication:** According to Section 3 of the Act, for the purpose of this Act, "Publication" means making a work available to the public by issue of copies by communicating the work to the public.

The amendment made in 1983 says "seeing the nature of the work make it ready for dissemination of that it fulfils the public need. Law of copyright is applicable to the unpublished work whether a work has been published as to the date on which a work was published for the purpose is decided by the Copyright Board.

According to Section 3 of the Act, in order to constitute publication of a literary work, copies of the work must be issued to the public in sufficient quantities.

From the definition in section 3 it would appear that anybody who issues copies of a work, in sufficient quantities, to the public would be a "publisher" of the work.

**Translation:** "Translation" is included as one of the incidents of copyright in a literary work in Section 14 (*i*) (*iv*). The owner of the Copyright in a work shall have the exclusive right to "produce, reproduce or publish any translation of the work". So the right over the translated work and original version of a work is one and the same Copyright Board is the authority authorized to issue license for translation under Section 32.

**Adaptation:** Adaptation means conversion of work into another form; conversion of a drama to work into non-dramatic work; the conversion of a literary or an artistic work into dramatic work, abridgment of literary or dramatic work for reproduction in book or in newspaper or similarly transcription of musical work, use of any work involving its re-arrangement or alteration. It is the right of the Copyright owner to make any adaptation. If somebody else does it without the owner's license it would constitute an infringement of the Copyright.

**Literary Work:** Under the Act, "Literary work" includes computer programmes, tables and compilations including computer. The Act does not give an exhaustive definition of a "literary" work. Since the Act does not say whether the work is to be writing or in print, it must be concluded that a literary work" is 'an expression of thought in print or in writing (University of London Vs University of Tutorial Press, 1916). According Durga Das Basu, 'the word "Literary work" is used in a sense similar to the world "literature" in political or electioneering literature, and thus refers to any written or printed matter (University of London press Vs University Tutorial Press), *e.g.,* book, Pamphlet, sheet of printing, table, lecture, sermon, novel, drama, question paper set by examiner, latter addressed by a manufacturer to his trade customer's writing of religious preacher, catalogue, printed form, a book of grammar.

**Compilation:** As in the English Act, a compilation is included within the definition of literary work. And if it can satisfy the test of originality under Section 13 (1) (*a*) of the Indian Act, it could claim Copyright. A compilation literally indicates that it is prepared from the materials extracted from other sources. Even though it may not offer any new idea or information, it can claim originality in the collection, arrangement and combination of existing materials in a new form; which involves the exercise of labour, taste, judgment and skill (Macmilan Vs Cooper, 1924). In short, originality is a "matter of degree in compilation, depending on the amount of skill, judgment or labour that has been involved in making the compilation (Ladbroke Vs William Hill, 1964). But no excellence of quality or style of writing is required to claim originality (Ladbroke Vs William Hill, 1964)

**Exceptions:** There are some exceptions to this rule. In case of a literary, dramatic or artistic work made by the author in the course of his employment by the proprietor of a newspaper, magazine or similar periodical under a contract of service or apprenticeship for the publication in the same publication, the proprietor of the publication will be the first owner of the Copyright. But in all other respects the author shall be the first owner of the Copyright in the work.

Any composition written on the request of somebody against any reward or honorarium, in that case, the person making any such a request to the author becomes the owner of Copyright.'

In the case of a photograph taken, or a printing or portrait drawn or an engraving or a cinematographic film made for valuable consideration at the instance of any person, such person shall be the first owner of the Copyright.

In the case of work made in the course of the author's employment under a contract of service or apprenticeship, the employer shall be the first owner of the Copyright.

In the case of a government work, the Government shall be the first owner of the Copyright.

In the case of a work made or first published by or under the direction or control of any public undertaking, such public undertaking shall be the first owner of the Copyright.

In the case of question papers, the question setter (examiner) will be the owner of the Copyright and not the college in which he is a professor or lecturer.

If writing a composition is not a duty, the newspaper proprietor will not be the first owner of the Copyright.

**Term of Copyright:** Copyright shall subsist in any literary, dramatic, musical or artistic work (other than a photograph) published within the lifetime of the author until sixty years from the beginning of the calendar year next following the year in which the author dies.

In the case of more than one author of a work, this sixty-years will be counted from the author who dies last. The words "fifty year" in the Act of 1957 had been substituted by "sixty years" by Act no 13 of 1992.

Where the author(s) died before January 21, 1958 *i.e.,* before the commencement of the Act of 1957, the law applicable would be section 3 of the Act of 1914.

In case of the work published anonymously or pseudonymously, Copyright shall subsist until sixty years from the beginning of the calendar year next following the year in which the work is first published.

Provided that where the Identity of the author is disclosed before the expiry of the said period Copyright shall subsist until sixty years from the beginning of the calendar year following the year in which the author dies.

**Term of Copyright in posthumous work:** In case where a work is not published before the death of the author (s), Copyright shall subsist until sixty years from the beginning of the calendar year next following the year in which the work is first published.

**Infringement of Copyright:** Section 51 of the Act of 1957 says that without a license from the owner of the Copyright or the Registrar of Copyright or in contravention of the term there of could constitute an "infringement of the Copyright" in a work. The following are the acts of the infringement of the Copyright of a work; when committed by a person not authorized by license :

(*a*) If the defendant reproduced the work in any material form.

(*b*) If the defendant makes a cinematograph film by reproducing or converting a substantial portion of the plaintiff's novel or drama.

**Certain acts not to be infringement of Copyright:** According to Section 52 (1) of the Act, the following acts shall not constitute and infringement of Copyright, namely:

(*a*) A fair dealing with a literary, dramatic, musical or artistic work for the purpose of

  (*i*) Private use including research

  (*ii*) Criticism or receive, whether of that work or any other work.

(*b*) A fair dealing works, mentioned in (*a*) above for the purpose of reporting current events :

  (*i*) In a newspaper or magazine, or

  (*ii*) By broadcast or in a cinematographic film or by means of Photographs

(*c*) The reproduction of any work for the purpose of a report of judicial proceeding;

(*d*) The reproduction of publication of any work for Secretariat or Legislative work.

Also the publication in collection for the use of educational institutions reproduction by a teacher or a pupil in the course of instruction, in answers to question in examinations. The Supreme Court in the case of Anand Vs Deluxe Films, 1978, has summarized the tests to determine whether there has been an infringement in a novel or drama by making a film. Mere similarity between the book and the film is not enough. There being no Copyright in an idea or a theme, some similarity is bound to occur where the book and the film are based on the same idea or theme.

(*a*) Were apart from similarities in the two works, there are also material dissimilarities which negative the intention to copy the original and the coincidences are clearly incidental, there is no infringement of Copyright.

(*b*) On the other hand, if the defendant's work is nothing but a literal imitation of the Copyright work with some variation here and there, it would amount to violation of Copyright.

(*c*) When the theme is the same, but it is presented and treated differently so that the subsequent work becomes a completely new work, no question of violation of Copyright arises.

(*d*) Since a film has a much broader perspective than a stage play or drama, the producer of a film can, by introducing a variety of incidents, give a colour and complexion different from the manner in which the Copyright work has expressed the idea.

**Remedies for infringement of Copyright:** The remedies for infringement of Copyright are as follows :

(*i*) Civil Remedies
- (*a*) Damages
- (*b*) Injuries
- (*c*) Accounts
- (*d*) Recovery of possession of infringing copies
- (*e*) Damages for conversion, on the footing that the sale proceeds of the infringing copies is the owner's property.

(*ii*) Criminal Proceedings.

Prosecution for offence of infringement is given here in after.

**Offence of infringement of Copyright or other rights conferred by this Act**

Any person who 'knowingly infringes' or abets the infringement

(*a*) The Copyright in a work or

(*b*) any other right conferred by this Act (substituted by the Copyright (Amendment) Act, 1994)

Shall be punishable with imprisonment for a term which shall not be less than six months, but which may be extended to three years and it fine which shall not be less than fifty thousand rupees but which may extend to two lakh rupees.

The word "knowingly infringes" clearly postulate a knowledge on the part of the accused that he infringed the Copyright in a work.

Where any offence under this Act has been committed by a company, every person who at the time of the offence was committed was in charge of and was responsible to the company for the conduct of the business of the company and shall be liable to be proceeded against and punished accordingly.

**Appeals:** Any person aggrieved by any order made under sub-section (2) of section 64 or section 66 may, within thirty days of the date of such order, appeal to the court, to which appeals from the court making the order ordinarily lie and such appellate Court may direct that the execution of the order be stayed pending disposal of the appeal.

Any person aggrieved by any final decision or order of the Copyright Board, may within three months from the date of such decision or order, appeal to the High Court within whose Jurisdiction the appellant actually and voluntarily resides or carries business.

# CHAPTER III

## COPYRIGHT ACT, 1957

**13. Works in which copyright subsists:** (1) Subject to the provisions of this section and the other provisions of this Act. copyright shall subsist throughout India in the following classes of works, that is to say:

(*a*) original literary, dramatic, musical and artistic works;

(*b*) cinematograph films: and

(*c*) sound recording.

(2) Copyright shall not subsist in any work specified in sub-section (1), other than a work to which the provisions of section 40 or section 41 apply, unless:

(*i*) in the case of a published work, the work is first published in India, or where the work is first published outside India, the author is at the date of such publication, or in a case where the author was dead at that date, was at the time of his death, a citizen of India;

(*ii*) in the case of an unpublished work other than work of architecture, the author is at the date of the making of the work a citizen of India or domiciled in India; and

(*iii*) in the case of work of architecture, the work is located in India.

*Explanation:* In the case of a work of joint authorship, the conditions conferring copyright specified in this sub-section shall be satisfied by all the authors of the work.

(3) Copyright shall not subsist :

(*a*) in any cinematograph film if a substantial part of the film is an infringement of the copyright in any other work:

(*b*) in any sound recording made in respect of a literary, dramatic or musical work, if in making the sound recording, copyright in such work has been infringed.

(4) The copyright in a cinematograph film or a sound recording shall not affect the separate copyright in any work in respect of which or a substantial part of which, the-film, or, as the case may be, the sound recording is made.

(5) In the case of work of architecture, copyright shall subsist only in the artistic character and design and shall not extend to processes or methods of construction.

**14. Meaning of copyright:** For the purposes of this Act, "copyright" means the exclusive right subject to the provisions of this Act, to do or authorise the doing of any of:

(*i*) to reproduce the work in any material form including the storing of it in any medium by electronic means;

(*ii*) to issue copies of the work to the public not being copies already in circulation;

(*iii*) to perform the work in public, or communicate it to the public;

(*iv*) to make any cinematograph film or sound recording in respect of the work;

(*v*) to make any translation of the work;

(*vi*) to make any adaptation of the work;

(*vii*) to do, in relation to a translation or an adaptation of the work, any of the acts specified in relation to the work in sub-clauses (i) to (vi);

(*b*) in the case of a computer programme,:

  (*i*) to do any of the acts specified in clause (a);

  (*ii*) to sell or give on commercial rental or offer for sale or for commercial rental any copy of the computer programme:

Provided that such commercial rental does not apply in respect of computer programmes where the programme itself is not the essential object of the rental;

(*c*) in the case of an artistic work,:

  (*i*) to reproduce the work in any material form including depiction in three dimensions of a two dimensional work or in two dimensions of a three dimensional work;

  (ii) to communicate the work to the public;

  (*iii*) to issue copies of the work to the public not being copies already in circulation;

  (*iv*) to include the work in any cinematograph film;

  (*v*) to make any adaptation of the work;

(*vi*) to do in relation to an adaptation of the work any of the acts specified in relation to the work in sub-clauses (i) to (iv);

(*d*) in the case of a cinematograph film,:

(*i*) to make a copy of the film including a photograph of any image forming part thereof;

(*ii*) to sell or give on hire or offer for sale or hire, any copy of the film, regardless of whether such copy has been sold or given on hire on earlier occasions;

(*iii*) to communicate the film to the public;

(*ii*) to sell or give on hire, or offer for sale or fire, any copy of the sound recording, regardless of whether such copy has been sold or given on hire on earlier occasions;

(*iii*) 10 communicate the sound recording to the public.

*Explanation*: For the purposes of this section, a copy which has been sold once shall be deemed to be a copy already in circulation.

**16.** No **copyright except as provided in this Act:** No person shall be entitled to copyright or any similar right in any work. whether published or unpublished, otherwise than under and in accordance with the provisions of this Act or of any other for the time being in force, but nothing in this section shall be construed as abrogating any right or jurisdiction to restrain a breach of trust or confidence.

## CHAPTER IV

## OWNERSHIP OF COPYRIGHT AND THE RIGHTS OF THE OWNER

**17. First owner of copyright:** Subject to the provisions of this Act, the author of a work shall be the owner of the copyright therein:

**Provided that:**

(*a*) in the case of a literary, dramatic or artistic work made by the author in the course of his employment by the proprietor of a newspaper, magazine or similar periodical under a contract of service or apprenticeship, for the purpose of publication in a newspaper, magazine or similar periodical, the said proprietor shall, in the absence of any agreement to the contrary, be the first owner of the copyright in the work in so far as the copyright relates to the publication of the work in any newspaper, magazine or similar periodical, or to the reproduction of the work for the purpose of its being so published, but in all other respects the author shall be the first owner of the copyright in the work;

(*b*) subject to the provisions of clause (a), in the case of a photograph taken, or a painting or portrait drawn, or an engraving or a cinematograph film made, for valuable consideration at the instance of any person, such person shall, in the absence of any agreement to the contrary, be the first owner of the copyright therein;

(*c*) in the case of a work made in the course of the author's employment under a contract of service or apprenticeship, to which clause (a) or clause (b) does not apply, the employer shall, in the absence of any agreement to the contrary, be the first owner of the copyright therein;

(*cc*) in case of any address or speech delivered in public, the person who has delivered such address or speech or if such person has delivered such address or speech on behalf of any other person, such other person shall be the first owner of the copyright therein notwithstanding that the person who delivers.

(*d*) in the case of a Government work. Government shall in the absence of any agreement to the conrrary, be the first owner of the copyright therein:

(*dd*) in the case of a work made or first published by or under the direction or control of any public undertaking, such public undertaking shall, in the absence of any agreement to the contrary, be the first owner of the copyright therein;

*Explanation:* For the purposes of this clause and section 28A, "public undertaking" means :

(*i*) an undertaking owned or controlled by Government; or

(*ii*) a Government company as defined in section 617 of the Companies Act, 1956(1 of 1956); or

(*iii*) a body corporate established by or under any Central, Provincial or State Act;

(*e*) in the case of a work to which the provisions of section 41 apply, the international organisation concerned shall be the first owner of the copyright therein.

**18. Assignment of copy right:** (1) The owner of the copyright in an existing worker the prospective owner of the copyright in a future work may assign to any person the copyright either wholly or partially and either generally or subject to limitations and either for the whole of the copyright or any part thereof :

Provided that in the case/of the assignment of copyright in any future work, the assignment shall take effect only when the work comes into existence.

(2) Where the assignee of a copyright becomes entitled to any right comprised in the copyright, the assignee as respects the rights so assigned, and the

assignor as respects the rights not assigned, shall be treated for the purposes of this Act as the owner of copyright and the provisions of this Act shall have effect accordingly.

(3) In this section, the expression "assignee" as respects the assignment of the copyright in any future work includes the legal representatives of the assignee, if the assignee dies before the work comes into existence.

**19. Mode of assignment:** (1) No assignment of the copyright in any work shall be valid unless it is in writing signed by the assignor or by his duly authorised agent.

(2) The assignment of copyright in any work shall identify such work, and shall specify the rights assigned and the 'duration and territorial extent of such assignment.

(3) The assignment of copyright in any work shall also specify the amount of royalty payable, if any, to the author or his legal heirs during the currency of the assignment and the assignment shall be subject to revision, extension or termination on terms mutually agreed upon by the parties.

(5) If the period of assignment is not stated, it shall be five from the date of assignment.

(6) If the territorial extent of assignment of the rights is; not specified, it shall be presumed to extend within India.

(7) Nothing in sub-section (2) or sub-section (3) or sub-section (4) or sub-section (5) or sub-section (6) shall be applicable to assignments made before the coming into force of the Copyright (Amendment) Act. 1994.

**20. Transmission of copy right in manuscript by testamentary disposition:** Where under a bequest a person is entitled to the manuscript of a literary, dramatic or musical work, or to an artistic work, and the work was not published before the death of the testator, the bequest shall, unless the contrary intention is indicated in the testator's will or any codicil thereto, be construed as including the copyright in the work in so far as the testator was the owner of the copyright immediately before his death.

*Explanation*: In this section, the expression "manuscript" means the original document embodying the work, whether written by hand or not.

**22. Term of copyright in published literary, dramatic, musical and artistic works:** Except as otherwise hereinafter provided, copyright shall subsist in any literary, dramatic, musical or artistic work (other than a photograph) published within the lifetime of the author until sixty years from the beginning of the calendar year next following the year in which the author dies.

*Explanation: In* this section the reference to the author shall, in the case of a work of joint authorship, be construed as a reference to the author who dies last.

**23. Term of copyright in anonymous and pseudonymous works:** (1) In the case of a literary, dramatic, musical or artistic work (other than a photograph), which, is published anonymously or pseudonymously, copyright shall subsist until sixty years from the beginning of the calendar year next following the year in which the work is first-published:

Provided that where the identity of the author is disclosed before the expiry of the said period, copyright shall subsist until sixty years from the beginning of the calendar year following the year in which the author dies.

(2) In sub-section (1), references to the author shall, in the case of an anonymous work of joint authorship, be construed:

(*a*) where the identity of the authors is disclosed, as references to that–author

(*b*) where the identity of more authors than one is disclosed, as references to the author who dies last from amongst such authors.

(3) In sub-section (1), references to the author shall, in the case of a pseudonymous work of joint authorship, be construed, :

(*a*) where the names of one or more (but not all) of the authors are pseudonymous and his or their identity is not disclosed, as references to the author whose name is not a pseudonym, or, if the names of two or more of the authors are not pseudonyms, as references to such of those authors who dies last :

(*b*) where the names of one or more (but not all) of the authors are pseudonyms and the identity of one or more of them is disclosed, as references to the authors who has dies last from amongst the authors whose names are not pseudonyms and the author whose names are pseudonyms and are disclosed; and

(*c*) where the names of all the authors are pseudonyms and the identity of one of them is disclosed, as references to the author whose identity is disclosed or if the identity of two or more of such authors is disclosed, as references to such of those authors who dies last.

*Explanation:* For the purposes of this section, the identity of an author shall be deemed to have been disclosed, if either the identity of the author is disclosed publicly by both the author and the publisher or is otherwise established to the satisfaction of the Copyright Board by that author.

**24. Term of copyright in posthumous work:** (1) In the case of a literary, dramatic or musical work or an engraving, in which copyright subsists at the date of the death of the author, or in the case of any such work of joint authorship, at or immediately before the date of the death of the author who dies last, but which, or any adaptation of which, has not been published before that date. copyright shall subsist unti1 sixty years from the beginning of the calendar year next following the year in which the work is first published or, where an adaptation of the work is published in any earlier year, from the beginning of the calendar year next following that year.

(2) For the purposes of this section a literary, dramatic or musical work or an adaptation of any such work shall be deemed to have been published, if it has been performed in public or if any sound recording made in respect of the work have been sold to the public or have been offered for sale to the public.

**30. Licences by owners of copyright:** The owner of the copyright in any existing work of the prospective owner of the copyright in any future work may grant any interest in the right by licence in writing signed by him or by his duty authorised agent:

Provided that in the case of a licence relating to copyright in any future work, the licence shall take effect only when the work comes into existence.

*Explanation*: Where a person to whom a licence relating to copyright in any future work is granted under this section dies before the work comes into existence, his legal representatives shall, in the absence of any provision to the contrary in the licence, be entitled to the benefit of the licence.

**32. Licence to produce and publish translations:** (l) Any person may apply to the Copyright Board for a licence to produce and publish a translation of a literary or dramatic work in any language after a period of seven years from the first publication of the work.

(1 A) Notwithstanding anything contained in sub-section (1), any person may apply to the Copyright Board for a licence to produce and publish a translation, in printed or analogous forms of reproduction, of a literary or dramatic work, other than an Indian work in any language in general use in India after a period of three years from the first publication of such work, if such translation is required for the purposes of teaching, scholarship or research.

Provided that where such translation is in a language not in general use in any developed country, such application may be made after a period of one year from such publication.

(2 ) Every application under this section shall be made in such form as may be prescribed and shall state the proposed retail price of a copy of the translation of the work.

(3) Every applicant for a licence under this section shall, along with his application deposit with the Registrar of Copyrights such fee as may be prescribed.

(4) Where an application is made to the Copyright Board under this section it may, after holding such inquiry as may be prescribed, grant to the applicant a licence, not being an exclusive licence. to produce and publish a translation of the work in the language mentioned. in the application :

(*i*) subject to the condition that the applicant shall pay to the owner of the copyright in the work royalties in respect of copies of the translation of the work sold to the public, calculated at such rate as the Copyright Board may. in the circumstances of each case, determine in the prescribed manner: and

(*ii*) where such licence is granted on an application under sub-section(lA) subject also to the condition that the licence shall not extend to the export of copies of the translation of the work outside India and every copy of such translation shall contain a notice in the language of such translation' that the copy is available for distribution only in India :

Provided that nothing in clause (*ii*) shall apply to export by Government or any authority under the Government of copies of such translation in a language other than English, French for Spanish in any country if:

(1) such copies are sent to citizens of India residing outside India or to any association of such citizens outside India; or

(2) such copies are meant to be used for purposes of teaching, scholarship or research and not for any commercial purpose; and

(3) in either case, the permission for such export has been given by the Government of that country:

Provided further that no licence under this section shall be granted, unless :

(*a*) a translation of the work in the language mentioned in the application has not been published by the owner of the copyright in the work or any person authorised by him, within seven years or three years or one year, as the case may be, of the first publication of the work, or if a translation has been so published, it has been out of print;

(*b*) the applicant has proved to the satisfaction of the Copyright Board that he had requested and had been denied authorisation by the owner of the copyright to produce and publish such translation, or that he was, after due diligence on its part, unable to find the owner of the copyright;

(*c*) where the applicant was unable to find the owner of the copyright, he has sent, *a* copy of his request for such authorisation by registered air mail post to the publisher whose name appears from the work, and in the case of an application for a licence under sub-section ('), not less than two months before such application;

(*cc*) a period of six months in the pase of an application under sub-section (I A) (not being an application under the proviso thereto), or nine months in the case of an application under the proviso to that sub–section, has elapsed from the date of making the request under clause (*b*) of this proviso or where copy of the request has been sent under clause (*c*) of this proviso, from the date of sending of such copy, and the translation of the work in the language mentioned in the application has not been published by the owner of the copyright in the work or any person authorised by him within the said period of six months or nine months, as the case may be :

(*ccc*) in the case of any application made under sub-section (IA),

(*i*) the name of the author and the title of the particular edition of the work proposed to be translated are printed on all the copies of the translation;

(*ii*) if the work is composed mainly of illustrations, the provisions of section 32A are also complied with;

(*d*) the Copyright Board is satisfied that the applicant is competent to produce and publish a correct translation of the work and possesses the means to pay to the owner of the copyright the royalties payable to him under this section;

(*e*) the author has not withdrawn from circulation copies of the work; and

(*f*) an opportunity of being heard is given, wherever practicable, to the owner of the copyright in the work.

(5) Any broadcasting authority may apply to the Copyright Board for a licence to produce and publish the translation of:

(*a*) a work referred to in sub-section (1A) and published in printed or analogous forms of reproduction;or

(*b*) any text incorporated in audio-visual fixations prepared and published solely for the purpose of systematic instructional activities, for broadcasting such translation for the purposes of teaching or for the dissemination ofthe results of specialised, technical or scientific research to the experts in any particular field.

(6) The provisions of sub-sections (2) to (4) in so far as they are relatable to an application under sub-section (1A), shall, with the necessary modifications, apply to the grant of a licence under sub-section (5) and such licence shall not also be granted unless:

(*a*) the translation is made from a work lawfully acquired;

(*b*) the broadcast is made through the medium of sound and visual recordings;

(*c*) such recording has been low of fully and exclusively made for the purpose of broadcasting in India by the applicant or by other broadcasting agency ; and (*d*) the translation and the broadcasting of such translation are not used for any commercial purposes.

*Explanation:* For the purposes of this section:

(*a*) "developed country" means a country which is not a developing country;

(*b*) "developing country" means a country which is for the time being regarded as such in conformity with the practice of the General Assembly of the United Nations:

(*c*) "purposes of research" does not inclucie purposes of industrial research, or purposes of research by bodies corporate (not being bodies corporate owned or controlled by Government or other association or body of persons forcom mercial purposes :

(*d*) "purposes of teaching, research or scholarship" includes:

(*i*) purposes of instructional activity at all levels in educational insiclenlins of including Schools, Colleges. Universities and tutorial institutions; and

(*ii*) purposes of all other types of organised educational activity.

**52. Certain acts not to be infringement of copyright:** (1) The follow in acts shall not constitute an infringement of copyright, namely:

(*a*) a fair dealing with a literary, dramatic, musical or artistic work not being a computer programme for the purposes of:

(*i*) Private use including research:

(*ii*) criticism or review, whether of that work or of any other work;

(*aa*) the making of copies or adaptation or a computer programme by the lawful possessor of a copy of such computer programme from such copy:

(*i*) in order to utilise the computer programme for the purpose for which it was supplied; or

(*ii*) to make back-up copies purely as a temporary protection, against loss, destruction or damage in order only to utilise the computer programme for the purpose for which it was supplied;

(*b*) a fair dealing with a literary, dramatic, musical or artistic work for the purpose of reporting current events:

(*i*) in a newspaper, magazine or similar periodical; or

(*ii*) by broadcast or in a cinematograph film or by means of photographs.

*Explanation:* The publication of a compilation of addresses or speeches delivered in public is not a fair dealing of such work within the meaning of this clause;

(*c*) the reproduction of a literary, dramatic musical or artistic work for the purpose ofajudicial proceeding or for the purpose of a report of a judicial proceeding,

(*d*) the reproduction or publication of a literary, dramatic, musical or artistic work in any work prepared by the Secretariat of a Legislature or, where the Legislature consists of two Houses, by the Secretariat of either House of the Legislature, exclusively for the use of the members of that Legislature;

(*e*) the reproduction of any literary, dramatic or musical work in a certified copy made or supplied in accordance with any law for the time being in force;

(*f*) the reading or recitation in public of any reasonable extract from a published literary or dramatic work;

(g) the publication in a collection, mainly composed of non-copyright matter *bonafide* intended for the use of educational institutions, and so described in the title and in any advertisement issued by or on behalf of the publisher, of short passages from published literary or dramatic works, not themselves published for the use of educational institutions, in which copyright subsists:

Provided that not more than two such passages from works by the same author are published by the same publisher during any period of five years

*Explanation*: In the case of a work of joint authorship, references in the clause to passage from works shall include references to passages from works by any one or more of the authors of those passages or by any one or more of those authors in collaboration with any other person;

(*h*) the reproduction of a literary, dramatic, musical or artistic work :

  (*i*) by a teacher or a pupil in the course of instruction; or

  (*ii*) as part of the questions to be answered in an examination; or

  (*iii*) in answers, to such questions;

(*i*) the performance, in the course of the activities of an educational institution, of a literary, dramatic or musical work by the staff and student of the institution, or of a cinematograph film or a sound recording, if the audience is limited to such staff and students, the parents and guardians of the students and persons directly connected with the activities of the institution or the communication to such an audience of a cinematograph film or sound recording;

(*j*) the making of sound recordings in respect of any literary, dramatic or musical work, if:

  (*i*) sound recordings of that work have been made by or with the licence or consent of the owner of the right in the work;

(*ii*) the person making the sound recordings has given a notice of his intention to make the sound recordings, has provided copies of all covers or labels with which the sound recordings are to be sold, and has paid in the prescribed manner to the owner of rights in the work royalties in respect of all *such* sound recordings to be made by him, at the rate fixed by the Copyright Board in this behalf:

Provided that :

(*i*) no alterations shall be made which have not been made previously by or with the consent of the owner of rights, or which are not reasonably necessary for the adaptation of the work for the purpose of making the sound recordings;

(*ii*) the sound recordings shall not be issued in any form of packaging or with any label which is likely to mislead or confuse the public as to their identity;

(*iii*) no such sound recording shall be made until the expiration of two calendar years after the end of the year in which the first recording of the work was made: and

(*iv*) the person making such sound recordings shall allow the owner of right or his duly auiliorised agent or representative to inspect all records and books of account relating to such sound recording:

Provided further that if on a complaint brought before the Copyright Board to the effect, that the owner rights has not been paid in full foranv sound recordings purporting to be made in pursuance of this clause, the Copyright Board *is prima facie* satisfied that the complaint is genuine, it may pass an order ex–parate directing the person making the sound recording to cease from making further copies and, after holding such inquiry as it considers necessary, make such further order as it may deem fit, including an order for payment of royalty;

(*k*) the causing of a recording to be heard in public by utilising it:

(*i*) in an enclosed room or hall meant for the common use of residents in any residential premises (not being a hotel or similar commercial establishment) as part of the amenities provided exclusively or mainly for residents therein; or

(*ii*) as part of the activities of a club or similar organisation which is not established or conducted for profit:

(*l*) the performance of a literary, dramatic or musical work by an amateur club or society, if the performance is given to a non-paying audience, or for the benefit of a religious institution;

(*m*) the reproduction in a newspaper, magazine or other periodical of an article on current economic, political, social or religious topics, unless the author of such article has expressly reserved to himself the right of such reproduction;

(*n*) the publication in a newspaper, magazine or other periodical of a report of a lecture delivered in public;

(*o*) the making of not more than three copies of a book (including a pamphlet, sheet of music, map, chart or plan) by or under the direction of the person in charge of a public library for the use ofthe library if such book is not available for sale in India;

(*p*) the reproduction, for the purpose of research or private study, or with a view to publication, of an unpublished literary, dramatic or musical works kept in a library, museum or other institution to which the public has access:

Provided that where the identity of the author of any such work or, in the case of a work of joint authorship, of any of the authors is known to the library, museum or other institution, as the case may be, the provisions of this clause shall apply only if such reproduction is made at a time more than fifty years from the date of the death of the author or, in the case of a work of joint authorship, from the death of the author whose identity is known or, if the identity of more authors than one is known from the death of such of those authors who died last:

(*q*) the reproduction or publication of:

(*i*) any matter which has been published in any Official Gazette except an Act of a Legislature;

(*ii*) any Act of a Legislature subject to the condition that such Act is reproduced or published together with any commentary thereon or any other original matter :

(*iii*) the report of any committee, commission, council, board or other like body appointed by the Legislature, unless the reproduction or publication of such report is prohibited by the Government;

(*iv*) any judgment or order of a court, Tribunal or other judicial authority. unless the reproduction or publication of such judgment or order is prohibited by the court, the Tribunal or other judicial authority, as the case may be;

(*r*) the production or publication of a translation in any Indian language of an Act of a Legislature and of any rules or orders made thereunder :

(*i*) if no translation of such Act or rules or orders in that language has been produced or published by the Government; or

(*ii*) where a translation of such Act or rules or orders in that language has been produced or published by the Government, if the translation is not available for sale to the public:

Provided that such translation contains a statement at a prominent place of the effect that the translation has not been authorised or accepted as authentic by the Government;

(*s*) the making or publishing of a painting, drawing, engraving or photograph of a work of architecture or the display of a work of architecture;

(*t*) the making or publishing of a painting, drawing, engraving or photograph of a sculpture, or other artistic work falling under sub-clause (iii) of clause (c) of section 2, if such work is permanently situate in a public place or any premises to which the public has access;

(*u*) the inclusion in a cinematograph film of:

   (*i*) any artistic work permanently situate in a public place or any premises to which the public has access; or

   (*ii*) any other artistic work, if such inclusion is only by way of background or is otherwise incidental to the principal matters represented in the film;

(*v*) the use by the author of an artistic work, where the author of such work is not the owner of the copyright therein, of any would, cast, sketch, plan, model or study made by him for the purpose of the work:

Provided that he does not thereby repeat or imitate the main design of the work;

(*x*) the reconstruction of a building or structure in accordance with the architectural drawings or plans by reference to which the building or structure was originally constructed:

Provided that the original construction was made with the consent or licence of the owner of the copyright in such drawings and plans;

(*y*) in relation to a literary, dramatic or musical work recorded or reproduced any cinematograph film. the exhibition of such film after the expiration of the tern of copyright therein:

Provided that the provisions of sub-clause (ii) of clause (a), sub-clause (i) of clause (b) and clauses (d), (f), (g), (m), and (p) shall not apply as respects any-act unless that act is accompanied by an acknowledgement:

   (*i*) identifying the work by its title or other description; and

   (*ii*) unless the work is anonymous or the author of the work has previously agreed or required that no acknowledgement of his name should be made. also identifying the author:

(*z*) the making of an ephemeral recording, by a broadcasting organisation using its own facilities for its own broadcast by a broadcasting organisation of a work which it has the right to broadcast; and the retention of such recording for achival purposes on the ground of its exceptional documentary character;

(*za*) the performance of a literary, dramatic or musical work or the communication to the public of such work or of a sound recording in the course of any bonafide religious ceremony or an official ceremony held by the Central Government or the State Government or any local authority.

*Explanation:* For the purpose of this clause, religious ceremony including a marriage procession and other social festivities associated with a marriage.

(2) The provisions of sub-section (1) shall apply to the doing of any act in relation to the translation of a literary, dramatic or musical work or the adaptation of a literary, dramatic, musical or artistic work as they apply in relation to the work itself.

**54. Definition:** For the purposes of this Chapter, unless the context otherwise requires, the expression "owner of copyright" shall include:

(*a*) an exclusive licensee;

(*b*) in the case of an anonymous or pseudonymous literary, dramatic, musical or artistic work, the publisher of the work, until the identity of the author or, in the case of an anonymous work of joint authorship, or a work of joint authorship published under names all of which are pseudonyms, the identity of any of the authors, is disclosed publicly by the author and the publisher or is otherwise to the satisfaction of the Copyright Board by that author or his legal representatives.

**55. Civil remedies for infringement of copyright:** (1) Where copyright in any work has been infringed, the owner of the copyright shall, except as otherwise provided by this Act, be entitled to all such remedies by way of injunction, damages, accounts and otherwise as are or may be conferred by law for the infringement of a right:

Provided that if the defendant proves that at the date of the infringement he was not aware and had no reasonable ground for believing that copyright subsisted in the work, the plaintiff shall not be entitled to any remedy other than an injunction in respect of the infringement and a decree for the whole or part of the profits made by the defendant by the sale of the infringing copies as the court may in the circumstances deem reasonable.

(2) Where, in the cased a literary, dramatic, musical or artistic work. a name purporting to be that to the author or the publisher, as the case may be, appears on copies of the work published, or. in the case *of an* artistic work. appeared on the work when it was made. the person whose name so appear or appeared shall, in any proceeding in respect of infringement of copyright in such w ork, be presumed, unless the contrary is proved, to be the author or the publisher of the work, as the case may be.

(3) The costs of all parties in any proceedings in respect of the in fringement of copyright shall be in the discretion of the court.

**56. Protection of separate rights:** Subject to the provisions of this Act. where the several rights comprising the copyright in any work are owned by different persons, the owner of any such right shall, to the extent of that right, be entitled to the remedies provided by this Act and may individually enforce such right by means of any suit, action or other proceeding without making the owner of any other right party to such suit, action or proceeding.

**57. Author's special right:** (1) Independently of the author's copyright and even after the assignment either wholly or partially of the said copyright, the author of a work shall have the right :

(*a*) to claim authorship of the work; and

(*b*) to restrain or claim damages in respect of any distortion, mutilation, modification or other act in relation to the said work which is done before the expiration of the term of copyright if such distortion, mutilation, modification or other act would be prejudicial to his honour or reputation:

Provided that the author shall not have any right to restrain of claim damages in respect of any adaptation of a computer programme to which clause (aa) of sub-section (1) of section 52 applies.

*Explanation*: Failure to display a work or to display it to the satisfaction ofthe author shall not be deemed to be an infringement of the rights conferred by this section.

(2) The right conferred upon an author of a work by sub-section (1), other than the right to claim authorship of the work, may be exercised by the legal representatives of the author.

**58. Rights of owner against persons possessing or dealing with infringing copies:** All infringing copies of any work in which copyright subsists, and all plates used or intended to be used for the production of such infringing copies, shall be deemed to be the property of the owner of the copyright, who accordingly may take proceedings for the recovery of possession thereof or in respect of the conversion thereof:

Provided that the owner of the copyright shall not be entitled to any remedy in respect of the co–version of any infringing copies if the opponent proves:

(*a*) that he was not aware and had no reasonable ground to believe that copyright subsisted in the work of which such copies are alleged to be infringing copies: or

(*b*) that he had reasonable grounds for believig that such copies or plates don not involve infringement of the copyright in any work.

**60. Remedy in the case of groundless threat of legal proceedings:** Where any person claiming to be the owner of copyright in any work, by circulars, advertisements or otherwise, threatens any other person with any legal proceedings or liability in respect of an alleged infringement of the copyright, any person aggrieved thereby may. not with standing anything contained in section 34 of the Specific Relief Act. 1963 (47 of 1963), institute a declaratory suit that the alleged infringement to which the threats related was not in fact an infringement of any legal rights of the person making such threats and may in any such suit :

(*a*) obtain an injunction against the continuance of such threats; and

(*b*) recover such damages, if any. as he has sustained by reason of such threats.

Provided that this section does not apply if the person making such threats, with due diligence, commences and prosecutes an action for infringement ofthe copyright claimed by him.

**61. Owners of copyright to be party to the proceeding:** (1) In every civil suit or other proceeding regarding infringement of copyright instituted by an exclusive licensee, the owner of the copyright shall, unless the court otherwise directs, be made a defendant and where such owner is made a defendant, he shall have the right to dispute the claim of the exclusive licensee.

(2) Where any civil suit or other proceeding regarding infringement of copyright instituted by an exclusive licensee is successful, no fresh suit or other proceeding in respect of the same cause of action shall lie at the instance of the owner of the copyright.

**63. Offence of infringement of copyright or other rights conferred by this Act:** Any person who knowingly infringes or abets the infringement of:

(a) the copyright in a work, or

(*b*) any other right conferred by this Act, except the right conferred by section 53A.

shall be punishable with imprisonment for a term which shall not be less than six months but which may extend to three years and with fine which shall not be less than fifty thousand rupees but which may extend to two lakh rupees:

Provided that where the infringement has not been made for gain on the course of trade or business the court may, for adequate and special reasons to be mentioned in the judgment, impose a sentence of imprisonment for a term of less than six months or a fine of less than fifty thousand rupees.

*Explanation*: Construction of a building or other structure which infringes or which, if completed, would infringe the copyright in some other work shall not be an offence under this section.

**64. Power of police to seize infringing copies:** (1) Any police officer, not below the rank of a sub-inspector, may, if he is satisfied that an offence under section 63 in respect of the infringement of copyright in any work has been, is being, or is likely to be coinmitied. seize without warrant, all copies of the work, and all plates used for the purpose of making infringing copies of the work, wherever found, and all copies and plates so seized shall, as soon as practicable, be produced before a Magistrate.

(2) Any person having an interest in any copies of a work or plates seized under subsection (I) may. within fifteen days of such seizure- make an application to the magistrate for such copies or plates being restored to him and the Magistrate, after hearing the applicant and the complainant and making such further inquiry as may be necessary, shall make such order on the application as he may deem fit.

**69. Offences by companies:** (I) Where any offence under this Act has been committed by a company, every person who at the time the offence was committed was in charge of, and was responsible to the company for, the conduct of the business of the company, as well as the company shall be deemed to be guilty of such offence, shall be liable to be proceeded against and punished accordingly:

Provided that nothing contained in this sub-section shall render any person fit to any punishment, if he proves that the offence was committed without his knowledge or that he exercised all due diligence to prevent the commission of such offence.

(2) Notwithstanding anything contained in sub-section (1), where an offence under this Act has been committed by a company, and it is proved that the offence was committed with the consent or connivance of, or is attributable to any negligence on the part of, any director, manager, secretary or other officer of the company, such director, manager, secretary or other officer shall also be deemed to be guilty of that offence and shall be liable to be proceeded against and punished accordingly.

*Explanation*: For the purposes of this section:

(*a*) "company" means any body corporate and includes a firm or other association of persons: and

(*b*) "director" in relation to a firm means a partner in the firm.

**70. Cognizance of offences:** No court in ferior to that of a Metropolitan Magistrate or a Judicial Magistrate of the first class shall try any offence under this Act.

**71. Appeals against certain order of Magistrate:** Any person aggrieved by an order made under sub-section(2) of section 64 or section 66 may, within thirty days of the date of such order appeal to (he court to which appeals from the court making the order ordinarily lie, and such appellate court may direct that execution of the order be stayed pending disposal of the appeal.

# 10

# Press Commission of India

**First Press Commission:** The First Press Commission was constituted in 1952, under the Chairmanship of Justice B.G. Rajadhyaksha. It was asked to look into the factors, which influence the establishment and maintenance of high standards of journalism in India. After independence the press was fast turning from a mission to a business. The commission remarked that whatever the law relating to the press may be there would still be a large quantity of objectionable journalism, which though not falling within the purview of the law, would still require some checking. The Commission desired that the best way of maintaining professional standards of journalism would be to establish a body of people principally connect with the industry and it should be given the responsibility to arbitrate on doubtful points and to ensure the punishment of any found guilty of infraction of good journalistic behaviour.

Rajadhyaksha Report did not recommend a revolution. But it recommended to introduce order into an industry which had known no law and respect none. The First Press Commission for the first time in India defined what a responsible press should be. An important recommendation of the commission was the setting up of a statutory Press Council at the national level, consisting of press people and other members.

**Second Press Commission:** The Government of India constituted a Second Press Commission in 1978 after the internal emergency in the country was lifted. The Second Press Commission desired that the press be neither a mindless adversary nor an unquestioning. The Commission wanted the press to play a responsible role in the development process. The Press should reflect it the aspirations and problems of the people and widely accessible to them. The Commission said that for development to take place, internal stability was as important as safeguarding national security. It also highlighted the role of the press in preventing and deflating communal conflict. The positive role of the press in bringing together diverse elements in the nation's life was as important as the avoidance of objectionable or communal writing. The Commission recommended that the Press Council of India should be given statutory power to recommend actions against the newspapers, which consistently violated the Council's ruling.

The appointment of the First Commission began with an educative process and continued as a fact finding Commission. It did really some work of lasting value for an industry which has been least organized and knew no self-regulation Public element was the most dominant approach of the Commission. The inquiry was to be an inquiry on behalf of the public into the working of the press. The place of the press in the social set up and its working were to be examined by the test of public interest. It was a commission which was equipped by its powers and composition to take evidence from all sections of the industry and the public and to assess its impartiality. It is the point of view of the public that dominates the report, and it is within this framework that the Commission dealt with the overriding social aspect, the true nature of freedom of expression, the need for restraint and regulation, the place of small newspapers, the working of news agencies or the meaning of editorial freedom and the healthy growth of the press. Even the recommendation on collective bargaining and service conditions had to be viewed within the framework of the public interest.

The report could be divided into three parts; (*i*) dealing with the social (*ii*) Industrial and (*iii*) legal; aspects of freedom of expression and press.

According to the findings of the report, of a total of three hundred and thirty dailies, five owners controlled twenty-nine newspapers and 312 percent of the circulation while fifteen owners controlled fifty four newspapers and 501 percent of the circulation. The Commission said that there already existed a considerable degree of concentration and that these were not the product of any evil design, but was largely attributed to economic and technological influences. They were in a monopolistic position in regard to newsprint, advertisements, financial resources, facilities, relations with the Government. When it was realized that they came from the same social and economic class, the extent of the impact could be known.

The list of unfair and restrictive practices which the report gave illustrated the kind of unholy competition which prevailed. But in the opinion of organized newspapers proprietors that it is not easier to recognize that public interest is higher than their right to run and use newspapers as they like. The Commission proposed that the principle of private ownership, as admittedly recognized by the Commission, must go with restraint. No reason has been advanced why there should not be a limitation on profits in an industry which avails postal and many other concessions in the pretension to be a public utility service. But it conveniently forgets public interest. The right to property is extended through manipulation and public opinion. This created as bad an impression on the Press Commission as they had on the public mind.

After independence the industrialists have made no distinction between the newspaper industry and other industries. Emphasizing the "freedom of press" for democracy, the Commission said that freedom of expression must be freed from the steam rollering of the commercial process. So that it may mean the maximum amount of freedom of expression, for the maximum number of people of course subject to constitutional restraint.

The Commission's recommendations are calculated to help the development of a healthy press. The appointment of a Press Registrar with the powers and responsibilities outlined by the Commission was to help in the improvement of financial standards, the maintenance of correct statistics and accurate surveying of the working of the press. The recommendation for separation of the accounts of multiple units was in the interest of the Government receiving the taxes that are due. The recommendations as a hole are to put an end to adventurism which had led to so much unsteadiness and insecurity. The recommendation was intended similarly in the interest of the soundness of each unit and check capricious diversions to the kind of adventure which ended in a closure of newspapers in Calcutta.

Newspapers are started with money dreams of power or wants by someone to have a share in public or wants by some one to have a share in public affairs which he is not otherwise entitled to. In such cases personal interest overrides public interest. For the development of Indian press and growth of small newspapers, the Commission sought to deal with the problem in the only way it could have dealt with it, short of asking the government to subsidize district press.

The Newspaper Society and certain other interests were visibly upset over the recommendations of the Commission about state trading in newsprint, a reasonable tariff for news services, a prince-page schedule, readjustment of advertisement allotments and rates and elimination of unfair and restrictive practices, including crossword and other prize competitions.

The Commission also stated that for ensuring equal conditions of competition not only should unfair and restrictive practices go but there should be a fair price paid by reader as a reasonable return for the cost of production of the paper. This would guarantee a minimum price.

It has been presented by certain interests that a price-page schedule would be against the readers' interest and that the guarantee of a certain price would mean compelling the reader to subsidize the newspaper. It would be better for the reader to subscribe the press than the press being subsidized by any other element. In the public interest, the reader would rather have a newspaper dependant upon this contribution rather than upon the direct or indirect contribution of interest whose working is not transparent. The reader should not mind paying for a newspaper adequately. It is for the reader to judge how far newspaper is essential for information and instruction for them. It is, rather, misleading to bring in the reader and oppose rice, age schedule in the name of his interest. The press should rather be subsidized by reader who is interested in the fairness of the supply of news, rather than at the behest of interested agency or party.

Those who have opposed the principle of price-page schedule in the name of the reader have failed to explain the interplay between the economic and social elements of the newspaper industry. Within certain price ranges the reader will have reading matter within the range of his choice and also a healthy and widely diffused up press. Price-page schedule is perhaps the best means to ensure fair competition and provide help to small newspapers. The smaller should exert themselves in favour of better economics and not for denying economic justice to their employees.

The Commission's observations on the maintenance and improvement of the standards of the Journalistic profession are intended as muscle for the practitioners of the profession as for the newspaper proprietors.

It was the duty of the press to work for the establishment of a Press Council and elimination of those factors separating power and responsibility.

For creation of the proper environment, the Commission laid down some healthy conditions necessary in the editorial sphere. For the editorial freedom, the managing editorships and other forms of managing agencies is required to end soon.

The principle of collective bargaining and trade unionism as recommended for the working journalists and their conditions by the Commission, industry people who want newspapers to be a special industry for some purposes, are not willing to accept the limitations that are inherent, like limitations on profit, but want this industry to be treated like any other industry.

The recommendations for the press made by two Press Commission could be summarized as follows:

(*i*) Help the country in its development process, both by making constructive suggestions a well as criticism of delays and distortion as in the development process.

(*ii*) Give the widest possible access to the people, reflecting the pluralistic composition of Indian society.

(*iii*) Maintain internal stability and safeguard external security.

(*iv*) Prevent and deflate social conflict.

The Advancement in communication and information technologies have provided greater strength to communication. Today the magnitude and economics of mass media operations have resulted in primacy being accorded to market objectives and change in media priorities. The editor's role is influenced by the advertisement and circulation department needs. The Press Council of India also advised that in reporting on communal or sensitive matters, newspapers should exercise proper restraint and caution and maintain objectivity. First Press Commission in India had recommended constitution of statutory Press Council in India.

The Second Press Commission too observed that one of the functions entrusted to the press Council as to build a code of conduct for newspapers, news agencies and Journalists with a high standard of journalism. The Council claims that attempts at framing an exhaustive code for journalist in India have either proved futile or resulted in the drawing of certain basic principles which have not proved helpful while applying the principles to individual cases.

All India Newspaper Editor's Conference in its code of ethics desired at Journalists to serve and guard public interest, to observe restraints in reports on public disorder and communal tension, to accept the responsibility for all informations published, voluntarily correct inaccurate information, not to allow personal interest to influence professional conduct, not to give currency to rumors concerning the private life of individuals. The declaration of National Union of Journalism 1981 also is largely on similar lines.

# 11

# Press Council Act, 1978

On the recommendations of the First Press Commission to establish a statutory Press Council, an Act was passed to establish a Press Council for the purpose of preserving the freedom of the press and of maintaining and improving the standards of newspapers and news agencies in India; it was found necessary that there should be some authority vested with the statutory powers. Hence the Press Council was established in July, 1966. The Press Council Act, 1965 as repealed by the Press Council (Repeal) Act, 1976 during the emergency. After the repeal of emergency a series of measures were taken by the Government to restore the freedom of the press and news agencies in the country. As a part of the same it was proposed to revive the Press Council of India. A bill was presented to establish a Press Council of India on the same lines of the Press Council Act, 1965, with some changes.

The Press Council Bill, 1977 was passed by both the Houses of Parliament and it came on the Statute Books as the Press Council Act, 1978 after receiving the assent of the President of India on 7th September, 1978.

The Press Council is being empowered to levy a fee from newspapers and news agencies for the services it proposes to render under the provision of the proposed measures and the amount realized thereby will be utilized to meet part of the expenses of the council.

The power to appoint the Chairman and a Member of the Press and Registration Appellate Board under the Press and Registration of Books Act, 1867, so far vested with the Government of India, is now proposed to confer on the Press Council of India.

### Composition of the Press Council

The Council shall consist of a Chairman and twenty-eight other members. The Chairman shall be nominated by a Committee consisting of the Chairman of Rajya Sabha, the Speaker of Lok Sabha and a person elected by the members of the Council under sub-section (6).

Out of the other twenty-eight Members ;

(*a*) Thirteen shall be nominated from journalists; of whom six shall be editors of newspapers and seven shall be working journalists other than editors. Again out of these not less than three editors and four journalists from Indian languages.

(*b*) Six shall be nominated from the proprietors out of which two each shall be of big newspapers, medium newspapers and small newspapers.

(*c*) One shall be nominated from the management of news agencies.

(*d*) Three shall be persons from the field of education and science, law and literature and culture, of whom one each shall be nominated by the University Grants Commission, Bar Council of India and the Sahitya Academy.

(*e*) Five shall be the Members of the Parliament; three to be nominated by the Speaker of the Lok Sabha from its Members, and to be nominated by the Chairman of Rajya Sabha from its Members. The Chairmen and other members shall hold office for a period of three years.

**Committee of the Council:** The Council may constitute from among its members such committees for general or specific purposes as it may deem necessary and every committee so constituted shall perform such functions as are assigned to it by the Council.

**Power and Functions of Council:** The object of the Council shall be to preserve the freedom of the press and to maintain and improve the standards of newspapers and news agencies in India.

The main functions of the Council are to help maintain independence, build a code of conduct with high professional standards, maintenance of high standard of public taste, growth of a scene of responsibility and public service among the news papers, news agencies and journalists.

The Council is also to review any restriction on the supply and dissemination of news of public interest. It is also to review any cases of assistance received by any newspaper or news agency in India from any foreign source. It is also to undertake the studies of foreign newspapers brought out in India, their circulation and other matter. The Council is also to see developments such as concentration of ownership of newspapers and news agencies, which may affect the independence of the press.

**Power to Censure:** On receipt of a complaint, if the council so believes that a newspapers or news agency has offended against the standards of journalistic ethics or public tastes, the Council may after giving an opportunity to the defendant, of being heard hold an inquiry. And on being satisfied that it is necessary to do so, it may for reasons to be recorded in writing, warn, admonish or censure the newspaper, the news agency, the editor or the journalist. The publication of the report of any inquiry by the Council is mandatory for the newspaper as asked to by the Council and in such manner as the Council thinks.

But the Council shall not hold any inquiry into any mater in respect of which any proceeding is in a court a law.

The decision of the Council in respect of offence against the standards of journalistic ethics or public taste or the publication of the inquiry report as mentioned above, shall be final and shall not be questioned in any court of law.

**Holding an Inquiry under the Act:** For holding any inquiry under this Act, the Council shall have the same powers throughout India as are vested in a civil court while trying a suit under the code of civil procedure, 1908 in respect of following matters; namely;

(a) Summoning and enforcing the attendance of persons and examining them on oath;
(b) Requiring the discovery and inspection of documents
(c) Receiving evidence on affidavit;
(d) Requisitioning any public record or copies thereof from any court or office;
(e) Issuing notices for the examination of witnesses or do documents; and
(f) Any other matter, which may be prescribed.

However, the journalist shall not be compelled to disclose the source of any news or information published by that newspaper or reported by that news agency, editor or journalist. Every inquiry held by the Council shall be deemed to be judicial proceeding within the meaning of sections 193 and 228 of the Indian Penal Code.

**Levy of Fees:** The Council may for the purpose of performing its functions under the Act, levy such fees, at such rates and in such manner, as may be prescribed from registered newspapers and news agencies. Different rates may be prescribed for different newspapers having regard to their circulation and other matters.

In addition, the Central Government may pay to the Council by way of grants necessary for the performance of the functions of the Council under this Act. The Council shall have its own fund and all payments by the Council shall be made from this fund.

**Annual Report:** The Council shall prepare once every year an annual report in a prescribed from and forward the same to the Central Government, for being laid on the tables of both houses of the Parliament. The Council may prepare report, at any time of the year, and shall forward the same to the Central Government for being laid on the tables of both Houses of the Parliament.

**Protection of action:** No suit or other legal proceeding shall be initiated against the Council or any Member of the Council in respect of anything which is in good faith done or intended to be done under this Act.

No suit or other legal proceeding shall lie against any newspaper in respect of the publication of any matter therein under the authority of the Council.

**Power to make rules :** The Central Government may, by notification in the official gazette, make rules to carry out the purposes of this Act. Such rules shall be made in consultation with the Council. Every rule made under this section shall be laid before both the Houses of the Parliament. Any modification in the rule by the Parliament, will come into effect only in the modified form.

Some changes have been incorporated and amendment made in the Act of 1978 through the following successive Acts.

(*i*) The Delegated Legislation Provision (Amendment) Act, 1983

(*ii*) The Repealing and Amending Act, 1988 and

(*iii*) The Press Council (Amendment) act, 1994

The standards of journalism profession do not depend upon press law or even Press Council though the machinery for self-regulation like Press Council is necessary. It is the duty of the press to work for the establishment of Press Council and the elimination of the factors which led to a divorce between power and responsibility. The best way of maintaining professional standards of journalism would be to bring in existence a body of people principally connected with the industry whose responsibility would be to arbitrate on doubtful points and to ensure the punishment to get guilty of infraction of good journalistic behaviour. An important recommendation of the First Press Commission was the setting up of statutory Press Council at the national level, consisting of press people and lay members. Though it did not say that the Council should have teeth. The Commission, by majority, recommended actions against the newspapers, which consistently violated the council's ruling.

In every country, there are always some sections of the press which misused the right to freedom of the press resulting in adverse consequences to the Society and the State. These led to the constitution of two Press Commissions in India and on its recommendation the constitution of statutory Press Council.

From time to time, complaints are heard throughout the world that a section of the press functions without any regard for its responsibilities to the society. There are some specific laws for the press. There are always areas, which are outside the jurisdiction of law. A vast area is not covered by any legal regime. Media ethics apply mostly to cases not specifically covered by law. This is where responsibility too should be important element of journalism.

The Press Institute of India has also cautioned the Fourth Estate against a decline in professional and ethical standards. Its director was very critical of what he called "partisan reporting" in Indian newspaper.

Some of the findings of the Press Council also call for objective journalism. The Council mildly chided the Times of India for its reporting of Indira Gandhi's assassination. The Council advised that in reporting on or writing about communal or other sensitive matters, newspapers should exercise proper restraint and caution.

The Second Press Commission also observed that one of the functions entrusted to the Press council was the building up of a code of conduct for newspaper, news agencies and journalists in accordance with high standards of journalism. But in a number of reports the Press Council preferred to build a code of conduct based on its previous decision rather than to frame a code. The Council claims that attempts at framing an exhaustive code for professional bodies of journalists in various countries, including India, have either proved futile or resulted in the mere enunciation of certain basic principles in general terms that had not proved helpful, when it came to applying the principles to individual cases.

The All India Newspaper Editors' Conference formulated a Code of Ethics and a Charter for Editors in 1953. The National Union Journalists, the All India Small and Medium Newspapers' Association, all drafted similar codes. But Editors' Guild of India refused to draft any code arguing that responsible do not need any such code.

Vir Singhvi has suggested that any Code of Ethics must cover five basic areas.

(*i*) Defamation and Privacy

(*ii*) Acceptance of gift and hospitality

(*iii*) Conflict or interest

(*iv*) Willingness of the investigative reporter to accept 'leak' and

(*v*) The role of the proprietor.

## (Act No. 37 of 1978)

*[7th September, 1978]*

*An Act to establish a Press Council for the purpose of preserving the freedom of the Press and of maintaining and improving the standards of newspapers and news agencies in India.*

**BE it enacted by Parliament in the Twenty-ninth Year of the Republic of India as follows:**

## CHAPTER I

## PRELIMINARY

Short title and extent.

**1. This Act may be called the *fress* Council Acl, 1978.**

(2) It extends to the whole of India.

Definitions.

**2. In this Act, unless the context otherwise requires:**

(*a*) "Chairman" means the Chairman of the Council;

(*b*) "Council" means the Press Council of India established under Section 4;

(*c*) "member means a member of the Council and includes its Chairman:

(*d*) "prescribed" means prescribed by rules made under this Act;

(*e*) the exprcssiois "editor" and "newspaper" have the meanings respectively assigned to them in the Press and Registration of Books ACT. 1857, and the expression "working journalist" has the meaning assigned to it in the Working Journalists and other Newspaper Employees (Conditions of Service) and Miscellaneous Provisions Act, 1955.

**3. Any reference in this Act to a law which is not in force in the State of Jammu and Kashmir or Sikrkim shall, in relation to that State be construed as a reference to the corresponding law, if any, in force in that State.**

## CHAPTER II

## ESTABLISHMENT OF THE PRESS COUNCIL

4.(1) With effect from such date as the Central Government may, by notification in Official Gazette, appoint there shall be established a Council by the name of the Press Council of India.

(2) The said Council shall be a body corporate having perpetual succession and a common seal and shall by the said name sue and be sued

5. (1) The Council shall consist of a Chairman and twenty-eight other members

(2) The Chairman shall be a person nominated by a Committee consisting of the Chairman of the Council of States (Rajya Sabha), the Speaker of the House of the People (Lok Sabha) and a person elected by the members of the Council under sub-section (6) and the nomination so made shall take effect from the date on which it is notified by the Central Government in the Official Gazette.

(3) Of the other members:

(*a*) thirteen shall be nominated in accordance with such procedure as may be prescribed from among the working journalists, of whom six shall be editors of newspapers and the remaining seven shall be working journalists other than editors; so, however, that *the* number of such editors and working journalists other than editors in relation to newspapers published in Indian languages shall be not less than three and four respectively;

(*b*) six shall be nominated in accordance with such procedure as may be prescribed from among persons who own or carry on the business of management of newspapers, so, however, that there shall be two representatives from each of the categories of big newspapers, medium newspapers and small newspapers;

(*c*) one shall be nominated in accordance with such procedure as may be prescribed from among persons who manage news agencies;

(*d*) three shall be persons having special knowledge or practical experience in respect of education and science, law, and literature and culture of whom respectively one shall be nominated by the University Grants Commissions, one by the Bar Council of India and one by the Sahitya Academy;

(*e*) five shall be members of Parliament of whom three shall be nominated by the Speaker from among the members of the house of the People (Lok Sabha) and two shall be nominated by the Chairman of the Council of States (Rajya Sabha) from among its members:

Provided that no working journalist who owns, or carries on the business of management of, any newspaper shall be eligible for nomination under clause (a):

Provided further that the nominations under clause (a) and clause (b) shall be so made that among the persons nominated there is not more than one person interested in any newspaper or group of newspapers under the same control or management.

(4) Before making any nomination under clause (a), clause (b) or clause (c) of sub-section (3), the Central Government in the case of the first Council and the retiring Chairman of the previous Council in the case of any subsequent Clause shall, in the prescribed manner, invite panels of names comprising twice the numlfaer of members to be nominated from such associations of persons off the categories referred to in the said clause (a), clause (b) or clause (c) as may be notified in this behalf by the Central Government in the case of the first Council and by the Council itself in the case of subsequent Councils:

Provided that where there is no association of persons of the category referred to in the said clause (c). the panels of names shall be invited from such news agencies as may be notified as aforesaid.

(5) The Central Government shall notify the names of persons nominated as members under sub–section (3) in the Official Gazette and every such nomination shall take effect from the date on which it is notified.

(6) The members of the Council notified under sub-section (5) shall elect from among themselves in accordance with such procedure as may be prescribed, a person to be is member of the Committee referred to in sub-section (2) and a meeting of the members of the Council for the purpose of such election shall be presided over by a person chosen from among themselves.

**6.** (1) Save as otherwise provided in this section the Chairman and other members shall hold office for a period of three years:

Provided that the Chairman shall continue to hold such office until the Council is reconstituted in accordance with the provisions of Section 5 or for a period of six months whichever is earlier.

(2) Where a person nominated as a member under clause (*a*), clause (*b*) or clause (*c*) of sub–section (3) of Section 5 is cansurea under the provisions of sub–section (1) of Section 14, he shall cease to be a member of the Council.

(3) The term of office of a member nominated under clause (e) of sub-section (3) of Section 5 shall come to an end as soon as he ceases to be a member of the House from which he was nominated.

(4) A member shall be deemed to have vacated his seat if he is absent without excuse, sufficient in the opinion of the Council, from three consecutive meetings of the Council.

(5) The Chairman may resign his office by giving notice in writing to the Central Government, and any other member may resign his office by giving notice in writing to the Chairman, and upon such resignation being accepted by the Central Government, or as the case may be, the Chairman, or the member shall be deemea to have vacated his office.

(6) Any vacancy arising under sub-section (2), sub-secttion (3), subsection (4) or sub-section (5) or otherwise shall be filled, as soon as may be, by nomination in the same manner in which the member vacating office was nominated and the member so nominated shall hold office for the remaining period in which the member in whose place he is nominated would have held office.

(7) A retiring member shall be eligible for re-nominaition for not more than one term.

7. (1) The Chairman shall be a whole-time officer and shall be paid such salary as the Central Government may think fit; and the other members shall receive such allowances or fees for attending the meeting of the Council, as may be prescribed.

(2) Subject to the provisions of sub-section (1), the conditions of service of members shall be such as may be prescribed.

(3) It is hereby declared that the office of a member of the Council shall not disqualify its holder for being chosen as, for being, a member, of either House of Parliament.

**8.** (1) For the purpose of performing its functions under this Act, the Council may constitute from among its members such committees for general or special purposes as it may deem necessary and every committee so constituted shall perform such junctions as are assigned to it by the Council.

(2) The Council shall have the power to co-opt as members of any committee constituted under sub–section (1) such other number of persons, not being members of the Council, as it thinks fit.

(3) Any such member-shall have the right to attend any meeting of the Committee on which he is so co–opted an to take part in the discussions thereat, but shall not have the right to vote and shall not be a member for any other purpose.

**9. The Council or any committee thereof shall meet at such times and places and shall observe such rules of procedure in regard to the transaction of business at its meetings as may be provided by regulations made under this Act.**

**10. No actor proceeding of the Council shall be deemed to be invalid by reasons merely of the existence of any vacancy in, or any defect in the Constitution of, the Cenancil.**

**11.** (1) Subject to such rules as may be made by the Central Government in this, behalf, the Council may appoint a Secretary and such other employees as it may think necessary for the efficient performance of its functions under this Act

(2) The terms and conditions of service of the employees shall be such as may be determined by regulations.

**12. All orders and decisions of the Council shall be authenticated by the signature of the Chairman or any other member authorised by the Council in this behalf and other instruments issued by the Council shall be authenticated by due signature of the Secretary or any other officer of the Council authorised in like manner in this behalf.**

## CHAPTER III

## POWERS AND FUNCTION OF THE COUNCIL

Objects and functions

**13.** (1) The objects of the Council shall be to preserve the freedom of the Press and to maintain and improve the standards of newspapers and news agencies in India.

(2) The Council may, in furtherance of its objects, perform the following functions, namely:

(*a*) to help newspapers and news agencies to maintain their independence;

(*b*) to build up a code of conduct for newspapers, news agencies and journalists in accordance with high professional standards;

(*c*) to ensure on the part of newspapers, news agencies and journalists, the maintenance of high standards of public taste and foster a due sense of both the rights and responsibilities of citizenship;

(*d*) to encourage the growth of a sense of responsibility and public service among all those engaged in the profession of journalism;

(*e*) to keep under review any development likely to restrict the supply and dissemination of news of public interest and importance;

(*f*) to keep under review cases of assistance received by any newspaper or news agency in India from any foreign source including such cases as are referred to it by the Central Government or are brought to its notice by any individual, association of persons or any other orgnisation:

Provided that nothing in this clause shall preclude the Central Government from dealing with any case of assistance received by a newspaper or news agency in India from any foreign source in any other manner it thinks fit;

(*g*) to undertake studies of foreign newspapers, including those brought out by any embassy or other representative in India of a foreign State, their circulation and impact.

*Explanation*: For the purposes of this clause, the expression "foreign State" has the meaning assigned to it in Section *87A* of the Cods of Civil Procedure, 1908;

(*h*) to promote a proper functional relationship among all classes of persons engaged in the production or publication of newspapers or in news agencies:

Provided that nothing in this clause shall be deemed to confer on the Council any functions in regard to dispute to which the Industrial Disputes Act, 1947, applies;

(*i*) to concern itself with developments such as concentration of or other aspects of ownership of newspapers and news agencies which may affect the independence of the Press;

(*j*) to undertake such studies as may be entrusted to the Council and to express its opinion in regard to any matter referred to it by the Central Government;

(*k*) to do such other acts as may be incidental or conducive to the discharge of the above functions.

**14.** (1) Where on receipt of a complaint made to it or otherwise, the Council has reason to believe that a newspapers or news agency has offended against the standards of journalistic ethics or public taste or that an editor or a working journalist has committed any professional misconduct, the Council may, after giving the newspaper, or news agency, the editor, or journalist concerned an opportunity of being heard, hold an inquiry in such manner as may be provided by regulations made under this Act and, if it is satisfied that it is necessary so to do, it may, for reasons to be recorded in writing, warn, admonish or censure the newspaper, the news agency, the editor or the journalist or disapprove the conduct of the editor or the journalist, as the case may be:

Provided that the Council may not take cognizance of a complaint if in the opinion of the Chairman, there is no sufficient ground for holding an inquiry.

(2) If the Council is of the opinion that it is necessary or expedient in the public interest so to do, it may require any newspaper to publish therein in such manner as the Council thinks fit, any particulars relating to any inquiry under this section against a newspaper or news agency, an editor or a journalist working therein, including the name of such newspaper, news agency, editor or journalist.

(3) Nothing in sub-section (1) shall be deemed to empower the Council! to hold an inquiry into any matter in respect of which any proceeding is pending in a court of law.

(4) The decision of the Council under sub-section (1), or subsection (2), as the case may be. shall be final and shall not be questioned in any court law.

The aggrieved petitioners were deprived of defending themselves effectively because the Council passed a Resolution without supplying copy of the complaint.

Mens publication of notice an the newspaper cannot be presumed to be sufficient compliance of mandatory provisions of the Regulations and the fundamental principles of natural justice ?

**15.** (1) For the purpose of performing its functions or holding any inquiry under this Act. The Council shall have the same powers throughout India as are vested in a civil court while trying a suit under the Code of Civil Procedure, 1908, in respect of the following matters, namely:

(*a*) summoning and enforcing the attendance of persons and examining them on oath;

(*b*) requiring the discovery and inspection of documents;

(*c*) receiving evidence on affidavits;

(*d*) requisitioning any public record or copies thereof from any court or office;

(*e*) issuing commissions for the examination of witnesses or documents; and

(*f*) any other matter, which may be prescribed.

(2) Nothing in sub-section (1) shall be deemed to compel any newspaper, news agency, editor or journalist to disclose the source of any news or information published by that newspaper or received or reported by that news agency, editor or journalist.

(3) Every inquiry held by the Council shall be deemed to be a judicial proceeding within the meaning of Sections 193 and 228 of the Indian Penal Code.

(4) The Council may, if it considers it necessary for the purpose of carrying out its objects or for the performance of any of its functions under this Act, make such observations, as it may think fit, in any of its decisions or reports, respecting the conduct of any authority, including Government.

**16.** (1) The Council may, for the purpose of performing its functions under this Act, levy such fees, at such rates and in such manner, as may be prescribed, from registered newspapers and news agencies and different rates may be prescribed for different newspapers having regard to their circulation and other matters.

(2) Any fees payable to the Council under sub-section (1) may be recovered & as an arrear of land revenue.

**17.** The Central Government may, after due appropriation made by Parliament by law in this behalf, pay to the Council by way of grants such sums of money as the Central Government may consider necessary for the performance of the functions of the Council under this Act.

**18.** (1) The Council shall have its own fund; and the fees collected by it, all such sums as may, from time to time, be paid to it by the Central Government and all grants and advances made to it by any other authority or person shall be credited to the Fund and all payments by the Council shall be made therefrom.

(2) All moneys belonging to the Fund shall be deposited in such banks or invested in such manner as may, subject to the approval of the Central Government, be decided by the Council.

(3) The, Council may spend such sums as it thinks fit for performing its functions under this Act, and such sums shall be treated as expenditure payable out of the Fund of the Council.

**19.** The Council shall prepare, in such form and at such time each year as may be prescribed, a budget in respect of the financial year next ensuing showing, the estimated receipts and expenditure, and copies thereof shall be forwarded to the Central Government.

**20.** The Council shall prepare once every year, in such from and at such time as may be prescribed, an annual report, giving a summary of its activities during the previous year, and giving an account of the standards of newspapers and news agencies and factors affecting them, and copies thereof, together with the statement of accounts audited in the manner prescribed under Section 22 shall be forwarded to the Central Government and the Government shall cause the same to be laid before both Houses of Parliament.

**21.** Without prejudice to the provisions of Section 20, the Council may prepare at any time during the course of a year, a report giving a summary of such of its activities during the year as it considers to be of public importance and copies thereof shall be forwarded to the Central Government and the Government shall cause the same to be laid before both Houses of Parliament.

**22.** The accounts of the Council shall be maintained and audited in such manner as may, in consultation with the Controller and Auditor-General of India, be prescribed.

## CHAPTER IV

## MISCELLANEOUS

**23.** (1) No suit or other legal proceeding shall lie against the Council or any member thereof or any person acting under the direction of the Council in respect of anything which is in good faith done or intended to be done under this Act.

(2) No suit or other legal proceeding shall lie against any newspaper in respect of the publication of any matter therein under the authority of the Council.

**24.** Every member of the Council and every officer or other employee appointed by the Council shall be deemed to be a public servant within the meaning of Section 21 of the India Penal Code.

**25.** (l) The Central Government may, by notification in the Official Gazette, make rules to carry out the purposes of this Act:

Provided that when the Council has been established, no such rules shall be made without consulting the Council.

(2) In particular, and without prejudice to the generality of the foregoing power, such rules may provide for all or any of the following matters, namely:

(*a*) the procedure for nomination of members of the Council under clauses (a), (b) and (c) of sub-seeffion (3) of Section 5;

(*b*) the manner in which panels of names may be invited under sub–section (4) of Section 5;

(*c*) the procedure for election of a member of the Committee referred to in sub-section (2) of Section 5 under sub-section (6) of that section;

(*d*) the allowances or fees to be paid to the members of the Council for attending the meetings of the Council, and other conditions of service of such members under sub-sections (1) and (2) of Section 7;

(*e*) the appointment of the Secretary and other employees of the Council under Section 11;

(*f*) the matters referred to in clause (f) of sub-section (1) of Section 15;

(*g*) the rates at which fees may be levied by the Council under Section 16 and the manner in which such fees may be levied;

(*h*) the form in which, and the time within which, the budget and annual report are to be prepared by the Council under Sections 19 and 20 respectively;

(*i*) the manner in which the accounts of the Council are to be maintained and audited under Section 22.

(3) Every rule made under this section shall be laid, as soon as may be after it is made, before each House of Parliament, while it is in session, for a total period of thirty days which may be comprised in one session or in two or more successive sessions, and if, before the expiry of the session immediately following the session or the successive sessions aforesaid, both Houses agree in making any modification in the rule or both Houses agree that the rule should not be made, the rule shall thereafter have effect only in such modified form or be of no effect, as the case may be; so however, that any such modification or annulment shall be without prejudice to the validity of anything previously done under that rule.

During 2005-2006, the Council formulated its opinion on several issues that pertained to the freedom of the Press or its standards, prominent among thein being:

1. National Policy for Consumers which inter alia seeks to regulate advertisements in newspaper and electronic media.
2. Amendments to the Rules under Tobacco Control Act, 2003 to control advertisements.
3. Platform for Action - 10 years after India Country Report—Action Taken Report on women empowerment.
4. Reference from Ministry of Information and Broadcasting regarding II-1II periodic report on the convention on the elimination of all forms of discrimination against women (CEDAW) 1997-2005
5. Matter raised by Mr. Rama Shulda, M.P. regarding "need to ban fake advertisement in newspaper inviting application for employment with a view to safeguard the interests of unemployed persons.

6. Reference from Ministry of Information and Broadcasting regarding Mechanism of regulation of print media in relation to M.A. No. 399 of 2005 Abu Salem Abdul Qayoom Ansari versus State Government of Maharashtra and the Secretary, Ministry of Information and Broadcasting filed in Designated Court for Bomb Blast cases in Greater Bombay (TADA Court)
7. Reference from Rajya Sabha Secretariat regarding opinion of the Hon'ble Chairman, on Contempt of Court (Amendment) Bill, 2004.
8. Indifference of the media towards publication of matters of public interest.
9. Formation of Uniform Accreditation Policy.
10. Controversial advertisement issued by the Star News and Dainik Jagran as a part of their Sting Operation to expose the racket of sale of Kidney.
11. Report on short-term measures to curb misleading advertisement-Presented to the Ministry of Consumer Affairs by the Working Group on Misleading Advertisements.

The Council had taken suo–motu cognisance of incidents of violation against media persons in the following cases.

1. Persistent threats, to professional journalists from militants organisations in Manipur.
2. Arrest of Chandigarh-based Principal Correspondent of Indian Express reportedly following his news report on a complaint against Police Officer before the Punjab State Human Rights Commission.
3. Arrest of some journalists of the State of M.P. reportedly on the directions of the State Education Minister.
4. Blockading of Statesman House by hawkers affiliated to CITU the obstruction of the supply of copies of the Statesman and Dainik Stateman (Bengali).
5. Incident of lathi-charge on the journalists of, print as electronic media at Jehanabed (Bihar) on 15 November 2005 after the Naxalities

## GUIDANCE TO THE MEDIA

1. The Council while considering a reference regarding the need to create awareness among the public for ascertaining medical compatibility while seeking matrimonial alliances advised the Press to amplify its caution note thus "while choosing the life partner one may also undertake health screening to prevent any genetic disorder in any future offspring."
2. The Council advised the media to refrain from identification of the victim of sexual abuse in their reports.

Discussion through Seminars and Workshops:

(*a*) 'Media Ethics: Fetters or Freedom on the occasion of National Press Day.

(*b*) Sensitisation of Media on Disaster Management; on 4 August 2005. c) "Trivialisation of Content in Media" in Pune on 10 February 2006. d) "Role of Media during Communal Strife" in Ayodhya on 25 March 2006 respectively.

During the period under review the Press Council of India was also represented at various other seminars/conferences/meets related to media world by its Chairman, Mr. Justice G.N. Ray.

In its adjudicatory role, during 2005–2006, Press Council of India received 726 complaints, of which the Press filed 150 cases while 576 were against the Press. 975 cases were already pending. Of these the Council adjudicated 193 cases, while 1508 cases were closed at the threshold without detailed inquiry. The Council thus disposed of 1701-mattere during 2005-2006.

**26.** 1[(1)] The Council may, 2[by notification in the Official Gazette, make regulations not inconsistent with this act and the rules made there under, for :

(*a*) regulating the meetings of the Council or any committee thereof and the proceduce for conducting the business thereat under Section 9.

(*b*) specifying the terms and conditions of service of the employees, appointed by the Council, under sub-section (2) of Section 11.

(*c*) regulating the manner of holding any inquiry under this Act;

(*d*) delegating to the Chairman or the Secretary of the Council, subject to such conditions as it may think fit to impose, any of its powers under sub-sectfion (3) of Section 18;

(*e*) any other matter for which provision may be made by regulations under this Act:

Provided that the regulation is made under clause (b) shall be made only with the prior approval of the Central Government.

[(2)] The Central Government shall cause every regulation made under this Act to be laid, as soon as may be after it is made, before each House of Parliament, while it is in session, for a total period of thirty days which may be comprised in one session or in two or more successive sessions, and if, before the expiry of the session immediately following the session or the successive sessions aforesaid, both Houses agree in making any modification in the regulation or both Houses agrees that the regulations should not be made, the regulation shall thereafter have effect only in such modified form or be of no effect, as the case may be; so, however, that any such modification or annulment shall be without prejudice to the validity of anything previously done under that regulation].

**27.** [Repealed by Repealing and Amending Act (19 of 1988, S. 2 Sch. (w.e.f. 4–4–1988)].

## NOTIFICATION NO. G.S.R. 633 (E) DATED 5TH AUGUST, 1994

In pursuance of sub–section (4) of Section 5 of the Act, the press Council of India has notified vide G.S.R. 633 (E), dated 5th August, 1994 the following associations of persons of the categories referred to in Clause (*a*) and Clause (*b*) and news agencies for the purpose of Clause (c) of sub–section (3) of that section, namely:

(I) Association of persons of category referred to in Clause (a) of sub–section (3) of Section 5:

(1) Editors Guild of India, Delhi,
(2) All India Newspapers Editors' Conference, Delhi
(3) The press Association, Delhi
(4) National Union of Journalists (I), Delhi
(5) Indian Federation of Working Journalists, Delhi
(6) Indian Journalists Union, Delhi

as representative bodies of Working Journalists–who are Editors

as representative bodies of Working Journalists–other than Editors

(II) Association of persons of category referred to in Clause (b) of sub–section (3) of Section 5:

(1) The Indian Newspapers Society, Delhi As representative body of Owners and Managers of big, medium and small newspapers
(2) All India Small and Medium Newspapers Federation, Delhi as representative bodies of Owners and
(3) All India Small and Medium Newspapers Association, Delhi Managers of small and medium newspapers
(4) Indian Federation Small and Medium Newspapers, Delhi

(III) News agencies for the purpose of nominating a person from the category of persons referred to in Clause (c) of sub–section (3) of Section 5 :

(1) The Press Trust of India Limited.

# 12

# Prasar Bharti Act, 1990

In order to organize and conduct broadcasting services to inform, educate and entertain the public and to ensure a balanced development of broadcasting on radio and television, a Public Broadcasting Corporation was established. The Act to provide for the establishment of Broadcasting Corporation for India was known as Prasar Bharti (Broadcasting Corporation of India) Act, 1990.

The Corporation shall be body corporate, having perpetual succession. The general superintendence, direction and management of the affairs of the Corporation shall vest in Prasar Bharti Board which may exercise all such powers and do all such acts and things as may be exercised or done by the Corporation under this Act.

The Board shall consist of:

A Chairman, one Executive Member, one Member (Finance), one Member (Personnel), six part time member, Director General (Akashavani) ex-officio, Director General (Doordarshan), ex-officio, one representative of the Union Ministry of Information and Broadcasting and two representatives of the employees of the Corporation.

The Chairman and other Members, except ex-officio Members, the nominated Member and the elected Members, shall be appointed by the President of India on the recommendations of a committee consisting of:

(*a*) The Chairman of the Council of States, who shall be the Chairmen of the Committee.

(*b*) The Chairman of the Press Council of India, and

(*c*) One Nominee of the President of India.

The Chairman shall be a part time Member and the Executive member, the Member (Finance) and the Member (Personnel) shall be whole time Member. All the whole time and part time Members shall hold office for a term of six years, and until attaining the age of sixty two years in case of whole time Members.

## FUNCTIONS AND POWERS OF THE CORPORATIONS

Under the provisions of the Act, it shall be the primary duty of the Corporation to organize and conduct public broadcasting services to inform, educate and entertain the public and to ensure a balanced development of broadcasting on radio and television.

**Explanation:** For the removal of doubts it is hereby declared that the provisions of this section shall be in addition to and not in derogation of, the provisions of the India Telegraph Act, 1885.

### *The Corporation may take steps*

To ensure that broadcasting is conducted as a public service to provide and produce programme, to establish a system for the gathering of news for radio and television, to establish and maintain a library or libraries of radio, television and other materials, to conduct or commission programmes, audience research, market or technical service, to provide such other services as may be specified by regulations, as also to purchase or acquire programme and rights in respect of sports and other events, films serial etc.

The Corporation shall have power to determine and levy feed ad other service charges for or in respect of the advertisements and such programmes as may be specified by regulations.

The Corporation shall not be subject to any civil liability on the ground merely that it failed to comply with any of the provisions of this section.

### *Objectives of the Corporation*

The Corporation shall in discharge of its functions, be guided by the following objectives, namely;

(*a*) Upholding the unity and integrity of the country and the values enshrined in the Constitution.

(*b*) Safeguarding the citizen's right to be informed freely, truthfully and objectively on all maters of public interest national or international and presenting a fair and balanced flow of information including contrasting views, without advocating any opinion or ideology of its own.

(*c*) Paying special attention to the field of education and spread of literacy, agriculture, rural development, environment, health and family welfare and science and technology;

(*d*) Providing adequate coverage to the diverse cultures and languages of the various regions of the country by broadcasting appropriate programmes;

(*e*) Providing adequate coverage to sports and games so as to encourage healthy competition and the spirit of sportsmanship;

(*f*) Providing appropriate programmes keeping in view the special needs of the youth;

(*g*) Informing and stimulating the national consciousness in regard to the status and problems of women and paying special attention to the up liftmen of women;

(*h*) Promoting social justice and combating exploitation, inequality and such evils as untouchability and advancing the welfare of the weaker sections of the society;

(*i*) Safeguarding the rights of the working classes and advancing their welfare;

(*j*) Serving rural and weaker sections of the people and those residing in boarder regions, backward or remote areas;

(*k*) Providing suitable programmes keeping in view the special needs of the minorities and tribal communities.

(*l*) Taking special steps to protect the interests of the children, the blinds, the aged, the handicapped and other vulnerable sections of the people;

(*m*) Promoting national integration by broadcasting in a manner that facilitates communication in languages in India, and facilitating the distribution of regional broadcasting services in every state in the languages of that state;

(*n*) Promoting research and development activities in order to ensure that the radio and television broadcasting technology are constantly updated, and

(*o*) Expanding broadcasting facilities by establishing additional channels of transmission at various levels.

There will be two committees to supervise the functioning of the Corporation.

1. **Parliamentary committee:** There shall be a Parliamentary Committee to oversee that the Corporation discharges its functions in accordance with the provisions of this Act and particularly shall consist of twenty two Members of Parliament, of whom fifteen from the House of the People and seven from the Council of States, to be elected by the respective Houses in accordance with the proportional representation by means of the single transferable vote.

2. **Broadcasting Council:** To receive and consider complaints from any person against certain programmes or broadcast or the functioning of the Corporation, a council shall be appointed which will be known as Broadcasting Council. The Council shall advise the Corporation in the discharge of its functions in accordance with the objectives with which the corporation has been established.

**Composition of the Broadcasting Council:** The Broadcasting Council shall consist of a President and ten other Members. They will be appointed by the President of India from amongst persons of immense in public life. There will be four Members of Parliament; two from the House of the people, to be nominated by the Speaker and two from the Council of States, to be nominated by the Chairman of Rajya Sabha. The President of the Broadcasting Corporation shall be a whole-time member and all other members shall be part-time members. All of them shall hold office for a period of three years.

**Jurisdiction of the Broadcasting Council:** The Broadcasting Council shall receive and consider complaints against certain programme or broadcast or the functioning of the Corporation in specific cases or in general, it is not in accordance with the objectives for which the Corporation is established, by any person claiming himself to have been treated unjustly or unfairly in any manner in connection with any programme broadcast by the Corporation.

If the complaint is found to the justified, either wholly or partly, the Broadcasting Council shall advise the executive Member to take appropriate action. If the Executive Member is unable to accept the recommendation of the Council, he shall place such recommendations before the Board for a decision. Where the Broadcasting Council deems it appropriate, it may, for reasons to be recorded in writing, require the Corporation to broadcast its recommendations with respect to a complaint in such manner as the Council may deem fit.

**Corporation not be liable to be taxed:** The Corporation shall not be liable to pay any income tax in respect of:

(*a*) Any income, profit or gain, accruing or arising out of the fund of the Corporation or any amount received in that fund, and

(*b*) Any income, profits or gains, derived or any amount received by the Corporation.

**Annual Report:** The Corporation shall prepare once in every calendar year an annual report giving a full account of its activities during the previous year and forward copies, to the Central Government, which shall be laid before each House of the Parliament. The Broadcasting Council shall also prepare in every calendar year an annual report giving full account of its activities during the previous year and forward its copies to the Central Government and it will be laid before each House of the Parliament.

## RULES AND REGULATIONS TO BE LAID BEFORE PARLIAMENT

Every rules and regulations made under this Act shall be laid before each House of the Parliament. If both Houses agree in making any modification in the rules or regulation, the rule or regulation shall thereafter have effect only in such modified form or be of no effect in case of annulment.

## POWER OF THE CENTRAL GOVERNMENT TO GIVE DIRECTION AND TO SEEK INFORMATION

The Central Government may issue to the Corporation such directions as it may think necessary in the interests of the sovereignty, unity and integrity of India or the security of the State or preservation of public order requiring it to broadcast on a mater specified in the direction or to make a broadcast on any matter of public importance. The Central Government may also require the Corporation to furnish such information as the government may also require the Corporation to furnish such information as the government may consider necessary.

**Supersession of the Board:** On the recommendations of the Parliament, the President of India, may supersede the Board for a period not exceeding six months. The President shall give a reasonable opportunity to the Board to show cause as to why it should not be superseded.

## PROTECTION OF ACTION TAKEN IN GOOD FAITH

No suit or other legal proceeding shall lie against the Corporation, the Chairman or any Member or official or the president or the member of the Broadcasting Council for anything which is done is good faith or intended to be done in pursuance of this Act or any rules or regulations made there under.

The idea of enacting Prasar Bharti Act was conceived on the basis of the autonomy and independent character of the "British Broadcasting Corporation". But certain provisions inserted in the Act provide enough scope to the Government and the people in power. For example, according to section 23 (1) of the act.

"The Central Government may from time to time, as and when occasion arises, issue to the Corporation such directions as it may think necessary in the interest of the sovereignty, unity and integrity of India, or the security of the State, or preservation of public order requiring it not to make a broadcast on a matter specified in the direction".

Similarly through Parliamentary Committee there is a tendency in different political parties to exercise some control over the Board.

Some change have been made in Prasar Bharti Act, 1990 thought "Prasar Bharti (Amendment) Ordinance, 1997.

# THE PRASAR BHARTI (BROADCASTING CORPORATION OF INDIA) ACT, 1990 (25 of 1990)

[*12th September, 1990*]

*An Act to provide for the establishment of a Broadcasting Corporation for India, to be known as Prasar Bharati, to define its composition, functions and powers and to provide for matters connected therewith or incidental thereto.*

Be it enacted by Parliament in the Forty–first Year of the Republic of India as follows:

## CHAPTER I

### PRELIMINARY I

**1. Short title, extent and commencement:**

(1) This Act may be called the Prasar Bharti (Broadcasting Corporation of India) Act, 1990.

(2) It extends to the whole of India.

(3) It shall come into force on such date as the Central Government may, by notification, appoint.

**2. Definitions:** In this Act, unless the context otherwise requires:

(*a*) "Akashvani" means the offices, stations and other establishments, by whatever name called, which, immediately before the appointed day, formed part of or were under the Director-General; All India Radio of the Union Ministry of Information and Broadcasting;

(*b*) "appointed day" means the date appointed under section 3;

(*c*) "broadcasting" means the dissemination of any form of communication like signs, signals, writing, pictures, images and sounds of all kinds by transmission of electro-magnetic waves through space or through, cables intended to be received by the general public either directly or indirectly through the medium of relay stations and all its grammatical variations and cognate expressions shall be construed accordingly;

(*d*) "Board" means-the Prasar Bharati Board;

(*e*) "Broadcasting Council" means the Council established under section 14;

(*f*) "Chairman" means the Chairman of the Corporation appointed under section 4;

(*g*) "Corporation" means the Prasar Bharati (Broadcasting Corporation *of* India) established under section 3;

(*h*) "Doordarshan" means the offices, kendras and other establishments, by whatever name called, which, immediately before the appointed day, formed part of or were under the Directorate–General, Doordarshan of the Union Ministry of Information and Broadcasting;

(*i*) "Elected Member" means a Member elected under section 3;

(*j*) "Executive Member" means the Executive Member appointed under section 4;

(*k*) "Kendra" means any telecasting centre with studios or transmitters or to the and includes a relay station;

(*l*) "Member" means a member of the Board;

(*m*) "Member (Finance)" means" the Member (Finance) appointed i section 4;

(*n*) "Member (Personnel)" means the Member (Personnel) appointed section 4;

(*o*) "Nominated Member" means the Member nominated by the Union minisly of Information and Broadcasting under section 3;

(*p*) "Non-lapsable Fund" means the Fund created from the commercial revenues of Akashvani and Doordarshan to meet expenditure on certain scheme;

(*q*) "notification" means a notification published in the Official Gazette;

(*r*) "Part-time Member" means a Part-time Member of the Board appointed under section 4, but does not include an ex officio Member, the Nominated Member or an elected Member;

(*s*) "prescribed" means prescribed by rules made under this Act;

(*t*) "Recruitment Board" means a board established under sub-section (1) of

(*u*) "regulations" means regulations made by the Corporation under this Act

(*v*) "station" means any broadcasting station with studios or transmitters or both and includes a relay station;

(*w*) "Whole-time Member" means the Executive Member, Member (Finance) Member (Personnel);

(*x*) "year" means the financial year.

## CHAPTER II

## PRASAR BHARATI (BROADCASTING CORPORATION OF INDIA)

**3. Establishment and Composition of Corporation:** (1) With effect from such date as the Central Government may by notification appoint in this behalf, there shall be established for the purposes of this Act a Corporation, to be known as the Prasar Bharati (Broadcasting Corporation of India).

(2) The Corporation shall be a body corporate by the name aforesaid, having perpetual succession and a common seal with power to acquire, hold and dispose of property, both movable and immovable, and to contract, and shall by the said name sue and be sued.

(3) The headquarters of the Corporation shall be at New Delhi and the Corporation may establish offices, kendras or stations at other places in India and, with the previous approval of the Central Government, outside India.

(4) The general superintendence, direction and management of the affairs of the Corporation shall vest in the Prasar Bharati Board which may exercise all such powers and do all such acts and things as may be exercised or done by the Corporation under this Act.

(5) The Board shall consist of:

(*a*) a Chairman;

(*b*) one Executive Member;

(*c*) one Member (Finance);

(*d*) one Member (Personnel);

(*e*) six Part-time Members;

(*f*) Director-General (Akashvani), ex officio;

(*g*) Director-General (Doordarshan), ex officio;

(*h*) one representative of the Union Ministry of information and Broadcasting, to be nominated by that Ministry and

(*i*) "two representatives of the employees of the Corporation, of whom one shall be elected by the engineering staff from amongst themselves and one "'shall be elected by the other employees from amongst themselves.

(6) The Corporation may appoint such committees as may be necessary for the efficient performance, exercise and discharge of its functions, powers and duties:

Provided that all or a majority of the members of each committee shall be Members and a member of any such committee who is not a Member shall have only the right to attend meetings of the committee and take part in the proceedings thereof, but shall not have the right to vote.

(7) The Corporation may associate with itself, in such manner and for such purposes as may be provided by regulations, any person whose assistance or advice it may need in complying with any of the provisions of this Act and a person so associated shall have the right to take part in the discussions of, the Board relevant to the purposes for which 'he has been associated, but shall not have the right to vote.

(8) No act or proceeding of the Board or of any committee appointed by it under sub-section (6) shall be invalidated merely by reason of:

(*a*) any vacancy in. or any defect in the constitution of the Board or such committee; or

(*b*) any defect in the appointment of a person acting as a Member or a member of such committee; or

(*c*) any irregularity in the procedure of the Board or such committee not affecting the merits of the case.

4. **Appointment of Chairman and Other Members:** (1) The Chairman and the other Members, except the ex officio Members, the Nominated Member and the elected Members shall be appointed by the President of India on the recommendation of a committee consisting of:

(*a*) the Chairman of the Council of States, who shall be the Chairman of the Committee;

(*b*) the Chairman of the Press Council of India established under section 4 of the Press Council Act, 1978 (37 of 1978); and

(*c*) one nominee of the President of India.

(2) No appointment of a Member shall be invalidated merely by reason of any vacancy in, or any defect in the constitution of, the committee appointed under sub-section (1).

(3) The Chairman and the Part-time Members shall be persons of eminence in public life; the Executive Member shall be a person having special knowledge or practical experience in respect of such matters as administration, management, broadcasting, education, literature, culture, arts, music, dramatics or journalism, the Member (Finance) shall be a person having special knowledge or practical experience in respect of financial matters ,and the Member (Personnel) shall be a person having special knowledge *or* practical-experience in respect, of personnel management and administration.

(4) The recommendations made by the committee constituted under sub-section. (1) shall be binding for the purposes of appointment under this section.

5. **Powers and functions of Executive Member:** The Executive Member shall be the Chief Executive of the Corporation and shall, subject to the control and supervision of the Board, exercise such powers and discharge such functions of the Board as it may delegate to him.

6. **Term of office, conditions of service, etc., of Chairman and other. Members :** (1) The Chairman shall be Part–time Member and shall hold office for a term of six years from the date on which he enters upon his office.

(2) The Executive Member, the Member (Finance) and the Member (Personnel) shall be Whole-time Members and every such Member shall hold office for a term of six years from the date on which he enters upon his office or until he attains the age of sixty-two years, whichever is earlier.

(3) The term of office of Part-time Members shall be six years, but one-third of such . 'Members shall retire on the expiration of every second year.

(4) The term of office of an elected Member shall be two years or till he ceases to be an employee of the Corporation, whichever is earlier.

(5) As soon as may be after the establishment of the Corporation, the President "of India may, by order, make such provision as he thinks fit for curtailing the term of :office of some of the Part-time Members then appointed in order that one-third of the Members holding office as such Part-time Members shall retire in every second year thereafter.

(6) Where before the expiry of the term of office of a person holding the office of Chairman, or any other Member, a vacancy arises, for any reason whatsoever, such vacancy shall be deemed to be a casual vacancy and the person appointed or elected to fill such vacancy shall hold office for the unexpired period of the term for which his predecessor in office would have held office if such vacancy had not arisen.

(7) The Whole-time Members shall be the employees of the Corporation and as such shall be entitled to such salaries and allowances and shall be subject to such conditions of service in respect of leave, pension-(if any), provident fund and other matters as may be prescribed:

Provided that the salaries and allowances and the conditions of service shall not be varied to their disadvantage after their appointment.

(8) The Chairman and Part-time Members shall be entitled to such allowances as "may be prescribed.

7. **Removal and suspension of Chairman and** Members: (1) Subject to the provisions of sub-section (3), the Chairman or any other Member, except an ex officio Member, the Nominated Member and an elected Member, shall only be removed from' his office by order of the President of India on the ground of misbehaviour after the Supreme Court, on a reference being made to it by the President, has, on inquiry held in; accordance with such procedure as the Supreme Court may by rules provide, reported that the Chairman or such other Member, as the case may be, ought, on such ground, be removed.

(2) The President may suspend from office the Chairman or other Member- except an ex officio Member, the Nominated Member or an elected Member, in respect of whom a reference has been made to the Supreme Court under sub-

section (1) until the President has passed orders on receipt of the report of the Supreme Court on such reference.

(3) Notwithstanding anything contained in sub-section (1). the President may, by order, remove the Chairman or any Whole-time Member from his office if such Chairman or such Whole-time Member :

(*a*) ceases to be a citizen of India ; or

(*b*) is adjudged an insolvent; or

(*c*) engages during his term of office in any paid employment out side the duties of his office; or

(*d*) is convicted of any offence involving moral turpitude: or

(*e*) is, in the opinion of the President, Unfit to continue in office by reason of infirmity of body or mind:

Provided that the President may, by order, remove any Part-time Member from his office if he is adjudged an insolvent or is convicted of any offence involving moral turpitude or where he is, in the opinion of the President, unfit to continue in office by reason of infirmity of body or mind.

(4) If the Chairman or any Whole-time Member, except any ex officio Member, the Nominated Member or any elected Member, is, or becomes in any way concerned or interested in any contract or agreement made by or on behalf of the Corporation or the Government of India or the Government of a State or, participates in any way in the profit thereof, or in any benefit or emolument arising therefrom than as a member, and in common with other members of an incorporated company, he shall, for the purposes of sub-section (1), be deemed to be guilty of misbehaviour.

(5) If a Part-time Member is, or becomes in any way concerned, or interested in any contract or agreement made by or on behalf of the Corporation, he shall, for the purposes of sub-section (1), be deemed to be guilty of misbehaviour.

(6) The Chairman or any other Member may resign his office by giving notice. thereof in writing to the President of India and on such resignation being accepted, the Chairman or other Member shall be deemed to have vacated his office.

**8. Meetings of Board:** (1) The Board shall meet at such times-and places and shall 'observe such rules of procedure in regard to the transaction of business at its meetings (including the quorum at meetings) as may be provided by regulations:

Provided that there shall not be less than six meetings every year but three months shall not intervene between one meeting and the next meeting.

(2) A Member-shall be deemed to have vacated his office if he absents himself for three consecutive meetings of the Board without the leave of the Chairman.

(3) The Chairman shall preside at the meetings of the Board and if for any is reason he is unable to attend any meeting, the Executive Member and in the absence of both, any other Member elected by the Members present at such meeting, shall preside at the meeting.

(4) All questions which come up before an meeting of the Board shall be decided by a majority of the votes of the Members present and voting and, in the event of an equality of votes, the Chairman, or in his absence, the person presiding, shall have and exercise a second or casting vote.

**9. Officers and other employees of Corporation:** (I) Subject to such control, restrictions and conditions as may be prescribed, the Corporation may point, after consultation with the Recruitment Board, the Director-General (Akashvani), the Director-General (Doordarshan) and such other officers and other employees as may be necessary.

(2) The method of recruitment of such officers and employees and all other matters connected therewith and the conditions of service of such officers and other employees shall be such as may be provided by regulations.

**10. Establishment of Recruitment Boards:** (1) The Corporation shall, as soon as may be, after the appointed day and in such manner and subject to such conditions and restrictions as may be prescribed, establish for the purposes of section 9, one or more Recruitment Boards consisting wholly of persons other than the Members, officers and 'other employees of the Corporation:

Provided that for the purposes of appointment to the posts carrying scales of pay which are not less than that of a Joint Secretary to the Central Government, the Recruitment Board shall consist of the Chairman, other Members, the ex officio Members, the Nominated Member and the elected Members.

(2) The qualifications and other conditions of service of the members constituting the Recruitment Board and the period for which such members shall hold office, shall be such as may be prescribed.

**11.** Transfer of service of existing employees to Corporation: (1) Where the Central Government has ceased to perform any functions which under section 12 are the functions of the Corporation, it shall be lawful for the Central Government to transfer, by order and with effect from such date or dates as may be specified in the order, to the Corporation any of the officers or other employees serving .in the Akashvani or Doordarshan and engaged in the performance of those functions:

Provided that no order under this sub-section shall be made in relation to any office or other employee in the Akashvani or Doordarshan who has, in respect of the proposal of the Central Government to transfer such officer or other employee to the Corporation, intimated within such time as may be specified in this behal by the Central. Government, his intention of not becoming an employee of the Corporation.

(2) The provisions of sub-section (I) shall also apply to the members of the Indian Information Service the Central Secretariat Service or any other service or to persons borne on cadres outside Akashvani and Doordarshan who where been working in Akashvani or Doordarshan immediately before the appointed day:

Provided that where any such member intimates, within the time specified in subsection (1) his intention of not becoming an employee of the Corporation but to continue on deputation, he may be allowed to continue on deputation in accordance with such terms and conditions as may be prescribed.

(3) In making an order under sub-section (I), the Central Government shall, as far as may be. take into consideration the functions which the Akashvani or, as the case may be, Doordarshan has ceased or ceases to perform and the area in which such functions have been or are performed.

(4) An officer or other employee transferred by an order under sub-section (I) shall, on and from the date of transfer, cease to be an employee of the Central Government and become an employee of the Corporation with such designation as the Corporation may determine and shall, subject to the provisions of sub-sections (5) and (6), be governed by such regulations as may be made as respects remuneration and other conditions of service including pension, leave and provident fund and shall continue to be an officer or other employee of the Corporation unless and until his employment is terminated by the Corporation.

(5) Ever.' officer or other employee transferred by an order made under sub-section (I) shall, within six months from the date of transfer, exercise his option, in writing, to be governed :

(*a*) by the scale of pay applicable to the post held by him in the Akshvani or Doordarshan immediately before the date of transfer or by the scale applicable to the post under the Corporation to which he is transferred;

(*b*) by the leave, provident, fund, retirement or other terminal benefits admissible to employees of the Central Government in accordance with the rules or orders of the Central Government, as amended from time to time, or the leave, provident fund or other terminal benefits admissible to the. employees of the Corporation under the regulations, and such option once exercised under this Act shall be final:

Provided that the option exercised under clause (a) by an officer or other employee shall be applicable only in respect of the post under the Corporation to which such officer or other employee is transferred and on appointment to a higher post under the Corporation he shall be eligible only for the scale of pay applicable to such higher post:

Provided further that if immediately before the date of his transfer any such officer or other employee is officiating in a higher post under the Government either in a leave vacancy or any other, vacancy of a specified duration, his pay on transfer shall be protected for the unexpired period of such vacancy and thereafter he shall be entitled to the scale of pay applicable to the post under the Government to which he would have reverted or to the scale of pay applicable to the post under the Corporation to which he is transferred whichever he may opt:

Provided also that when an officer or other employee serving in the Union Ministry of Information and Broadcasting or in. any of its attached or subordinate offices is promoted to officiate in a higher post in the Ministry or office subsequent to the transfer to the Corporation of any other officer or employee senior to him in that Ministry or office before such transfer, the officer or other employee who is promoted to officiate in such higher post shall, on transfer to the Corporation, be entitled only to the scale of pay applicative to the post he would have held but for such promotion or the scale of pay applicable .to the post under the Corporation to which he is transferred, whichever he may opt.

(6) No officer or other employee transferred by an order made under sub-section (I) or sub-section (2) :

(*a*) shall be dismissed or removed by an authority subordinate to that competent to make a similar or equivalent appointment under the Corporation as may be specified in the regulations;

(*b*) shall be dismissed or removed or reduced in rank except after an inquiry in which he has been informed of the charges against him and given a reasonable opportunity of being heard in respect of those charges:

Provided that where it is proposed after such inquiry to impose upon him any such penalty, such penalty may be imposed on the basis of evidence adduced during such inquiry and it shall not be necessary to give such person an opportunity of making representation on the proposed penalty:

Provided further that clause (b) shall not apply where an officer or other employee is dismissed or removed or reduced in rank on the ground of conduct which has led to his conviction on a criminal charge.

**12. Functions and powers of Corporation:** (1) Subject to the provisions of this Act, it shall be the primary duty of the Corporation to organise and conduct public [broadcasting services to inform, educate and entertain the public and to ensure a balanced development of broadcasting on radio and television.

Explanation: For the removal of doubts, it is hereby declared that the provisions of this section shall be in addition to, and not in derogation of, the provisions of the Indian Telegraph Act, 1885 (13 of 1885).

(2) The Corporation shall, in the discharge of its functions, be guided by the following objectives, namely :

(*a*) unholding the unity and integrity of the country and the values enshrined in the Constitution :

(*b*) safeguarding the citizen's right to be informed freely, truthfully and objectively on all matters of public interest, national or international, and presenting a fair and balanced flow of information including contrasting views without advocating any opinion or ideology of its own;

(*c*) paying special attention to the fields of education and spread of literacy, agriculture rural development, environment, health and family welfare and science and technology;

(*d*) providing adequate coverage to the diverse cultures and languages of the, various regions of the country by broadcasting appropriate programmes;

(*e*) providing adequate coverage to sports and games so as to encourage healthy;. competition and the spirit of sportsmanship;

(*f*) providing appropriate programmes keeping in view the special needs of the youth;

(*g*) informing and stimulating the national consciousness in regard to the status' and problems of women and paying special attention to the upliftment of women;

(*h*) promoting social justice and combating exploitation, inequality and such evils as untouchability and advancing the welfare of the weaker sections of the society;

(*i*) safeguarding the rights of the working classes and advancing their welfare;

(*j*) serving the rural and weaker sections of the people and those residing in border regions, backward or remote areas;

(*k*) providing suitable programmes keeping in view the special needs of the minorities and tribal communities;

(*l*) taking special steps to protect the interests of children, the blind, the aged, the handicapped and other vulnerable sections of the people;

(*m*) promoting national integration by broadcasting in a manner that facilitates communication in the languages in India; and facilitating the distribution of regional broadcasting services in every State in the languages of that State;

(*n*) providing comprehensive broadcast coverage through the choice of appropriate technology and the best utilisation of the broadcast frequencies available and ensuring high quality reception;

(*o*) promoting research and development activities in order to ensure that radio and television broadcast technology are constantly updated; and

(*p*) expanding broadcasting facilities by establishing additional channels of transmission at various levels.

(3) In particular, and without prejudice to the generality of the foregoing provisions, the Corporation may take such steps as it thinks fit :

(*a*) to ensure that broadcasting is conducted as a public service to provide and produce programmes;

(*b*) to establish a system for the gathering of news for radio and television;

(*c*) to negotiate for purchase of, or otherwise acquire, programmes and rights or privileges in respect of sports and other events, films, serials, occasions, meetings, functions or incidents of public interest for broadcasting and to establish procedures for the allocation of such programmes, rights or privileges to the services;

(*d*) to establish and maintain a library or libraries of radio, television and other materials;

(*e*) to conduct or commission, from time to time, programmes, audience research, market or technical service, which may be released to such persons and in such manner and subject to such terms and conditions as the Corporation may think fit;

(*f*) to provide such other services as may be specified by regulations.

(4) Nothing in sub-sections (2) and (3) shall prevent the Corporation from managing on behalf of the Central Government and in accordance with such terms and conditions as may be specified by that Government the broadcasting of External Services and monitoring of broadcasts made by organisations outside India on the basis of arrangements made for reimbursement of expenses by the Central Government.

(5) For the purposes of ensuring that adequate time is made available for the promotion of the objectives set out in this section, the Central Government shell have the power to determine the maximum limit of broadcast time in respect of the advertisement.

(6) The Corporation shall be subject to no civil liability on the ground merely that it failed to comply with any of the provisions of this section.

(7) The Corporation shall have power to determine and levy fees and other service charges for or in respect of the advertisements and such programmes as may be specified by regulations:

Provided that the fees and other service charges levied and collected under this subsection shall not exceed such limits as may be determined by the Central Government, from time to time.

**13. Parliamentary Committee :** (1) There shall be constituted a Committee consisting of twenty-two Members of Parliament, of whom fifteen from the House of the People to be elected by the Members thereof and seven from the Council of States to be elected by the Members thereof in accordance with the system of proportional representation by means of the single transferable vote, to oversee that the Corporation discharges its functions in accordance with the provisions of this Act and, in particular, the objectives set out in section 12 and submit a report thereon to Parliament.

(2) The Committee shall function in accordance with such rules as may be made by the Speaker of the House of the People.

**14. Establishment of Broadcasting Council, term of office and removal, etc., of members thereof:** (1) There shall be established, by notification, as soon as may be after the appointed day, a Council, to be known as the Broadcasting Council, to receive and consider complaints referred to in section 15 and to advise the Corporation in the discharge of its functions in accordance with the objectives set out in section 12.

(2) The Broadcasting Council shall consist of:

(*i*) a President and ten other members to be appointed by the President of India from amongst persons of eminence in public life;

(*ii*) four Members of Parliament, of whom two from the House of the People to be nominated by the Speaker thereof and two from the Council of States to be nominated by the Chairman thereof.

(3) The President of the Broadcasting Council shall be a whole-time member and every other member shall be a part-time member and the President or the part-time member shall hold office as such for a term of three years from the date on which he enters upon his office.

(4) The Broadcasting Council may constitute such number of Regional Councils as it may deem necessary to aid and assist the Council in the discharge of its functions.

(5) The President of the Broadcasting Council shall be entitled to such salary and allowances and shall be subject to such conditions of service in respect of leave, pension (if any), provident fund and other matters as may be prescribed:

Provided that the salary and allowances and the conditions of service shall not be varied to the disadvantage of the President of the Broadcasting Council after his appointment.

(6) The other members of the Broadcasting Council and the members of the Regional Councils constituted under sub-section (4) shall be entitled to such allowances as may be prescribed.

**15. Jurisdiction of, and the procedure to be followed by. Broadcasting Council:** (1) The Broadcasting Council shall receive and consider complaints from :

(*i*) any person or group of persons alleging that a certain programme or broadcast or the functioning of the Corporation in specific cases or in general is not in accordance with the objectives for which the Corporation is established;

(*ii*) any person (other than an officer or employee of the Corporation) claiming himself to have been treated unjustly or unfairly in any manner (including unwarranted invasion of privacy, misrepresentation, distortion or lack of objectivity) in connection with any programme broadcast by the Corporation.

(2) A complaint under sub-section (1) shall be made in such manner and within such period as may be specified by regulations.

(3) The Broadcasting Council shall follow such procedure as, it thinks fit for the disposal of complaints received by it.

(4) If the complaint is found to be justified either wholly or in part, the Broadcasting Council shall advise the Executive Member to take appropriate action.

(5) If the Executive Member is unable to accept the recommendation of the Broadcasting Council, he shall place such recommendation before the Board for its decision thereon.

(6) If the Board is also unable to accept the recommendation of the Broadcasting Council, it shall record its reasons therefor and inform the Broadcasting Council .accordingly.

(7) Notwithstanding anything contained in sub-sections (5) and (6), where the Broadcasting Council deems it appropriate, it may, for reasons to be recorded in writing, require the Corporation to broadcast its recommendations with respect to a complaint in such manner as the Council may deem fit.

## CHAPTER III

## ASSETS, FINANCES AND ACCOUNTS

**16. Transfer of certain assets, liabilities, etc. of Central Government to Corporation** As from the appointed day :

(*a*) all property and assets (including the Non-lapsable Fund) which immediately before that day vested in the Central Government for the purpose of Akashvani or Doordarshan or both shall stand transferred to the

Corporation on such terms and conditions as may be determined by the Central Government and the book value of all such property and assets shall be treated as the capital provided by the Central Government to the Corporation;

(*b*) all debts, obligations and liabilities incurred, all contracts .entered into and all matters and things engaged to be done by, with or for the Central .Government immediately before such day for or in connection with the purposes of Akashvani or Doordarshan or both shall be deemed to have been incurred, entered into and engaged to be done by, with or for the Corporation;

(*c*) all sums of money due to the Central Government in relation to the Akashvani or Doordarshan or both immediately before such day shall be deemed to be due to the Corporation;

(*d*) all suits and other legal proceedings instituted or which could have been instituted by or against the Central Government immediately before such day for any matter in relation to the Akashvani or Doordarshan or both may be continued or instituted by or against the Corporation.

**17. Grants, etc. by Central Government:** For the purposes of enabling the Corporation to discharge its functions efficiently under this Act, the Central Government may, after due appropriation made by Parliament by law in this behalf, pay to the Corporation in each financial year:

(*i*) the proceeds of the broadcast receiver licence fees, if any, as reduced by the collection charges; and

(*ii*) such other sums of money as that Government considers necessary, by way of equity, loan.

**18. Fund of Corporation:** (1) The Corporation shall have its own Fund and all the receipts of the Corporation (including the amounts which stand transferred to the Corporation under section 16) shall be credited to the Fund and all payments by the Corporation shall be made therefrom.

(2) All moneys belonging to the Fund shall be deposited in one or more nationalised banks in such manner as the Corporation may decide.

(3) The Corporation may spend such sums as it thinks fit for performing its functions under this Act and such sums shall be treated as expenditure payable out of the Fund of the Corporation.

**Explanation:** For the purposes of this section, "nationalised bank" means a 'corresponding new bank specified in the First Schedule to the Banking Companies (Acquisition and .Transfer of Undertakings) Act, 1970 or a corresponding new bank specified in the First Schedule to the Banking Companies (Acquisition and Transfer of Undertakings) Act, 1980.

**19. Investment of moneys:** The Corporation may invest its moneys in the securities of the Central Government or any State Government or in such other manner as may be prescribed.

**20. Annual Financial Statement of the Corporation:** (I) The Corporation shall prepare, in each financial year, an Annual Financial Statement for the next financial year showing separately :

(*a*) the expenditure which is proposed to be met from the internal resources of the Corporation; and

(*b*) the sums required from the Central Government to meet other expenses, and distinguishing :

(*i*) revenue expenditure from other expenditure; and

(*ii*) non-plan expenditure from plan expenditure.

(2) The Annual Financial Statement shall be prepared in such form and forwarded at such time to the Centra! Government for its approval as may be agreed to by that Government and the Corporation.

**21. Accounts and audit of Corporation:** (1) The Corporation shall maintain proper accounts and other relevant records and prepare an annual statement of accounts in such form and in such manner as may be prescribed.

(2) The accounts of the Corporation shall be audited by the Comptroller and Auditor-General of India at such intervals as may be specified by him and any expenditure incurred in connection with such audit shall be payable by the Corporation to the Comptroller and Auditor-General.

(3) The Comptroller and Auditor-General and any person appointed by him in connection with the audit of the accounts of the Corporation shall have the same rights and privileges and authority in connection with such audit as the Comptroller and Auditor-General has in connection with the audit of Government accounts and, in particular, shall have the right to demand the production of books, accounts, connected vouchers and other documents and papers and to inspect any of the offices of the Corporation.

(4) The accounts of the Corporation as certified by the Comptroller and Auditor-General of India or any other person appointed by him in this behalf together with the audit report thereon shall be forwarded annually to the Central Government and that Government shall cause the same to be laid before each House of Parliament.

**22. Corporation not liable to be taxed:** Notwithstanding anything contained in the Income-tax Act, 1961, (43 of 1961) or any other enactment for the time being in force relating to income-tax or any other tax on income, profits or gains, the Corporation shall not be liable to pay any income-tax or any other tax in respect of:

(*a*) any income, profits or gains, accruing or arising out of the Fund of the Corporation or any amount received in that Fund; and

(*b*) any income, profits or gains, derived or any. amount, received, by the Corporation

## CHAPTER IV

## MISCELLANEOUS

**23. Power of Central Government to give directions:** (1) The Central Government may, from time to time as and when occasion arises, issue to the Corporation such directions as it may think necessary in the interests of the sovereignty, unity and integrity of India or the security of the State or preservation of public order requiring it not to make a broadcast on a matter specified in the direction or to make a broadcast on any matter of public importance specified in the direction.

(2) Where the Corporation makes a broadcast in pursuance of the direction issued under sub-section (1), the fact that such broadcast has been made in pursuance of such direction may also be announced along with such broadcast, if the Corporation so desires.

(3) A copy of every direction issued under sub-section (1) shall be laid before each House of Parliament.

**24. Power of Central Government to obtain information:** The Central Government may require the Corporation to furnish such information as that Government may consider necessary.

**25. Report to Parliament in certain matters and recommendations as to action against the Board:** (1) Where the Board persistently makes default in complying with any directions issued under section 23 or fails to supply the information required under section 24, the Central Government may prepare a report thereof and lay it before each House of Parliament for any recommendation thereof as to any action (including supersession of the Board) which may be taken against the Board.

(2) On the recommendation of the Parliament, the President may by notification supersede the Board for such period not exceeding six months as may be specified in the notification:

Provided that before issuing the notification under this sub-section, the President shall give a reasonable opportunity to the Board to show cause as to why it should not be superseded- and shall consider the explanations and objections, if any, of the Board.

(3) Upon the publication of the notification under sub-section (2):

(*a*) all the Members shall, as from the date of supersession, vacate their offices as such;

(*b*) all the powers, functions and duties which may, by or under the provisions ; of this Act be exercised or discharged by or on behalf of the Board, shall, until the Board is reconstituted under this Act, be exercised and discharged ... by such person or persons as the President may direct.

(4) On the expiration of the period of supersession specified in the notification issued under sub-section (2), the President may reconstitute the Board by fresh appointments, and in such a case any person who had vacated his office under clause (a) of sub-section (3) shall not be disqualified for appointment:

Provided that the President may, at any time before the expiration of the period of supersession, take action under this sub-section.

(5) The Central Government shall cause the notification issued under sub-section (2) and a full report of the action taken under this section to be laid before each House of Parliament.

**26. Office of member not to disqualify a Member of Parliament:** It is hereby declared that the office of the member of the Broadcasting Council or of the Committee constituted under section 13 shall not disqualify its holder for being chosen as, or for being, a Member of either House of Parliament.

**27. Chairman, Members, etc. to be public servants:** The Chairman and every other Member, every officer or other employee of the Corporation and every member of a Committee thereof, the President and every member of the Broadcasting Council or every member of a Regional Council or a Recruitment Board shall be deemed to be a public servant within the meaning of section 21 of the Indian Penal Code (45 of 1860).

**28. Protection of action taken in good faith:** No suit or other legal proceeding shall lie against the Corporation, the Chairman or any Member or officer or other employee thereof or the President or a member of the Broadcasting Council or a member of a Regional Council or a Recruitment Board for anything which is in good faith done or intended to be done in pursuance of this Act or of any rules or regulations made hereunder.

**29. Authentication of orders and other instruments of Corporation:** All orders and decisions of the Corporation shall be authenticated by the signature of the Chairman or any other Member authorised by the Corporation in this behalf and all other instruments executed by the Corporation shall be authenticated by the signature of the Executive Member or by any officer of the Corporation authorised by him in this behalf.

**30. Delegation of powers:** The Corporation may, by general or special order, delegate to the Chairman or any other Member or to any officer of the Corporation, subject to such conditions and limitations, if any, as may be specified therein, such of its powers and duties under this Act as it may deem fit.

**31. Annual report:** (1) The Corporation shall prepare once in every calendar year, in such Form and within such time as may be prescribed an annual report giving a full account of its activities (including the recommendations and suggestions made by the Broadcasting Council and the action taken thereon) during the previous year and copies thereof shall be forwarded to the Central Government and that Government shall cause the same to be laid before each House of Parliament.

(2) The Broadcasting Council shall prepare once in every calendar year, in such form and within such time as may be prescribed, an annual report giving a full a count of its activities during the previous year and copies thereof shall be forwarded to the Central Government and that Government shall cause the same. to be laid before each House of Parliament.

**32. Power to make rules:** (1) The Central Government may, by notification, make rules for carrying out the provisions of this Act.

(2) In particular, and without prejudice to the generality of the foregoing, power, such rules may provide for all or any of the following matters, namely:

(*a*) the salaries and allowances and conditions of service in respect of leave, pension (if any), provident fund and other matters in relation to the Whole-time Members under sub-section (7) of section 6;

(*b*) the allowances payable to the Chairman and Part-time Members under sub-section (8) of section 6;

(*c*) the control, restrictions and conditions subject to which the Corporation may appoint officers and other employees under sub-section (I) of section 9;

(*d*) the manner in which and the conditions and restrictions subject to which a Recruitment Board may be established under sub-section (1) of section 10;

(*e*) The qualifications and other conditions of service of the members of a Recruitment Board and their period of office under sub-section (2) of section 10;

(*f*) the terms and conditions in accordance with which the deputation may be regulated under sub-section (2) of section 11;

(*g*) the salary and allowances and conditions of service in respect of leave, pension (of any), provident fund and other matters in relation to the President of the Broadcasting Council under sub-section (5) of section 14;

(*h*) the allowances payable to other members of the Broadcasting Council and the members of the Regional Councils, under sub-section (6) of section 14;

(*i*) the manner in which the Corporation may invest its moneys under section 19;

(*j*) the form and the manner in which the annual statement of accounts shall be prepared under sub-section (1) of section 21;

(*k*) the form, in which, and the time within which the Corporation and the Broadcasting Council shall prepare their annual report under section 31;

(*l*) any other matter which is required to be, or may be, prescribed.

**33. Power to make regulations:** (1) The Corporation may, by notification, make regulations not inconsistent with this Act and the rules made thereunder for enabling it to perform its functions under this Act.

(2) Without prejudice to the generality of the foregoing power such regulations may provide for all or any of the following matters, namely:

(a) the manner in which and the purposes for which the Corporation may associate with itself any person under sub-section (7) of section 3;

(b) the times and places at which meetings of the Board shall be held and, the procedure to be followed there at, and the quorum necessary for the transaction of the business at a meeting of the Board under sub-section (1) of section 8;

(c) the methods of recruitment and conditions of service of officers and other employees of the Corporation under sub-section (2) of section 9;

(d) the remuneration and other conditions of service, including pension, leave and provident fund in relation to an officer or other employee of the Corporation under sub-section (4) of section 11;

(e) the authority competent to make certain appointments referred to in clause (a) of sub-section (6) of section 11;

(f) the services which may be provided by the Corporation under clause (f) of sub-section (3) of section 12;

(g) the determination and levy of fees and other service charges in respect of advertisements and other programmes under sub-section (7) of section 12;

(h) the manner in which and the period within which complaints may be made under sub-section (2) of section 15;

(i) any other matter in respect of which provision is, in the opinion of the Corporation, necessary for the performance of its functions under this Act:

Provided that the regulations under clause (c) or clause (d) shall be made only with the prior approval of the Central Government.

**34. Rules and regulations to be laid before Parliament:** Every rule and every regulation made under this Act shall be laid, as soon as may be after it is made, before each House of Parliament, while it is in session for a total period of thirty days which may be comprised in one session or in two or more successive sessions, and if, before the expiry of the session immediately following the session or the successive sessions aforesaid, both Houses agree in making any modification in the rule or regulation, or both Houses agree .that the rule or regulation should not be made, the rule or regulation shall thereafter have effect only in such modified form or be of no effect, as the case may be; so, however, that any such modification or annulment shall be without prejudice to the validity of anything previously done under that rule or regulation.

**35. Power to remove difficulties:** If any difficulty arises in giving effect to the provisions of this Act, the Centra! Government may, by order, published in the Official Gazette, make such provisions, not inconsistent with the provisions of this Act, as it may deem necessary, for the removal of the difficulty:

Provided that no such order shall be made after the expiry of a period of three years from the appointed day.

# 13

# Broadcasting Act, 1997

The Supreme Court in one of its decisions in 1975 viewed that there should be some authority to regulate the broadcasting system in the country and any single agency can have the authority on broadcasting. The broadcasting should be under the control of the people and not the Government. Radio waves are public property and it use can be regulated and controlled by any public authority, so that the right of the people are not hampered.

On the basis of this decision of the Supreme Court, "Broadcasting Bill" was placed before the Indian Parliament in 1977. The "Broadcasting Bill" is divided into six parts. There is a provision of "Indian Broadcasting Authority" in the second chapter of the Bill.

## COMPOSITION OF THE INDIAN BROADCASTING AUTHORITY

The Indian Broadcasting Authority will consist of a Chairman and not more that 11 part-time Members, the Secretary of the Deptt. of Information and Broadcasting will be ex-officio, Member, the Secretary, the Deptt. of Telecommunication, Government of India ex-official Secretary. The Government of India will make available a panel of five officers in the rank of the Secretary and the Authority will select one of them as Secretary General. The Secretary General will be the Chief Executive Officer of the Authority. The Chairman of the Authority shall be appointed by the President of India on the advice of a Committee consisting of the Chairman of the Council of States, Minister for Information and Broadcasting and the Chairman of the Press Council of India . The Chairman shall hold office for a period of five years or attainment of the age of 65 and other members for three years.

**Functions of the Authority:** The Authority will issue licenses for broadcasting services. After the enactment of this Act, no body can provide broadcasting services for any services mentioned in sub-section (1), of section (9) under the provision of the Act, without obtaining the license.

The Authority shall have the powers to issue licenses for the following broadcasting services:

1. Community radio broadcast
2. Community television broadcast;
3. Satellite radio broadcast;
4. Satellite television broadcast;
5. Direct to home broadcast
6. Local relay services and
7. Such other services, as may be prescribed

The Authority would ensure the availability of the broadcasting services on wide range throughout India, to ensure the proper and effective competition in establishment of broadcasting services, to ensure the arrangement of high quality services and to present wide range of programmes to attract multiple takes and choices. It shall also fix programme code and standard through regulations. The Authority shall also have the powers to receive complaints against the violation of the rules and regulations and the conditions of the license and take corrective measures, as it may deem necessary. It shall also be the functions of the Authority to execute radio wave scheme of such radio waves or band of waves allotted for broadcasting services to the Government of India by Wireless Adviser.

The Authority will appoint a committee of experts to advise on the system being followed regarding the depiction of violence in the programmes, the system being followed regarding depiction of sex and the standard of choice and ethics for programmes generally.

The Authority will also appoint a Committee of experts to monitor the programmes and to report on the standard in the depictions of violence and sex in the programmes and the choice and ethics followed in it.

## CONDITIONS FOR ISSUANCE OF LICENSES

The licenses will be issued under the following conditions:

1. The licensee will ensure that the programme of the licensee does not include any such mater which is against good choice or ethics or exaggerated or from which there is probability that it will encourage and instigate crime or spread disorder or will hurt the feelings of the people.
2. The licensee will ensure that news stories given in their programmes are presented with facts and impartially.
3. The licensee will ensure that proper impartiality is being maintained with respect to the subjects related to social or political issue or public policy.

4. The licensee will ensure that proper responsibility is being observed in respect of religious programmes from the stand point of its observance of the following:
   (*a*) Misuse of religious sentiments, and
   (*b*) Crime against religious views and faith of the person of any particular area religious community.
5. The licensee will ensure that proper importance is given for the proper development of the values of national unity, religious harmony, scientific viewpoint and Indian culture.
6. The licensee will ensure that the time allotted by the authority is fixed for the following:
   (*a*) Children's programme, education programme, development programme and programme of Indian origin.
   (*b*) Range of varieties in independent presentation.
7. The licensee will follow the prescribed programmes standards and codes decided by the Authority.
8. The licensee will not, without the prior permission of the Authority, execute the network of the local or regional broadcasting services.
9. The Authority can change the conditions of the license after giving proper opportunity of hearing.

## THE LICENSE IS NON–TRANSFERABLE

Any aggrieved person can appeal against any action of the Authority within 30 days in the High Court having the jurisdiction. The High Court having the Jurisdiction means such a High Court under whose Jurisdiction the aggrieved person normally resides, or conducts any business or works for personal benefits.

The person, found guilty of unauthorized broadcast, can be punished with imprisonment, extending upto five years or a fine upto rupees ten lacs, any act of repeated crime the fine can be extended upto rupees 50 lacs or both.

While presenting the Bill, the then Minister for Information and Broadcasting had declared that this Bill is for the establishment of an independent broadcasting authority of the purpose of regulating and facilitating broadcasting services in the country, so that along with being an incentive for creating model view point and improvement in the values of Indian culture, social changes, quality of service, investment in service and making the use of new technologies competitive.

The bill is for the fulfillment of these purposes.

# 14

# Cable Television Networks Rules, 1994

The invention of satellite brought a sort of revolution in the field of broadcasting. The satellite transmits the message received from one part of the earth to different parts of the earth. First of all Cable News Network (CNN) started the satellite broadcast by showing the gulf–war, after that a number of satellites were put in the orbit. In 1992 Star Television introduced Digital Video Compression in which six channels could be broadcast through a singly transponder. In addition to Doordarshan being controlled by Prasar Bharti, Star Plus, Zee TV, Discovery channel, BBC, Sony, etc. more than 90 (ninety) channels became available to Indian audience.

This conglomeration of satellite channels necessitated the framing of some rules to regulate them.

The Cable Television Networks Rules 1994: The Cable Television Networks, (Regulations) rules, 1994 came into being after it was published in the Gazette of India dated 19th September, 1994. The Rules defined "Cable Service", "Cable Television Networks" and "Programme".

**Programme Code:** Under the provision of the Rules, no programme should be carried in the cable service which;

(a) Offends against good taste and decency.

(b) Contains criticism of friendly countries.

(c) Contains attacks on religion or communities or visuals or words contemptuous of religious groups or which promotes communal attitudes.

(d) Contains anything obscene, defamatory, deliberate, false and suggestive innuendos and half–truths.

(e) Is likely to encourage or incite violence or contains anything against maintenance of law and order or which promotes anti–national attitudes.

(f) Contains anything amounting to contempt of Court;

(g) Contains aspersions against the integrity of the President or Judiciary;

(h) Contains anything affecting the integrity of the Nation;

(i) Criticizes, maligns or slanders any individual in person or certain groups, segments of social, public and moral life of the Country;

(j) Encourage superstition or blind belief

(k) Denigrates women through the depiction in any manner of the figure of a woman, her form or body or any part there of in such a way as to have the effect of being indecent or derogatory to woman or is likely to corrupt or injure the public morality or morals.

(l) Denigrades children.

(m) Contains visuals or words which reflect a slandering, ironical and snobbish attitude in the portrayal of certain ethnic, linguistic and regional groups.

(n) Contravenes the provisions of the Cinematographic Act, 1952

Programmes meant for children should not contain any bad language or explicit scenes of violence programmes unsuitable for children, must not be carried in the cable service at times when the largest numbers of children are viewing.

Advertising carried to the cable service should conform to the laws of the country and should not offend morality, decency and religious susceptibility of the subscribers. The advertisements must not be directed towards any religions or political end. Indecent, vulgar, suggestive, repulsive or offensive themes or treatment shall be avoided in all advertisements. The advertisements to be carried in the cable service should conform to the standards of practice for advertising agencies as approved by the Advertising Association of India, Bombay.

## CABLE TELEVISION NETWORK (REGULATION) ACT, 1995

Cable Television Networks (Regulation) Bill was passed by both the Houses of the Parliament and was assented by the president on 25th March 1995. The Cable Television Networks (Regulation) Act, 1995, was deemed to have come into force on 29th September 1994, when the notification for Cable Television Networks Rules, 1994 was published in the Gazette of India. It also contains the definition of certain terminology like “Cable Service”, “Cable Television Networks” as given in the Rules of 1994.

**Power to prohibit transmission of certain programmes in public interest:** Any authorized officer may, by order, prohibit any cable operator from transmitting or retransmitting any programme or channel if it is not is conformity with prescribed programme code and advertisement code or it is likely to promote on grounds of religions, race, language, cast or community, disharmony or feeling of enmity, hatred or ill–will, between different religious, racial, linguistic or regional groups or castes or communities or which disturbs or is likely to disturb the public tranquility.

The Central Government may regulate or prohibit the transmission or retransmission of any channel or programme in the interest of the;

(*i*) Sovereignty or integrity of India; or

(*ii*) Security of India; or

(*iii*) Friendly relations of India with any foreign State; or

(*iv*) Public order, decency or morality;

The Central Government, if so considers that any programme of any channel is not in conformity with the prescribed programme code in section (5) or the prescribed advertisement code in section (6) of the Act (also detailed in Rule of 1994, it may order, regulate or prohibit the transmission or re–transmission of such programme.

However, the Act shall not have any of the provisions of the following existing Acts;

(a) The Drugs and Cosmetics Act, 1940

(b) The Emblems and Names (Prevention of Improper Use) Act, 1950

(c) The Drugs (Control) Act, 1950

(d) The Cinematographic Act, 1952

(e) The Drugs and Magic Remedies (Objectionable Advertisement) Act, 1954

(f) The Prevention of Food Adulteration Act, 1954

(g) The Prize Competition Act, 1955

(h) The Copyright Act, 1957

(i) The Trade and Merchandise Marks Act, 1958

(j) The Indecent Representation of Women (Prohibition) Act, 1986 and

(k) The Consumer Protect Act, 1986.

## THE CABLE TELEVISION NETWORKS RULES, 1994

[*29th September, 1994*]

In exercise of the powers conferred by sub-section (1) of Section 22 of the Cable Television news works (Regulation) Ordinance, 1994 (9 of 1994)[2], the Central Government makes the following rules, namely:

**1.** (1) These rules may be called the Cable Television Networks Rules, 1994.

(2) They shall come into force on the date of their publication in the Official Gazette.

### *Definitions*

**2. In these rules, unless the context otherwise requires :**

(*a*) "Cable service" means the transmission by cables of programmes including re-transmission by cables of any broadcast television singnals ;

(*b*) "Cable television network" means any system consisting of a set of closed transmission paths and associated signals generation, control and distribution equipment, designed to provide cable service for reception by multiple subscribers;

(*c*) "Programme" means any television broadcast and includes:

(*i*) exhibition of films, features, dramas, advertisements and serials through video cassette recorders or video cassette players;

(*ii*) any audio or visual or audio–visual live performance or presentation; and the expression "programming service" shall be construed accordingly;

**6.** (1) No programme should be carried in the cable service which:

(a) offends against good taste or decency;

(b) contains criticism of friendly countries;

(c) contains attack on religions or communities or visusals or words contemptuous of religious groups or which promote communal attitudes;

(d) contains anything obscene, defamatory, deliberate, false and suggestive innuendos and half-truths;

(e) is likely to encourage or incite violence or contains anything against maintenance of law and order or which promote anti-national attitudes;

(f) contains anything amounting to contempt of Court;

(g) contains aspersions against the integrity of the President and Judiciary;

(h) contains anything affecting the integrity of the Nation:

(i) criticises, maligns or slanders any individual in person or certain groups, segments of social, public and moral life of the country;

(j) encourages superstition or blind belief;

(k) denigraes women through the depiction in any manner of the figure of a woman, her form or body or any therefor in such a way as to have the effect of being or derogatory to women, or is likely to deprave, corrupt or injure the public morality or morals;

(l) denigraes children;

(m) contains visuals or words which reflect a slandering' ironical and snobbish attitude in the portrayal of certain ethnic, linguistic and regional groups;

(n) contravenes the provisions of the Cinematograph **Act, 1952**.

(2) The cable operator should strive to carry programmes in his cable service which project women in a positive, leadership role of sobriety, moral and character building qualities.

(3) Programmes meant for adults should normally be carried in the cable service after 11 p.m and before 6 a.m.

(4) Care should be taken to ensure that programmes meant for children do not contain any bad language or explicit seenes of violence.

(5) Programmes unsuitable for children must not be carried in the cable service at times when the largest numbers of children are viewing.

7. (1) Advertising carried in the cable service shall be so designed as to conform to the laws of the country and should not offend morality, decency and religious susceptibilities of the subscribers.

(2) No advertisement shall be permitted which:

(*i*) derides any race, caste, colour, creed and nationality;

(*ii*) is against any provision of the Constitution of India;

(*iii*) teads to incite people to crime, cause disorder or violence or breach of law or glorifies violence or obscenity in any way;

(*iv*) presents criminality as desirable;

(*v*) exploits the national emblem, or any part of the Constitution or the person or personality of a national leader or a State dignitary;

(*vi*) in its deception of women violates the Constitutional guarantees to all citizens. In particular, no advertisement shall be permitted which projects a derogatory image of women. Women must not be portrayed in a manner that emphasises passive, submissive qualities and encourages them to play a subordinate, secondary role in the family and society. The cable operator shall ensure that the portrayal of the female form, in the programmes carried in his cable service is tasteful and aesthetic and is within the well established norms of good taste and decency;

(*vii*) exploits social evils like dowry, child marriage.

(3) No advertisement shall be permitted the objects whereof are wholly or mainly of a religious or political nature; advertisements must not be directed towards any religious or political end.

(4) The goods or services advertised shall not suffer from any defect or deficiency as mentioned in Consumer Protection Act, 1986.

(5) No advertisement shall contain references which are likely to lead the public to infer that the product advertised or any of its ingredients has some special or miraculous or super–natural property or quality, which is difficult of being proved.

(6) The picture and the audible matter of the advertisement shall not be excessively "loud".

(7) No advertisement which endangers the safety of children or creates in

them any interest in unhealthy practices or shows them begging or in an undignified or indecent manner shall not be carried in the cable service.

(8) Indecent, vulgar, suggestive, repulsive or offensive themes or treatment shall be avoided in all advertisements.

(9) No advertisement which violates the standards of practice for advertising agencies as approved by the Advertising Agencies Association of India, Bombay, from time to time shall be- carried in the cable service.

(10) All advertisements should be clearly distinguishable from the programme and should not in any manner interfere with the programme viz., use of lower part of screen to carry captions, static or moving alongside the programme.

## THE CABLE TELEVISION NETWORKS (REGULATION) ACT 1995

### Act 7 of 1995

The Bill titled Cable Television Networks Regulation Bill, 1995 was passed by both the Houses of Parliament and the same was assented by the President on 25th March, 1995. It came on the statute book *as* "The Cable Television Networks (Regulation) Act, 1995 (7 of 1995)" deemed to have come into force on 29th September, 1994.

### CHAPTER I

### PRELIMINARY

**1.** (1) This Act may be called the Cable Television Networks (Regulation) Act, 1995.

(2) It extends to the whole of India.

(3) It shall be deemed to have come into force on the 29th day of September, 1994.

**2. In this Act, unless the context otherwise requires:**

(*a*) "cable service" means the transmission by cables of programmes including re–transmission by cables of any broadcast television signals ;

(*b*) "cable television network" means any system consisting of a set of closed transmission paths and associated signal generation, control and distribution equipment designed to provide cable service for reception by multiple subscribers;

## CHAPTER V

## MISCELLANEOUS

**19.** Where [any authorised officer], thinks it transmission of necessary or expedient so to do in the public certain programmes interest, he may, by order, prohibit any cable operator from transmitting or re-transmitting [3][any programme or channel if it is not in conformity with the prescribed programme code referred to in Section 5 and advertisement code referred to in Section 6 or if it is] likely to promote, on grounds of religion, race, language, caste or community or any other ground whatsoever, disharmony or feelings of enmity, hatred or ill-will between different religious, racial, linguistic or regional groups or castes or communities or which disturbs or is likely to disturb the public tranquillity.

**20.** (1) Where the Central Government thinks it operation of cable necessary or expedient so to do in the public interest, it may prohibit the operation of any cable public interest television network in such areas as it may, by notification in the Official Gazette, specify in this behalf.

"(2) Where the Central Government thinks it necessary or expedient so to do in the interest of the:

(*i*) sovereignty or integrity of India; or

(*ii*) security of India: or

(*iii*) friendly relations of India with any foreign State: or

(*iv*) public order, decency or morality, it may, by order, regulate or prohibit the transmission or retransmission of any channel or programme.

(3) Where the Central Government considers that any programme of any channel is not in conformity with the prescribed programme code referred to in Section 5 or the prescribed advertisement code referred to in **Section 6**, it may by order, regulate or prohibit the transmission or re–tranmission of such programme".

**21.** The provisions of this Act shall be in addition to and not in derogation of, the Drugs and Cosmetics Act, 1940 (23 of 1940), the Pharmacy Act, 1948 (8 of 1948), the Emblems and Names (Prevention of Improper Use) Act, 1950 (12 afl950), the Drugs (Control) Act, 1950 (26 of 1950), the Cinematograph *Act,* 1952 (37 of 1952), the Drugs and Magic Remedies (Objectionable Advertisements) Act, 1954 (21 of 1954), the Prevention of Food Adulteration Act, 1954 (37 of 1954), the Prize Competitions Act, 1955 (42 of 1955), the Copyright Act, 1957 (14 of 1957), the Trade and Merchandise Marks Act, 1958 (43 of 1958), the Indecent Representation of Women (Prohibition) Act, 1986 (60 of 1986) and the Consumer Protection Act, 1986 (68 of 1986).

# 15

# The Freedom of Information Act, 2002

This is a Bill to provide freedom to every citizen to secure access to information under the control of public authorities, consistent with public interest, in order to promote openness, transparency and accountability in administration and in relation to matters connected therewith or incidental there to.

The Bill was enacted by both the Houses of Parliament and was called the Freedom of Information Act, 2002.

The freedom of information has been defined under the provisions of the Act as the right to obtain information from any public authority by means of;

(*i*) Inspection, taking of extracts and notes;

(*ii*) Certified copies of any records of such public authority

(*iii*) Diskettes, floppies or in any other electronic mode or through printouts where such information is stored in a computer or any other device.

"Information" means any material in any form relating to the administration, operations or decision of a public authority.

Under the provisions of the Act all citizens shall have freedom of information. Every public authority is required to maintain all its records, in such a manner and form as is consistent with all operational requirements duly catalogued and indexed and publish at such intervals as may be prescribed by the appropriate Government or competent authority. The records will include, among others, rules, regulations, instructions, manuals and other categories of records under its control used by its employees for discharging its functions.

## Request for obtaining Information and Disposal of Requests

A person desirous of obtaining information shall make a request in writing or through electronic means, to concerned public Information Officer specifying the particulars of the information sought by him. Public Information Officer shall also render all reasonable assistance to the person making such request rally, where such a request cannot be made in writing.

On receipt of the request the Public Information Officer shall, as expeditiously as possible, and in any case within thirty days of the receipt of the request, either provide the information requested on payment of such fee as may be prescribed or reject the request for any other reasons mentioned in sections listing information exempted.

## INFORMATION EXEMPTED FROM DISCLOSURE

The following information shall be exempted from disclosure under sub-section (1) of section (8) of the Act:

(a) Information, the disclosure of which would prejudicially affect the sovereignty and integrity of India, security of the State, strategic scientific or economic interest of India or conduct of international relations,

(b) Information, the disclosure of which would prejudicially affect public safety and order, detection and investigation of an offence, or which may lead to an incitement to commit an offence or prejudicially affect fair trial or adjudication of a pending case.

(c) Information, the disclosure of which would prejudicially affect the conduct of Centre–State relations, including information exchanged in confidence between the Central Government and State Government or any of their authorities or agencies.

(d) Cabinet papers including records of deliberations of the Council of Ministers, Secretaries or other officers.

(e) Minutes or records of advice including legal advice, opinions or recommendations made by any officer of a public authority during the decision making process prior to the executive decision or policy formulation.

(f) Trade of Commercial secrets protected by law or information, the disclosure of which would prejudicially affect the legitimate economic or commercial interests or the competitive position of a public authority, or would cause unfair gain or loss to any person, and

(g) Information, the disclosure of which may result in breach of privileges of Parliament of Legislature or a State, or Contravention of a lawful order of a Court.

However according sub–section (2) of sections (8) of the Act any information, relating to any occurrence, event or matter, which has taken place, occurred or happened twenty–five years before the date on which any request in made shall be provided to any person making a request.

## OTHER GROUNDS FOR REFUSAL OF INFORMATION

An Information Officer may reject a request for information also on the ground that;

(a) The information sought is too general in nature or is of such a nature that having regard to the volume of information required to be retrieved or processed would involve disproportionate diversion of the resources of a public authority or would adversely interfere with the functioning of such authority;

(b) It relates to information that is required by law, rules, regulations or orders to be published at a particular time and such information is likely to be so published within thirty days of the receipt of such request.

(c) It relates to information that is contained in published material available to public

(d) It relates to information, which would cause unwarranted invasion of the privacy of any person.

## THIRD PARTY INFORMATION

Where a public authority intends to disclose information on a request made by a party, which relates to, or has been supplied by a third party and has been treated as confidential by that third party, the Public Information Officer shall by notice to such third party, invite representation against the proposed disclosure, if any, within fifty days from the date of the receipt of such notice. However, the public interest outweighs in importance to any possible harm or injury to the interests of such third party.

## PROTECTION OF ACTION TAKEN IN GOOD FAITH

No suit, prosecution or other legal proceeding shall lie against any person for anything which is done in good faith or intended to be done under this Act or any rule made there under.

## OVERRIDING EFFECT OF THE ACT

The provisions of the Official Secrets Act, 1923 and every other Act in force shall cease to be operative to the extent to which they are inconsistent with the provisions of Freedom of Information Act, 2002.

## BAR ON JURISDICTION OF COURTS

No Court shall entertain any suit, application or other proceeding in respect of any order made under this Act and no such order shall be called in questions otherwise than by way of appeal under this Act.

### NON–APPLICATION OF THE ACT TO CERTAIN ORGANIZATIONS

The provisions of the Act shall not;

(*a*) Apply to the intelligence and security organizations specified in the schedule, being organizations established by the Central or State Government or any information furnished by such organizations to the respective Governments.

(*b*) Apply to the intelligence and security organizations discharging their functions as such under State Governments.

The Central Government and State Government, by notification in their respective official gazette, make rules to carry out the provisions of this Act.

Every notification issued to amend the schedule by the Central Government shall be laid before each House of the Parliament.

Every rule made by the Central Government under this Act shall be laid, as soon as possible, before each House of the Parliament. In case both Houses decide to make any modification in the rule, the rule shall have effect only in such modified form or be of no effect in case of its annulment. The same procedure has to be followed in cases of rule made by a State Government, which shall lay before its respective legislature.

However, the Act failed in the purposes for which enacted due to some inherent shortcomings Firstly, there was no provision of an independent agency to adjudicate in case of any dispute in non–supply of information sought for. Secondly, there was no provision of any fine to be imposed on any Government officer refusing to give information.

## THE FREEDOM OF INFORMATION BILL, 2000

A bill to provide for freedom to every citizen to secure access to information under the control of public authorities, consistent with public interest, in order to promote openness, transparency and accountability in administration and in relation to matters connected therewith or incidental thereto.

Be it enacted by Parliament in the Fifty–first Year of the Republic of India as follows:

### CHAPTER II

### PRELIM1NARY

**1.** (1) This Act may be called the Freedom of Information Act, 2000.

(2) It extends to the whole of India except the State of Jammu and Kashmir.

(3) It shall come into force on such date as the Central Government may, by notification in the Official Gazette, appoint.

*Definitions*

2. **In this Act, unless the context otherwise requires:**

(b) "competent authority" means:

- (*i*) the Speaker in the case of the House of the People or the Legislative Assembly and the Chairman in the case of the Council of States or the Legislative Council;
- (*ii*) the Chief Justice of India in the case of the Supreme Court;
- (*iii*) the Chief Justice of the High Court in the case of a High Court;
- (*iv*) the President or the Governor, as the case may be, in case of other authorities created by or under the Constitution;

(c) "freedom of information" means the right to obtain information from any public authority by means of:

- (*i*) inspection, taking of extracts and notes;
- (*ii*) certified copies of any records of such public authority;
- (*iii*) diskettes, floppies or in any other electronic mode or through printouts where such information is stored in a computer or in any other device;

(d) "information" means any material in any form relating to the administration, operations or decisions of a public authority;

(g) "Public Information Officer" means the Public Information Officer appointed under sub-section (1) of Section 5;

(h) "record" includes :

- (*i*) any document, manuscript and file;
- (*ii*) any microfilm, microfiche and facsimile copy of a document;
- (*iii*) any reproduction of image or images embodied in such microfilm (whether enlarged or not); and
- (*iv*) any other material produced by a computer or by any other device;

(i) "third party" means a person other than the person making a request for information and includes a public authority.

## CHAPTER II
## FREEDOM OF INFORMATION AND OBLIGATIONS OF PUBLIC AUTHORITIES

3. Subject to the provisions of this Act, all citizens shall have freedom of information.

4. Every public authority shall :

(a) maintain all its records, in such manner and form as is consistent with its operational requirements duly catalogued and indexed;

(b) publish an such intervals as may be prescribed by the appropriate Government or competent authority,:

   (*i*) the particulars of its organisation, functions and duties;

   (*ii*) the powers and duties of its officers and employees and the procedure followed by them in the decision making process;

   (*iii*) the norms set by the public authority for the discharge of its functions;

   (*iv*) rules, regulations, instructions, manuals and other categories of records under its control used by its employees for discharging its functions;

   (*v*) the details of facilities available to citizens for obtaining information; and

   (*vi*) the name, designation and other particulars of the Public Information Officer;

(*c*) publish all relevant facts concerning important decisions and policies that affect the public while announcing such decisions and policies;

(*d*) give reasons for its decisions, whether administrative or quasi-judicial to those affected by such decisions;

(*e*) before initiating any project, publish or communicate to the public generally or to the persons affected or likely to be; affected by the project in particular, the facts available to it or to which it has reasonable access which in its opinion should be known to them in the best interests of maintenance of democratic principles.

6. A person desirous of obtaining information shall make a request in writing or through electronic means, to the concerned Public Information Officer specifying the particulars of the information sought by him:

Provided that where such request cannot be made in writing, the Public Information Officer shall render all reasonable assistance to the person making the request orally to reduce it in writing.

7. (1) On receipt of a request under Section 6, the Public Information Officer shall, as expeditiously as possible, and in any case within thirty days of the receipt of the request, either provide the information requested on payment of such fee as may be prescribed or reject the request for any of the reasons specified in Sections 8 and 9 :

Provided that where it is decided to provide the information on payment of any further fee representing the cost of providing the information, he shall send an intimation to the person making the request, giving the details of the fees determined by him, requesting him to deposit the fees and the period intervening between the despatch of the said intimation and payment of fees shall be excluded for the purpose of calculating the period of thirty days referred to above,

**8.** (1) Notwithstanding anything herein before contained, the following information not being information relating to any matter referred to in sub-section (2), shall be exempted from disclosure, namely :

(a) In formation, the disclosure of which would prejudicially affect the sovereignty and integrity of India, security of the State, strategic scientific or economic interest of India or conduct of international relations;

(b) information, the disclosure of which would prejudicially affect public safety and order, detection and investigation of an offence or which may lead to an incitement to commit an offence or prejudicially affect fair trial **or** adjudication of a pending case;

(c) information, the disclosure of which would prejudicially affect the conduct of Centre-State relations, including information exchanged in confidence between the Central and State Governments or any of their authorities or agencies;

(d) Cabinet papers including records of deliberations of the Council of Ministers, Secretaries and other officers;

(e) minutes or records of advice including legal advice, opinions or recommendations made by any officer of a public authority during the decision making process prior to the executive decision or policy formulation;

(f) trade or commercial secrets protected by law or information, the disclosure of which would prejudicially affect the legitimate economic and commercial interests or the competitive position of a public authority; or would cause unfair gain or loss to any person; and

(g) information, the disclosure of which may result in the breach of privileges of Parliament or the Legislature of a State, or contravention of a lawful order of a Court.

(2) Any information relating to any occurrence, event or matter which has taken place, occurred or happened twenty-five years before the date on which any request is made under Section 6 shall be provided to any person making a request under that section :

Provided that where any question arises as to the date from which the said period of twenty–five years has to be computed, the decision of the Central Government shall be final.

**9. Without prejudice io the provisions of Section 8, a Public Information Officer may reject a request for information also where such request :**

(a) is too general in nature or is of such a nature that, having regard to the volume of information required to be retrieved or processed would involve volume of information required to be retrieved or processed would involve disproportionate diversion of the resources of a public authority or would adversely interfere with the functioning of such authority :

Provided that where such request is rejected on the ground that the request is too general, it shall be the duly of the Public Information Officer to render help as far as possible to the person making request to reframe his request in such a manner as may facilitate compliance with it;

(b) relates to information that is required by law, rules, regulations or orders to be published at a particular time and such information is likely to be so published within thirty days of the receipt of such request; or

(c) relates to information that is contained in published material available to public;

(d) relates to information which would came unwarranted invasion of the privacy of any person.

**10.** If a request for access to information is rejected on the ground that it is in relation to information which is exempted from disclosure, then not with standing anything contained in this Act, access may be given to that part of the record which does not obtain any information that a exempted from disclosure under this Act and which can reasonably be severed from any part that contains exempted information.

**11.** Where a public authority intends to disclose information on a request made by a party which relates to, or has been supplied by a third party and has been treated as confidential by that third party, the public Information Officer s»hall by notice to such third party invite representation against the proposed disclosure, if any within fifty days from the date of receipt of such notice:

Provided that except in the case of trade or commercial secrets protected by law, disclosure may be allowed if the public interest in disclosure outweighs in importance any possible harm or injury to the interests of such third party.

## CHAPTER III

## MISCELLANEOUS

Protection of action taken in good faith.

**13.** No suit, prosecution or other legal proceeding shall lie against any person for anything which is in good faith done or intended to be done under this Act or any rule made thereunder.

14. The Provisions of Official Secrets Act, 1923 (19 of 1923), and every other Act in force shall cease to be operative to the extent it which they are inconsistent with the provisions of this Act.

15. No Court shall uncertain any suit, application or other proceeding in respect of any order made under this Act and no such order shall be called in question other wise than by way of an appeal under this Act.

16. Nothing contained in this Act:

(a) shall apply to the intelligence and security organisations, specified in the Schedule being organisations established by the Central or a State Government or any information furnished by such organisations to the respective Governments ;

(b) shall until Part B of the Schedule is amended under subsection (2), apply to (fee intelligence and security organisations by whatever name called discharging their functions as such under the State Governments.

(2) The Central Government may, by notification in the Official Gazette, amend the Schedule by including therein any other intelligence or security organisation established by the Central or a State Government or omitting therefrom any organisation already specified therein and on the publication of such notification, such organisation shall be deemed to be included in or, as the case may be, omitted from the Schedule.

**17.** (1) The Central Government may, by notification in the Official Gazette, make rules to carry out the provisions of this Act.

**18.** (1) The State Government may, by notification in the Official Gazette, make rules to carry out the provisions of this Act.

**19.** (1) The competent authority may, notification in the Official Gazette, make rule carry out the provisions of this Act.

## LAYING OF RULES

**20.** (1) Every rule made by the Central Government under this Act shall be laid, as soon as may be after it is made, before each. House of Parliament, while it is in one session or in two or more successive sessions, and if, before the expiry of the session immediately following the session or the successive session aforesaid, both Houses agree in making any modification in the rule or both Houses agree that the rule should not be made, the rule shall thereafter have effect only in such modified form or be of no effect, as the case may be; so, however, that any such modification or annulment shall be without prejudice to the validity of anything previously done under that rule.

# 16

# Right to Information Act, 2005

Right to Information Act, 2005 is an epoch making Act to provide the right to the people at the grass root level to seek information from public authorities and inspect the works, documents and records of public authorities.

No such information could be denied to the people, which cannot be denied to Parliament in case of Central Government and to State Legislature in case of concerned State Government.

On the persistent demands of the people and intellectuals, the Government of India passed the Right to Information Act, 2005 and this came into effect after the President of India accorded his assent on June 15, 2005. However the process of obtaining the application began from October 12, 2005 after notified.

Under the provisions of the Act, all citizens shall have the right to information. "Right to Information" means the right to information accessible under this Act which is held by or under the control of any public authority and includes rights to

(*i*) Inspection of work, documents, records;

(*ii*) Taking notes, extract or certified copies of documents or records;

(*iii*) Taking certified samples of material

(*iv*) Obtaining information in the form of diskettes, floppies, tapes, videocassettes or any other electronic mode or through print only where such information is stored in a computer or any other device.

Some of the distinguishing features of this Act are constitution of independent agencies both at the Central and State levels to adjudicate in the matter of non–supply of information to the public. These will be Central Information Commission and State information Commission at the Central and State levels respectively.

No court shall entertain any suit, application or other proceeding in respect of any order made under this Act and no such order shall be called in question otherwise than by an appeal under this Act.

The provisions of this Act shall have effect notwithstanding inconsistent therewith contained in the Official Secrets Act, 1923 and any other law for the time being in force or in any instrument having effect by virtue of any law other than this Act.

The Act also defines various terminology to be used while implementing the various provisions of the Act.

**Information:** Information means any material in any form, including records, documents, memos, advices, press–releases, circulars, orders, contracts, reports, data materials held in any electronic form and information relating to any private body which can be accessed by a public authority under any other law for the time being in force.

**Public Authority:** Public authority means any authority or body or institution of self–government established or constituted; by or under the Constitution, any other law made by Parliament or made by State Legislature or by notification issued by the appropriate Government.

It also includes body or non–Government organization substantially financed directly or indirectly by funds provided by the appropriate Government.

**Records:** Record includes, any document, manuscript an file; any microfilm and facsimile copy of a document, or any other material produced by a computer or any other device.

**Central Information Commission:** A body constituted by the Central Government, through a notification constituting of the Chief Information Commissioners and such number of Information Commissioners, not exceeding ten.

**State Information Commission:** A body constituted by the concerned State Government, under sub-section(3) of the section 15 of the Act and consisting of the State Chief Information Commissioner and such numbers of State Information Commissioners, not exteeding ten, as may be deemed necessary.

**Third Party:** Third party means a person other than the citizen making a request for information and includes a public authority.

## RIGHT TO INFORMATION

Subject to the provisions of this Act, all citizens shall have the right to information. Right to Information means the right to information accessible under this Act which is held by or under the control of any public authority.

For this every public authority shall maintain all its records duly catalogued and indexed in a manner and form, which facilitates the right to information under the Act and access to such records is facilitated.

Every public authority shall disseminate every information in such a form and manner, which is easily accessible to the public with minimum resort to obtain information for use under the Act.

Every public Authority shall put within one hundred days of the enactment of this Act, as many officers as the Central Public Information Officers or State Public Information Officers, in all administrative units or offices under it to provide information to persons requesting for the information under the Act.

As also, every public authority shall designate within the stipulated time at each Sub–divisional level as a Central Assistant Public Information Officer or a State Assistant Public Information Officer to receive the application for information or appeals under the Act.

## PROCEDURE FOR OBTAINING INFORMATION

A person, who desires to obtain any information under this Act, shall make a request in writing or through electronic means in English or Hindi or in the official language of the area in which the application is being made, along with such fee as may be prescribed to the concerned Information Officer, specifying the particulars of the information sought by him or her.

## DISPOSAL OF THE REQUEST

On receipt of the request the concerned Information Officer, shall as expeditiously as possible, and in any case within thirty days of the receipt of the request either provide the information on payment of prescribed fee or reject the request for any of the reason specified under this Act.

Where the information sought for concerns the life or liberty of a person, the same shall be provided within forty–eight hours of the receipt of the request.

If the Central Public Information Officer or the State Public Information Officer fails to give a decision on the request for information within the stipulated period, he or she shall be deemed to have refused the request;

Where a request has been rejected, the concerned Public Information Officer shall communicate to the person making the request;

(*a*) The reasons for such rejection;

(*b*) The period within which an appeal against such rejection may be preferred; and

(*c*) The particulars of the appellate authority.

## EXEMPTION FROM DISCLOSURE OF INFORMATION

However, no information could be given to any citizens;

(a) disclosure of which would affect the sovereignty and integrity of India, security of the State, relations with foreign State or lead to incitement of an offence.

Provided that the information which cannot be denied to the Parliament Or a State Legislature shall not be denied to any citizen.

Any information relating to any occurrence, event or matter which has taken place, occurred or happened twenty years before the date on which any request is made, shall be provided to any person making a request.

**Third Party Information:** Where the concerned Public Information Officer intends to disclose any information or record on a request made under this Act, which relates to or has been supplied by a third party confidentially, the concerned Public Information Officer within five days on the receipt of request, give a written notice to such a third party and invite the third party to make a submission about his intention and the same shall be kept in view while taking a decision about disclosure of information.

## CENTRAL INFORMATION COMMISSION

The Central Information Commission shall consist of the Chief Information Commissioner and such number of Central Information Commissioners, as may be deemed necessary, subject to a maximum numbers of ten. The Chief Information Commissioner and Information Commissioners shall be appointed by the President of India on the recommendations of a committee consisting of the Prime Minister, as the Chairperson, the Leader of the Opposition in the Lok Sabha and a Union Cabinet Minister, to be nominated by the Prime Minister.

The general superintendence, direction and management of the affairs of the Central Information Commission shall vest in the Chief Information Commissioner who shall be assisted by the Information Commissioners and may exercise all such powers and do all such acts and things which may be exercised or done by the Central Information Commission autonomously without being subjected to directions by any other authority under this Act.

The Chief Information Commissioner and every Information Commissioner shall hold office for a term of five years or up to attaining the age of sixty–five, whichever is earlier.

## STATE INFORMATION COMMISSION

The State Information Commission shall consist of the State Chief Information Commissioner and such number of State Information Commissioners, as may be deemed necessary subject to a limit of ten members. The State Chief Information Commissioner and Information Commissioners shall be appointed by the Government on the recommendations of a committee consisting of, the Chief Minister, as chairperson, the Leader of the Opposition in the Legislative Assembly and a State Cabinet Minister nominated by the Chief minister.

The terms and conditions of service of the State Chief Information Commissioner and State Information Commissioners are the same at the State level and of the same as incase of Chief Information Commissioner and Central Information Commissioners at the central level.

## POWERS AN FUNCTIONS OF INFORMATION COMMISSIONS

The Central Information Commission or State Information Commission shall receive and inquire into a complaint from any person who has been unable to submit a request to the concerned Public Information Officer by any reason or the concerned Assistant Public Information Officer has refused to accept his or her application for information or appeal under this Act.

The concerned Information Commission if so satisfied, that there are reasonable grounds to inquire into the matter; it may initiate an inquiry in respect thereof. The Central Information Commission or State Information Commission have the same power as and vested in a Civil Procedure, 1908. The concerned Commission may summon and enforce the attendance of persons and compel them to give oral or written evidence on oath; to produce the document or things, may require the discovery and inspection of documents; may receive evidence on affidavit; may require any public record or copies thereof from any court or office; may issue summons for examination of witness or documents and any other matter as may be prescribed. During the inquiry of any complaint no record required for inquiry may be withheld from it on any grounds.

## APPEAL

Any person aggrieved by the decision of the concerned Public Information Officer, may within thirty days from the day of the receipt of such a decision, prefer an appeal to such Officer who is senior to the concerned Public Information Officer in each public authority.

A second appeal against the decision of the Sr. Officer as mentioned above shall lie within ninety days from the day on which the decision should have been made or was actually received with the concerned Information Commission. The concerned Information Commission may admit the appeal after the expiry of the period of ninety days if it is satisfied that the appellant was prevented by sufficient cause from filing the appeal in time.

If any appeal proceedings, the ones to prove that a denial of a request was justified, shall be on the concerned Public Information Officer who denied the request.

Both the first and second appeal shall be disposed within thirty days of the receipt of the appeal or within such extended period not exceeding forty five days from the date of filing thereof, for reasons to be recorded in writing.

The decision of the Central Information Commission or State Information Commission shall be binding on the concerned public authority.

## PENALTIES

The Central Information Commission or State Information Commission in its decision shall impose a penalty of two hundred and fifty rupees for each day till application is received or information is furnished. However, the total amount of such penalty shall not exceed twenty five thousand rupees. If the concerned Information Commission, at the time of deciding any complaint or appeal is of the opinion that the concerned Public Information Officer has without any reasonable cause and persistently failed to receive an application for information or has not furnished the information within the specified time, or malafidely denied the request for information or obstructed in any manner in furnishing the information, it may recommend for disciplinary action against the concerned Public Information Officer under the service rules applicable to him or her.

Some other Features of the Act:

(*i*) **Protection of action taken in good faith:** No suit, prosecution or other legal proceedings shall lie against any person for anything which is done in good faith or intended to be done under this Act or any rule made there under.

(*ii*) **Act to have over riding effect:** The provisions of this Act shall have effect on the provisions contained in the Official Secrets Act, 1923

(*iii*) **Bar of Jurisdiction of Courts:** No Courts shall entertain any suit, application or other proceeding in respect of any order made under this Act and no such order shall be called in question or otherwise than by way of an appeal under this Act.

(*iv*) **Non–application of Act:** The provisions of the Act shall not apply to the intelligence and security organization specified in second schedule.

However, the information pertaining to the allegations of corruption and human rights violations shall not be excluded under the Act.

Similarly, nothing contained in this Act shall apply to intelligence and security organizations established by the State Government. However, information pertaining to the allegations of corruption and human rights violations shall not be excluded under this Act.

The Central Government or State Government may, by notification in their respective Official gazette amend the schedule by including therein or deleting there from therein any intelligence or security organizations established by that Government. Every notification issued under the relevant sub-clause of the act shall be laid before the Parliament or concerned State Legislature.

## REPORTING

The Central Information Commission or State Information Commission after the end of each year shall prepare a report on the implementation of the provisions of this Act during that year and forward a copy thereof to the appropriate Government to be laid before each House of the Parliament or before each Hose of the State Legislature.

Each Ministry or Department shall, collect the information concerning public authorities within their jurisdiction and provide such information to the Central Information Commission or State Information Commission, mentioning the year to, which the report relates.

The concerned Information Commission, if so thought, may also, give to the public authority a recommendation specifying the steps, which in its opinion are to be taken for promoting the conformity to the provisions of this Act.

## POWER TO MAKE RULES

The appropriate Government may, by notification in their Official Gazette make rules to carry out the provisions of this Act, particularly relating to the cost of the medium or print cost price of the materials, fee payable, the procedure to be adopted by the Central Information Commission in deciding the appeal under relevant section of this Act.

## LAYING OF RULES BEFORE LEGISLATURE

Every rule made by the Central Government under this Act shall be laid before each House of the Parliament and by the State Government before each House of State Legislature as soon as possible.

If both the Houses agree in making any modification, in the rule shall thereafter have effect only in such modified form. If both the Houses agree that the rule should not be made, it shall be of no effect.

Every order made therein, shall be laid before each House of Parliament or State Legislature.

**Repeal :** The Freedom of Information Act, 2002 is now repealed.

**Implementation of the Act:** From the scenario of the implementation it seems that during the last two years after it was enacted, it is passing through a crucial phase. On the one hand the Central Information Commission has started penalizing Sarkari Babus for their lack lustre approach in giving information to the people, Govt.. Babus are trying to put spanners in the way of its full implementation. The Central Information Commission has penalized a Delhi government official with fine for making undue delay in making available information requested by an applicant. Chief Information Commissioner, Wajat Hbibullah, in one of his decisions, penalized a former Deputy Director (Education) Dharamveer Singh with a fine of Rs. 3500 in a case for delay in giving information to the applicant Manju and others.

On the other hand, even after four years from October 2005, when this Act was enacted public authority is not giving information about noting on files. Actually, the Personnel and Training Department of the Government of India, has put on its website "File notings are exempted from this Act". The Information Officers are confused in its implementation.

In July 2006, the Central Cabinet decided to make the amendment in the Act to this effect that file noting only relating to social and developmental projects could be provided on the request of public. The amendment was to be passed in the Monsoon session of the Parliament. But on the protests being made by public, intellectuals and some NGO's it was dropped.

The Chief Information Commissioner, is instructing to remove the information from the website. In a letter sent to the Secretary, Deptt. Of Personnel and Training, the Chief Information Commissioner has asked to ensure the presences of an authorized representative and Addl. Solicitor General during the next hearing, so that it can decide this issue in the next hearing.

## RIGHT TO INFORMATION ACT (2005)

**Short title, extent and commencement.**

1. (1) This Act may be called the Right to Information Act, 2005.

(2) It extends to the whole of India except the State of Jammu and Kashmir.

(3) The provisions of sub-section (1) of section 4, sub-sections (1) and (2) of section 5, sections 12, 13, 15,16,24, 27 and 28 shall come into force at once, and the remaining provisions of this Act shall come into force on the one hundred and twentieth day of its enactment.

*Definitions*

**2. In this Act, unless the context otherwise requires :**

(a) "appropriate Government" means in relation to a public authority which is established, constituted, owned, controlled or substantially financed by funds provided directly or indirectly :

(*i*) by the Central Government or the Union territory administration, the Central Government;

(*ii*) by the State Government, the State Government;

(b) "Central Information Commission" means the Central Information Commission constituted under sub-section (1) of section 12;

(c) "Central Public Information Officer" means the Central Public Information Officer designated under sub-section (1) and includes a Central Assistant Public Information Officer designated as such under sub-section (2) of section 5;

(d) "Chief Information Commissioner" and "Information Commissioner" mean the Chief Information Commissioner and Information Commissioner appointed under sub-section (3) of section 12;

(e) "competent authority" means :

(*i*) the Speaker in the case of the House of the People or the Legislative. Assembly of a State or a Union territory having such Assembly and the Chairman in the case of the Council of States or Legislative Council of a State;

(*ii*) the Chief Justice of India in the case of the Supreme Court;

(*iii*) the Chief Justice of the High Court in the case of a High Court;

(*iv*) the President or the Governor, as the case may be, in the case of other authorities established or constituted by or under the Constitution;

(*v*) the administrator appointed under article 239 of the Constitution;

(f) "information" means any material in any form, including records, documents, memos, e-mails, opinions, advices, press releases, circulars, orders, logbooks, contracts, reports, papers, samples, models, data material held in any electronic form and information relating to any private body which can be accessed by a public authority under any other law for the time being in force;

(g) "prescribed" means prescribed by rules made under this Act by the appropriate Government or the competent authority, as the case may be;

(h) "public authority" means any authority or body or institution of self-government established or constituted :

(*a*) by or under the Constitution;

(*b*) by any other law made by Parliament;

(*c*) by any other law made by State Legislature;

(*d*) by notification issued or order made by the appropriate Government, and includes any :

(i) body owned, controlled or substantially financed;

(ii) non-Government organisation substantially financed, directly or indirectly by funds provided by the appropriate Government;

(i) "record" includes :

(*a*) any document, manuscript and file;

(*b*) any microfilm, microfiche and facsimile copy of a document;

(*c*) any reproduction of image or images embodied in such microfilm (whether enlarged or not); and

(*d*) any other material produced by a computer or any other device;

(j) "right to information" means the right to information accessible under this Act which is held by or under the control of any public authority and includes the right to :

(i) inspection of work, documents, records;

(*ii*) taking notes, extracts or certified copies of documents or records;

(*iii*) taking certified samples of material;

(*iv*) obtaining information in the form of diskettes, floppies, tapes, video cassettes or in any other electronic mode or through printouts where such information is stored in a computer or in any other device;

(k) "State Information Commission" means the State Information Commission constituted under sub–section (1) of section 15;

(l) "State Chief Information Commissioner" and "State Information Commissioner mean the State Chief Information Commissioner and the State Information Commissioner appointed under sub-section (3) of section 15;

(m) "State Public Information Officer" means the State Public Information Officer designated under sub-section (1) and includes a State Assistant Public Information Officer designated as such under sub-section (2) of section 5;

(n) "third party" means a person other than the citizen making a request for information and includes a public authority.

## CHAPTER II

### Right to information and obligations of public authorities

**3. Subject to the provisions of this Act, all citizens shall have the right to information.**

**Right to Information**

4. (1) Every public authority shall :

(a) maintain all its records duly catalogued and indexed in a manner and the form which facilitates the right to information under this Act and ensure that all records that are appropriate to be computerised are, within a reasonable time and subject to availability of resources, computerised and connected through a network all over the country on different systems so that access to such records is facilitated

(b) publish within one hundred and twenty days from the enactment of this Act:

- (*i*) the particulars of its organisation, functions and duties;
- (*ii*) the powers and duties of its officers and employees;
- (*iii*) the procedure followed in the decision making process, including channels of supervision and accountability;
- (*iv*) the norms set by it for the discharge of its functions;
- (*v*) the rules, regulations, instructions, manuals and records, held by it or under its control or used by its employees for discharging its functions;
- (*vi*) a statement of the categories of documents that are held by it or under its control;
- (*vii*) the particulars of any arrangement that exists for consultation with, or representation by, the members of the public in relation to the formulation of its policy or implementation thereof;
- (*viii*) a statement of the boards, councils, committees and other bodies consisting of two or more persons constituted as its part or for the purpose of its advice, and as to whether meetings of those boards, councils, committees and other bodies are open to the public, or the minutes of such meetings are accessible for public;
- (*ix*) a directory of its officers and" employees;
- (*x*) the monthly remuneration received by each of its officers and employees, including the system of compensation as provided in its regulations;

(*xi*) the budget allocated to each of its agency, indicating the particulars of all plans, proposed expenditures and reports on disbursements made;

(*xii*) the manner of execution of subsidy programmes, including the amounts allocated and the details of beneficiaries of such programmes;

(*xiii*) particulars of recipients of concessions, permits or authorisations granted by it;

(*xiv*) details in respect of the information, available to or held by it, reduced in an electronic form;

(*xv*) the particulars of facilities available to citizens for obtaining information, including the working hours of a library or reading room, if maintained for public use;

(*xvi*) the names, designations and other particulars of the Public Information Officers;

(*xvii*) such other information as may be prescribed; and thereafter update these publications every year;

(c) publish all relevant facts while formulating important policies or announcing the decisions which affect public;

(d) provide reasons for its administrative or quasi-judicial decisions to affected persons.

(2) It shall be a constant endeavour of every public authority to take steps in accordance with the requirements of clause (b) of sub-section (1) to provide as much information suo motu to the public at regular intervals through various means of communications, including internet, so that the public have minimum resort to the use of this Act to obtain information.

(3) For the purposes of sub-section (1), every information shall be disseminated widely and in such form and manner which is easily accessible to the public.

(4) All materials shall be disseminated taking into consideration the cost effectiveness, local language and the most effective method of communication in that local area and the information should be easily accessible, to the extent possible in electronic format with the Central Public Information Officer or State Public Information Officer, as the case may be, available free or at such cost of the medium or the print cost price as may be prescribed.

**Explanation:** For the purposes of sub-sections (3) and (4), "disseminated" means making known or communicated the information to the public through notice boards, newspapers, public announcements, media broadcasts, the internet or any other means, including inspection of offices of any public authority.

**5.** (1) Every public authority shall, within one hundred days of the enactment of this Act, designate as many officers as the Central Public Information Officers or State Public Information Officers, as the case may be, in all administrative units or offices under it as may be necessary to provide information to persons requesting for the information under this Act.

(2) Without prejudice to the provisions of sub-section (1), every public authority shall designate an officer, within one hundred days of the enactment of this Act, at each sub-divisional level or other sub-district level as a Central Assistant Public Information Officer or a State Assistant Public Information Officer, as the case may be, to receive the applications for information or appeals under this Act for forwarding the same forthwith to the Central Public Information Officer or the State Public Information Officer or senior officer specified under sub-section (1) of section 19 or the Central Information Commission or the State Information Commission, as the case may be:

Provided that where an application for information or appeal is given to a Central Assistant Public Information Officer or a State Assistant Public Information Officer, as the case may be, a period of five days shall be added in computing the period for response specified under sub-section (1) of section 7.

(3) Every Central Public Information Officer or State Public Information Officer, as the case may be, shall deal with requests from persons seeking information and render reasonable assistance to the persons seeking such information.

(4) The Central Public Information Officer or State Public Information Officer, as the case may be, may seek the assistance of any other officer as he or she considers it necessary for the proper discharge of his or her duties.

(5) Any officer, whose assistance has been sought under sub-section (4), shall render all assistance to the Central Public Information Officer or State Public Information Officer, as the case may be, seeking his or her assistance and for the purposes of any contravention of the provisions of this Act, such other officer shall be treated as a Central Public Information Officer or State Public Information Officer, as the case may be

**Designation of Public Information Officers**

**6.** (1) A person, who desires to obtain any information under this Act, shall make a request in writing or through electronic means in English or Hindi or in the official language of the area in which the application is being made, accompanying such fee as : may be prescribed, to :

(a) the Central Public Information Officer or State Public Information Officer, as the case may be, of the concerned public authority;

(*b*) the Central Assistant Public Information Officer or State Assistant Public Information Officer, as the case may be, specifying the particulars of the information sought by him or her:

Provided that where such request cannot be made in writing, the Central Public Information Officer or State Public Information Officer, as the case may be, shall render all reasonable assistance to the person making the request orally to reduce the same in writing.

(2) An applicant making request for information shall not be required to give any reason for requesting the information or any other personal details except those that may be necessary for contacting him.

(3) Where an application is made to a public authority requesting for an information:

(*i*) which is held by another public authority; or

(*ii*) the subject matter of which is more closely connected with the functions of another public authority,

the public authority, to which such application is made, shall transfer the application or such part of it as may be appropriate to that other public authority and inform the applicant immediately about such transfer:

Provided that the transfer of an application pursuant to this sub-section shall be made as soon as practicable but in no case later than five days from the date of receipt of the application.

**Disposal of Request**

7. (1) Subject to the proviso to sub-section (2) of section 5 or the proviso to sub-section (3) of section 6, the Central Public Information Officer or State Public Information Officer, as the case may be, on receipt of a request under-section 6 shall, as expeditiously as possible, and in any case within thirty days of the receipt of the request, either provide the information on payment of such fee as may be prescribed or reject the request for any of the reasons specified in sections 8 and 9:

Provided that where the information sought for concerns the life or liberty of a person, the same shall be provided within forty-eight hours of the receipt of the request.

(2) If the Central Public Information Officer or State Public Information Officer, as the case may be, fails to give decision on the request for information within the period specified under sub-section (1), the Central Public Information Officer or State Public Information Officer, as the case may be, shall be deemed to have refused the request.

(3) Where a decision is taken to provide the information on payment of any further fee representing the cost of providing the information, the Central Public Information Officer or State Public Information Officer, as the case may be, shall send an intimation to the person making the request, giving :

(a) the details of further fees representing the cost of providing the information as determined by him, together with the calculations made to arrive at the amount in accordance with fee prescribed under subsection (1), requesting him to deposit that fees, and the period intervening between the despatch of the said intimation and payment of fees shall be excluded for the purpose of calculating the period of thirty days referred to in that sub-section;

(b) information concerning his or her right with respect to review the decision as to the amount of fees charged or the form of access provided, including the particulars of the appellate authority, time limit, process and any other forms.

(4) Where access to the record or a part thereof is required to be provided under this Act and the person to whom access is to be provided is sensorily disabled, the Central Public Information Officer or State Public Information Officer, as the case may be, shall provide assistance to enable access to the information, including providing such assistance as may(be appropriate for the inspection.

(5) Where access to information is to be provided in the printed or in any electronic format, the applicant shall, subject to the provisions of sub-section (6), pay such fee as may be prescribed:

Provided that the fee prescribed under sub-section (1) of section 6 and sub-sections (1) and (5) of section 7 shall be reasonable and no such fee shall be charged from the persons who are of below poverty line as may be determined by the appropriate Government.

(6) Notwithstanding anything contained in sub-section (5), the person making request for the information shall be provided the information free of charge where a public authority fails to comply with the time limits specified in sub-section (1).

(7) Before taking any decision under sub-section (1), the Central Public Information Officer or State Public Information Officer, as the case may be, shall take into consideration the representation made by a third party under section 11.

(8) Where a request has been rejected under sub-section (1), the Central Public Information Officer or State Public Information Officer, as the case may be, shall communicate to the person making the request :

(*i*) the reasons for such rejection;

(*ii*) the period within which an appeal against such rejection may be preferred; and

(*iii*) the particulars of the appellate authority.

(9) An information shall ordinarily be provided in the form in which it is sought unless it would disproportionately divert the resources of the public authority or would be detrimental to the safety or preservation of the record in question.

**8.** (1) Notwithstanding anything contained in this Act, there shall be no obligation to give any citizen:

(a) information, disclosure of which would prejudicially affect the sovereignty and integrity of India, the security, strategic, scientific or economic interests of the State, relation with foreign State, or lead to incitement of an offence;

(b) information which has been expressly forbidden to be published by any court, of law or tribunal or the disclosure of which may constitute contempt of court;

**Exemption from disclosure of information**

(c) information, the disclosure of which would cause a breach of privilege of Parliament or the State Legislature;

(d) information including commercial confidence, trade secrets or intellectual property, the disclosure of which would harm the competitive position of a third party, unless the competent authority is satisfied that larger public interest warrants the disclosure of such information;

(e) information available to a person in his fiduciary relationship, unless the competent authority is satisfied that the larger public interest warrants the disclosure of such information;

(f) information received in confidence from foreign Government;

(g) information, the disclosure of which would endanger the life or physical safety of any person or identify the source of information or assistance given in confidence for law enforcement or security purposes;

(h) information which would impede the process of investigation or apprehension or prosecution of offenders;

(i) cabinet papers including records of deliberations of the Council of Ministers, Secretaries and other officers:

Provided that the decisions of Council of Ministers, the reasons thereof, and the material on the basis of which the decisions were taken shall be made public after the decision has been taken, and the matter is complete, or over:

Provided further that those matters which come under the exemptions specified, in this section shall not be disclosed;

(j) information which relates to personal information the disclosure of which has no relationship to any public activity or interest, or which would cause unwarranted invasion of the privacy of the individual unless the Central Public Information Officer or the State Public Information Officer or the appellate authority, as the case may be, is satisfied that the larger public interest justifies the disclosure of such information:

Provided that the information which cannot be denied to the Parliament or a State Legislature shall not be denied to any person.

**19 of 1923**

(2) Notwithstanding anything in the Official Secrets Act, 1923 nor any of the exemptions permissible in accordance with sub-section (1), a public authority may allow access to information, if public interest in disclosure outweighs the harm to the protected interests.

(3) Subject to the provisions of clauses (a), (c) and (i) of sub-section (1), any information relating to any occurrence, event or matter which has taken place, occurred or happened twenty years before the date on which any request is made under section 6 shall be provided to any person making a request under that section:

Provided that where any question arises as to the date from which the said period of twenty years has to be computed, the decision of the Central Government shall be final, subject to the usual appeals provided for in this Act.

**Grounds for rejection to access in certain cases.**

**9. Without prejudice to the provisions of section 8, a Central Public Information Officer or a State Public Information Officer, as the case may be, may reject a request for information where such a request for providing access would involve an infringement of copyright subsisting in a person other than the State.**

**Severability**

**10.** (1) Where a request for access to information is rejected on the ground that it is in relation to information which is exempt from disclosure, then, notwithstanding anything contained in this Act, access may be provided to that part of the record which does not contain any information which is exempt from disclosure under this Act and which can reasonably be served from any part that contains exempt information.

(2) Where access is granted to a part of the record under sub-section (1), the Central Public Information Officer or State Public Information Officer, as the case may be, shall give a notice to the applicant, informing :

(a) that only part of the record requested, after severance of the record containing information which is exempt from disclosure, is being provided;

(b) the reasons for the decision, including any findings on any material question of fact, referring to the material on which those findings were based;

(c) the name and designation of the person giving the decision;

(d) the details of the fees calculated by him or her and the amount of fee which the applicant is required to deposit; and

(e) his or her rights with respect to review of the decision regarding non-disclosure of part of the information, the amount of fee charged or the form of access provided, including the particulars of the senior officer specified under sub-section (1) of section 19 or the Central Information Commission or the State Information Commission, as the case may be, time limit, process and any other form of access.

**Third Party Information**

**11.** (1) Where a Central Public Information Officer or a State Public Information Officer, as the case may be, intends to disclose any information or record, or part thereof on a request made under this Act, which relates to or has been supplied by a third party and has been treated as confidential by that third party, the Central Public Information Officer or State Public Information Officer, as the case may be, shall, within five days from the receipt of the request, give a written notice to such third party of the request and of the fact that the Central Public Information Officer or State Public Information Officer, as the case may be, intends to disclose the information or record, or part thereof, and invite the third party to make a submission in writing or orally, regarding whether the information should be disclosed, and such submission of the third party shall be kept in view while taking a decision about disclosure of information:

Provided that except in the case of trade or commercial secrets protected by law, disclosure may be allowed if the public interest in disclosure outweighs in importance any possible harm or injury to the interests of such third party.

(2) Where a notice is served by the Central Public Information Officer or State Public Information Officer, as the case may be, under sub-section (1) to a third party in respect of any information or record or part thereof, the third party

shall, within ten days from the date of receipt of such notice, be given the opportunity to make representation against the proposed disclosure.

(3) Notwithstanding anything contained in section 7, the Central Public Information Officer or State Public Information Officer, as the case may be, shall, within forty days after receipt of the request under section 6, if the third party has been given an opportunity to make representation under sub-section (2), make a decision as to whether or not to disclose the information or record or part thereof and give in writing the notice of his decision to the third party.

(4) A notice given under sub-section (3) shall include a statement that the third party to whom the notice is given is entitled to prefer an appeal under section 19 against the decision.

## CHAPTER III

## The Central Information Commission

### Constitution of Central Information Commission

**12.** (1) The Central Government shall, by notification in the Official Gazette, constitute a body to be known as the Central Information Commission to exercise the powers conferred on, and to perform the functions assigned to, it under this Act.

(2) The Central Information Commission shall consist of:

(a) the Chief Information Commissioner; and

(b) such number of Central Information Commissioners, not exceeding ten, as may be deemed necessary.

(3) The Chief Information Commissioner and Information Commissioners shall be appointed by the President on the recommendation of a committee consisting of:

(*i*) the Prime Minister, who shall be the Chairperson of the committee;

(*ii*) the Leader of Opposition in the Lok Sabha; and

(*iii*) a Union Cabinet Minister to be nominated by the Prime Minister.

**Explanation:** For the purposes of removal of doubts, it is hereby declared that where the Leader of Opposition in the House of the People has not been recognised as such, the Leader of the single largest group in opposition of the Government in the House of the People shall be deemed to be the Leader of Opposition.

(4) The general superintendence, direction and management of the affairs of the Central Information Commission shall vest in the Chief Information

Commissioner who shall be assisted by the Information Commissioners and may exercise all such powers and do all such acts and things which may be exercised or done by the Central Information Commission autonomously without being subjected to directions by any other authority under this Act.

(5) The Chief Information Commissioner and Information Commissioners shall be persons of eminence in public life with wide knowledge and experience in law, science and technology, social service, management, journalism, mass media or administration and governance.

(6) The Chief Information Commissioner or an Information Commissioner shall not be a Member of Parliament or Member of the Legislature of any State or Union territory, as the case may be, or hold any other office of profit or connected with any political party or carrying on any business or pursuing any profession.

(7) The headquarters of the Central Information Commission shall be at Delhi and the Central Information Commission may, with the previous approval of the Central Government, establish offices at other places in India.

**Term of office and conditions of service**

**13.** (1) The Chief Information Commissioner shall hold office for a term of five years from the date on which he enters upon his office and shall not be eligible for reappointment:

Provided that no Chief Information Commissioner shall hold office as such after he has attained the age of sixty-five years.

(2) Every Information Commissioner shall hold office for a term of five years from the date on which he enters upon his office or till he attains the age of sixty-five years, whichever is earlier, and shall not be eligible for reappointment as such Information Commissioner:

Provided that every Information Commissioner shall, on vacating his office under this sub-section be eligible for appointment as the Chief Information Commissioner in the manner specified in sub-section (3) of section 12:

Provided further that where the Information Commissioner is appointed as the Chief Information Commissioner, his term of office shall not be more than five years in aggregate as the Information Commissioner and the Chief Information Commissioner.

(3) The Chief Information Commissioner or an Information Commissioner shall before he enters upon his office make and subscribe before the President or some other person appointed by him in that behalf, an oath or affirmation according to the form set out for the purpose in the First Schedule.

(4) The Chief Information Commissioner or an Information Commissioner may, at any time, by writing under his hand addressed to the President, resign from his office:

Provided that the Chief Information Commissioner or an Information Commissioner may be removed in the manner specified under section 14.

(5) The salaries and allowances payable to and other terms and conditions of service of:

(a) the Chief Information Commfssioner shall be the same as that of the Chief Election Commissioner;

(b) an Information Commissioner shall be the same as that of an Election Commissioner:

Provided that if the Chief Information Commissioner or an Information Commissioner, at the time of his appointment is, in receipt of a pension, other than a disability or wound pension, in respect of any previous service under the Government of India or under the Government of a State, his salary in respect of the service as the Chief Information Commissioner or an Information Commissioner shall be reduced by the amount of that pension including any portion of pension which was commuted and pension equivalent of other forms of retirement benefits excluding pension equivalent of retirement gratuity.

Provided further that if the Chief Information Commissioner or an Information Commissioner if, at the time of his appointment is, in receipt of retirement benefits in respect of any previous service rendered in a Corporation established by or under any Central Act or State Act or a Government company owned or controlled by the Central Government or the State Government, his salary in respect of the service as the Chief Information Commissioner or an Information Commissioner shall be reduced by the amount of pension equivalent to the retirement benefits:

Provided also that the salaries, allowances and other conditions of service of the Chief Information Commissioner and the Information Commissioners shall not be varied to their disadvantage after their appointment.

(6) The Central Government shall provide the Chief Information Commissioner and the Information Commissioners with such officers and employees as may be necessary for the efficient performance of their functions under this Act, and the salaries and allowances payable to and the terms and conditions of service of the officers and other employees appointed for the purpose of this Act shall be such as may be prescribed.

**Removal of Chief Information Commissioner or Information Commissioner**

**14.** (1) Subject to the provisions of sub-section (3), the Chief Information Commissioner or any Information Commissioner shall be removed from his office only by order of the President on the ground of proved misbehaviour or incapacity after the Supreme Court, on a reference made to it by the President, has, on inquiry, reported that the Chief Information Commissioner or any Information Commissioner, as the case may be, ought on such ground be removed.

(2) The President may suspend from office, and if deem necessary prohibit also from attending the office during inquiry, the Chief Information Commissioner or Information Commissioner in respect of whom a reference has been made to the Supreme Court under sub-section (1) until the President has passed orders on receipt of the report of the Supreme Court on such reference.

(3) Notwithstanding anything contained in sub-section (1), the President may by order remove from office the Chief Information Commissioner or any Information Commissioner if the Chief Information Commissioner or a Information Commissioner, as the case may be :

(a) is adjudged an insolvent; or

(b) has been convicted of an offence which, in the opinion of the President, involves moral turpitude; or

(c) engages during his term of office in any paid employment outside the duties of his office; or

(d) is, in the opinion of the President, unfit to continue in office by reason of infirmity of mind or body; or

(e) has acquired such financial or other interest as is likely to affect prejudicially his functions as the Chief Information Commissioner or a Information Commissioner.

(4) If the Chief Information Commissioner or a Information Commissioner in any way, concerned or interested in any contract or agreement made by or on behalf of the Government of India or participates in any way in the profit thereof or in any benefit or emolument arising therefrom otherwise than as a member and in common with the other members of an incorporated company, he shall, for the purposes of sub-section (1), be deemed to be guilty of misbehaviour.

## CHAPTER IV

## The State Information Commission

**Constitution of State Information Commission**

**15.** (1) Every State Government shall, by notification in the Official Gazette, constitute a body to be known as the ... (name of the State) Information

Commission to exercise the powers conferred on, and to perform the functions assigned to, it under this Act.

(2) The State Information Commission shall consist of:

(a) the State Chief Information Commissioner, and

(b) such number of State Information Commissioners, not exceeding ten, as may be deemed necessary.

(3) The State Chief Information Commissioner and the State Information Commissioners shall be appointed by the Governor on the recommendation of a committee consisting of:

(*i*) the Chief Minister, who shall be the Chairperson of the committee;

(*ii*) the Leader of Opposition in the Legislative Assembly; and (iii) a Cabinet Minister to be nominated by the Chief Minister

**Explanation:** For the purposes of removal of doubts, it is hereby declared that where the Leader of Opposition in the Legislative Assembly has not been recognised as such, the

Leader of the single largest group in opposition of the Government in the Legislative Assembly shall be deemed to be the Leader of Opposition.

(4) The general superintendence, direction and management of the affairs of the State Information Commission shall vest in the State Chief Information Commissioner who shall be assisted by the State Information Commissioners and may exercise all such powers and do all such acts and things which may be exercised or done by the State Information Commission autonomously without being subjected to directions by any other authority under this Act.

(5) The State Chief Information Commissioner and the State Information Commissioners shall be persons of eminence in public life with wide knowledge and experience in law, science and technology, social service, management, journalism, mass media or administration and governance.

(6) The State Chief Information Commissioner or a State Information Commissioner shall not be a Member of Parliament or Member of the Legislature of any State or Union territory, as the case may be, or hold any other office of profit or connected with any political party or carrying on any business or pursuing any profession.

(7) The headquarters of the State Information Commission shall be at such place in the State as the State Government may, by notification in the Official Gazette, specify and the State Information Commission may, with the previous approval of the State Government, establish offices at other places in the State.

**Term of office and conditions of service**

**16.** (1) The State Chief Information Commissioner shall hold office for a term of five years from the date on which he enters upon his office and shall not be eligible for reappointment.

Provided that no State Chief Information Commissioner shall hold office as such after he has attained the age of sixty-five years.

(2) Every State Information Commissioner shall hold office for a term of five years from the date on which he enters upon his office or till he attains the age of sixty-five years, whichever is earlier, and shall not be eligible for reappointment as such State Information Commissioner:

Provided that every State Information Commissioner shall, on vacating his office under this sub-section, be eligible for appointment as the State Chief Information Commissioner in the manner specified in sub-section (3) of section 15:

Provided further that where the State Information Commissioner is appointed as the State Chief Information Commissioner, his term of office shall not be more than five years in aggregate as the State Information Commissioner and the State Chief Information Commissioner.

(3) The State Chief Information Commissioner or a State Information Commissioner, shall before he enters upon his office make and subscribe before the Governor or some other person appointed by him in that behalf, an oath or affirmation according to the form set out for the purpose in the First Schedule.

(4) The State Chief Information Commissioner or a State Information Commissioner may, at any time, by writing under his hand addressed to the Governor, resign from his office;

Provided that the State Chief Information Commissioner or a State Information Commissioner may be removed in the manner specified under section 17.

(5) The salaries and allowances payable to and other terms and conditions of service of:

(a) the State Chief Information Commissioner shall be the same as that of an Election Commissioner;

(b) the State Information Commissioner shall be the same as that of the Chief Secretary to the State Government:

Provided that if the State Chief Information Commissioner or a State Information Commissioner, at the time of his appointment is, in receipt of a pension, other than a disability or wound pension, in respect of any previous service under the Government of India or under the Government of a State, his salary in respect of the service as the State Chief Information Commissioner or a State Information Commissioner shall be reduced by the amount of that pension including any portion of pension which was commuted and pension equivalent of other forms of retirement benefits excluding pension equivalent of retirement gratuity:

Provided further that where the State Chief Information Commissioner or a State Information Commissioner if, at the time of his appointment is, in receipt of retirement benefits in respect of any previous service rendered in a Corporation established by or under any Central Act or State Act or a Government company owned or controlled by the Central Government or the State Government, his salary in respect of the service as the State Chief Information Commissioner or the State Information Commissioner shall be reduced by the amount of pension equivalent to the retirement benefits:

Provided also that the salaries, allowances and other conditions of service of the State Chief Information Commissioner and the State Information Commissioners shall not be varied to their disadvantage after their appointment.

(6) The State Government shall provide the State Chief Information Commissioner and the State Information Commissioners with such officers and employees as may be 'necessary for the efficient performance of their functions under this Act, and the salaries and allowances payable to and the terms and conditions of service of the officers and other employees appointed for the purpose of this Act shall be such as may be prescribed.

**Removal of State Chief Information Commissioner or State Information Commissioner**

**17.** (1) Subject to the provisions of sub-section (3), the State Chief Information Commissioner or a State Information Commissioner shall be removed from his office only by order of the Governor on the ground of proved misbehaviour or incapacity after the Supreme Court, on a reference made to it by the Governor, has on inquiry, reported that the State Chief Information Commissioner or a State Information Commissioner, as the case may be, ought on such ground be removed.

(2) The Governor may suspend from office, and if deem necessary prohibit also from attending the office during inquiry, the State Chief Information Commissioner or a State Information Commissioner in respect of whom a reference has been made to the Supreme Court under sub-section (1) until the Governor has passed orders on receipt of the report of the Supreme Court on such reference.

(3) Notwithstanding anything contained in sub-section (1), the Governor may by order remove from office the State Chief Information Commissioner or a State Information Commissioner if a State Chief Information Commissioner or a State Information Commissioner, as the case may be :

(a) is adjudged an insolvent; or

(b) has been convicted of an offence which, in the opinion of the Governor, involves moral turpitude; or

(c) engages during his term of office in any paid employment outside the duties of his office; or

(d) is, in the opinion of the Governor, unfit to continue in office by reason of infirmity of mind or body; or;

(e) has acquired such financial or other interest as is likely to affect prejudicially his functions as the State Chief Information Commissioner or a State Information Commissioner.

(4) If the State Chief Information Commissioner or a State Information Commissioner in any way, concerned or interested in any contract or agreement made by or on behalf of the Government of the State or participates in any way in the profit thereof or in any benefit or emoluments arising therefrom otherwise than as a member and in common with the other members of an incorporated company, he shall, for the purposes of sub-section.

(1) be deemed to be guilty of misbehaviour.

## CHAPTER V

## Powers and functions of the Information Commissions, Appeal and Penalties

### Powers and functions of Information Commissions

**18.** (1) Subject to the provisions of this Act, it shall be the duty of the Central Information Commission or State Information Commission, as the case may be, to receive and inquire into a complaint from any person:

(a) who has been unable to submit a request to a Central Public Information Officer or State Public Information Officer, as the case may be, either by reason that no such officer has been appointed under this Act, or because the Central Assistant Public Information Officer or State Assistant Public Information Officer, as the case may be, has refused to accept his or her application for information or appeal under this Act for forwarding the same to the Central Public Information Officer or State Public Information Officer or senior officer specified in subsection (1) of section 19 or the

Central Information Commission or the State Information Commission, as the case may be;

(b) who has been refused access to any information requested under this Act;

(c) who has not been given a response to a request for information or access to information within the time limit specified under this Act;

(d) who has been required to pay an amount of fee which he or she considers unreasonable;

(e) who believes that he or she has been given incomplete, misleading or false information under this Act; and

(f) in respect of any other matter relating to requesting or obtaining access to records under this Act.

(2) Where the Central Information Commission or State Information Commission, as the case may be, is satisfied that there are reasonable grounds to inquire into the matter, it may initiate an inquiry in respect thereof.

(3) The Central Information Commission or State Information Commission, as the case may be, shall, while inquiring into any matter under this section, have the same powers as are vested in a civil court while trying a suit under the Code of Civil Procedure, 1908, in respect of the following matters, namely:

**5 of 1908**

(a) summoning and enforcing the attendance of persons and compel them to give oral or written evidence on oath and to produce the documents or things;

(b) requiring the discovery and inspection of documents;

(c) receiving evidence on affidavit;

(d) requisitioning any public record or copies thereof from any court or office;

(e) issuing summons for examination of witnesses or documents; and

(f) any other matter which may be prescribed.

(4) Notwithstanding anything inconsistent contained in any other Act of Parliament or State Legislature, as the case may be, the Central Information Commission or the State Information Commission, as the case may be, may, during the inquiry of any complaint under this Act, examine any record to which this Act applies which is under the control of the public authority, and no such record may be withheld from it on any grounds.

### Appeal

**19.** (1) Any person who, does not receive a decision within the time specified in subsection (1) or clause (a) of sub-section (3) of section 7, or is aggrieved by a decision of the Central Public Information Officer or State Public Information Officer, as the case may be may within thirty days from the expiry of such period or from the receipt of such a decision prefer an appeal to such officer who is senior in rank to the Central Public Information Officer or State Public Information Officer as the case may be, in each public authority:

Provided that such officer may admit the appeal after the expiry of the period of thirty days if he or she is satisfied that the appellant was prevented by sufficient cause from filing the appeal in time.

(2) Where an appeal is preferred against an order made by a Central Public Information Officer or a State Public Information Officer, as the case may be, under ; section 11 to disclose third party information, the appeal by the concerned third party shall be made within thirty days from the date of the order.

(3) A second appeal against the decision under sub-section (1) shall lie within ninety days from the date on which the decision should have been made or was actually received with the Central Information Commission or the State Information Commission:

Provided that the Central Information Commission or the State Information Commission, as the case may be, may admit the appeal after the expiry of the period of ninety days if it is satisfied that the appellant was prevented by sufficient cause from filing the appeal in time.

(4) If the decision of the Central Public Information Officer or State Public Information Officer, as the case may be, against which an appeal is preferred relates to information of a third party, the Central Information Commission or State Information Commission, as the case may be, shall give a reasonable opportunity of being heard to that third party.

(5) In any appeal proceedings, the onus to prove that a denial of a request was justified shall be on the Central Public Information Officer or State Public Information Officer, as the case may be, who denied the request.

(6) An appeal under sub-section (1) or sub-section (2) shall be disposed of within thirty days of the receipt of the appeal or within such extended period not exceeding a total of forty-five days from the date of filing thereof, as the case may be, for reasons to be recorded in writing.

(7) The decision of the Central Information Commission or State Information Commission, as the case may be, shall be binding.

(8) In its decision, the Central Information Commission or State Information Commission, as the case may be,.has the power to:

(a) require the public authority to take any such steps as may be necessary to secure compliance with the provisions of this Act, including :

(*i*) by providing access to information, if so requested, in a particular form;

(*ii*) by appointing a Central Public Information Officer or State Public Information Officer, as the case may be;

(*iii*) by publishing certain information or categories of information;

(*iv*) by making necessary changes to its practices in relation to the maintenance, management and destruction of records;

(*v*) by enhancing the provision of training on the right to information for its officials;

(*vi*) by providing it with an annual report in compliance with clause (b) of subsection (1) of section 4;

(b) require the public authority to compensate the complainant for any loss or other detriment suffered;

(c) impose any of the penalties provided under this Act;

(d) reject the application.

(9) The Central Information Commission or State Information Commission, as the case may be, shall give notice of its decision, including any right of appeal, to the complainant and the public authority.

(10) The Central Information Commission or State Information Commission, as the case may be, shall decide the appeal in accordance with such procedure as may be prescribed.

## Penalties

**20.** (1) Where the Central Information Commission or the State Information Commission, as the case may be, at the time of deciding any complaint or appeal is of the opinion that the Central Public, Information Officer or the State Public Information Officer, as the case may be, has, without any reasonable cause, refused to receive an application for information or has not furnished information within the time specified under sub-section

(1) of section 7 or malafidely denied the request for information or knowingly given incorrect, incomplete or misleading information or destroyed information which was the subject of the request or obstructed in any manner in furnishing the information, it shall impose a penalty of two hundred and fifty rupees each day till application is received or information is furnished, so however, the total amount of such penalty shall not exceed twenty-five thousand rupees:

Provided that the Central Public Information Officer or the State Public Information Officer, as the case may be, shall be given a reasonable opportunity of being heard before any penalty is imposed on him:

Provided further that the burden of proving that he acted reasonably and diligently shall be on the Central Public Information Officer or the State Public Information Officer, as the case may be.

(2) Where the Central Information Commission or the State Information Commission, as the case may be, at the time of deciding any complaint or appeal is of the opinion that the Central Public Information Officer or the State Public Information Officer, as the case may be, has, without any reasonable cause and persistently, failed to receive an application for information or has not furnished information within the time specified under subsection (1) of section 7 or malafidely denied the request for information or knowingly given incorrect, incomplete or misleading information or destroyed information which was the subject of the request or obstructed in any manner in furnishing the information, it shall recommend for disciplinary action against the Central Public Information Officer or the State Public Information Officer, as the case may be, under the service rules applicable to him.

## CHAPTER VI

## MISCELLANEOUS

### Protection of action taken in good faith

**21. No suit, prosecution or other legal proceeding shall lie against any person for anything which is in good faith done or intended to be done under this Act or any rule made thereunder.**

### Act to have overriding effect

**22. The provisions of this Act shall have effect notwithstanding anything inconsistent therewith contained in the Official Secrets Act, 1923, and any other law for the time being in force or in any instrument having effect by virtue of any law other than this Act.**

### Bar of jurisdiction of courts

**23. No court shall entertain any suit, application or other proceeding in respect of any order made under this Act and no such order shall be called in question otherwise than by way of an appeal under this Act.**

### Act not to apply to certain organisations

24. (1) Nothing contained in this Act shall apply to the intelligence and security organisations specified in the second schedule, being organisations established by

the Central Government or any information furnished by such organisations to that Government:

Provided that the information pertaining to the allegations of corruption and human rights violations shall not be excluded under this sub-section:

Provided further that in the case of information sought for is in respect of allegations of violation of human rights, the information shall only be provided after the approval of the Central Information Commission, and notwithstanding anything contained in section 7, such information shall be provided within forty-five days from the date of the receipt of request.

(2) The Central Government may, by notification in the Official Gazette, amend the Schedule by including therein any other intelligence or security organisation established by that Government or omitting therefrom any organisation already specified there in and on the publication of such notification, such organisation shall be deemed to be included in or, as the case may be, omitted from the Schedule.

(3) Every notification issued under sub-section (2) shall be laid before each House of Parliament.

(4) Nothing contained in this Act shall apply to such intelligence and security organisation being organisations established by the State Government, as that Government may, from time to time, by notification in the Official Gazette, specify:

Provided that the information pertaining to the allegations of corruption and human rights violations shall not be excluded under this sub-section:

Provided further that in the case of information sought for is in respect of allegations of violation of human rights, the information shall only be provided after the approval of the State Information Commission and, notwithstanding anything contained in section 7, such information shall be provided within forty-five days from the date of the receipt of request.

(5) Every notification issued under sub-section (4) shall be laid before the State Legislature.

**Monitoring and Reporting**

**25.** (1) The Central Information Commission or State Information Commission, as the case may be, shall, as soon as practicable after the end of each year, prepare a report on the implementation of the provisions of this Act during that year and forward a copy thereof to the appropriate Government.

(2) Each Ministry or Department shall, in relation to the public authorities within their jurisdiction, collect and provide such information to the Central

Information Commission or State Information Commission, as the case may be, as is required to prepare the report under this section and comply with the requirements concerning the furnishing of that information and keeping of records for the purposes of this section.

(3) Each report shall state in respect of the year to which the report relates :

(a) the number of requests made to each public authority;

(b) the number of decisions where applicants were not entitled to access to the documents pursuant to the requests, the provisions of this Act under which these decisions were made and the number of times such provisions were invoked;

(c) the number of appeals referred to the Central Information Commission or State Information Commission, as the case may be, for review, the nature of the appeals and the outcome of the appeals;

(d) particulars of any disciplinary: action taken against any officer in respect of the administration of this Act;

(e) the amount of charges collected by each public authority under this Act;

(f) any facts which indicate an effort by the public authorities to administer and implement the spirit and intention of this Act;

(g) recommendations for reform, including recommendations in respect of the particular public authorities, for the development, improvement, modernisation, reform or amendment to this Act or other legislation or common law or any other matter relevant for operationalising the right to access information.

(4) The Central Government or the State Government, as the case may be, may, as soon as practicable after the end of each year, cause a copy of the report of the Central Information Commission or the State Information Commission, as the case may be, referred to in sub-section (1) to be laid before each House of Parliament or, as the case may be, before each House of the State Legislature, where there are two Houses, and where there is one House of the State Legislature before that House.

(5) If it appears to the Central Information Commission or State Information Commission, as the case may be,,that the practice of a public authority in relation to the exercise of its functions under this Act does not conform with the provisions or spirit of this Act, it may give to the authority a recommendation specifying the steps which ought in its opinion to be taken for promoting such conformity.

**Appropriate Government to prepare programmes**

**26.** (1) The appropriate Government may, to the extent of availability of financial and other resources:

(a) develop and organise educational programmes to advance the understanding of the public, in particular of disadvantaged communities as to how to exercise the rights contemplated under this Act;

(b) encourage public authorities to participate in the development and organisation of programmes referred to in clause (a) and to undertake such programmes themselves;

(c) promote timely and effective dissemination of accurate information by public authorities about their activities; and

(d) Train Central Public Information Officers or State Public Information Officers, as the case may be, of public authorities and produce relevant training materials for use by the public authorities themselves.

(2) The appropriate Government shall, within eighteen months from the commencement of this Act, compile in its official language a guide containing such information, in an easily comprehensible form and manner, as may reasonably be required by a person who wishes to exercise any right specified in this Act.

(3) The appropriate Government shall, if necessary, update and publish the guidelines referred to in sub-section (2) at regular intervals which shall, in particular and without prejudice to the generality of sub-section (2), include :

(a) the objects of this Act;

(b) the postal and street address, the phone and fax number and, if available, electronic mail address of the Central Public Information Officer or State Public Officer, as the case may be, of every public authority appointed under sub-section (1) of section 5;

(c) the manner and the form in which request for access to an information shall be made to a Central Public Information Officer, or State Public Information Officer, as the case may be;

(d) the assistance available from and the duties of the Central Public Information Officer or State Public Information Officer, as the case may be, of a public authority under this Act;

(e) the assistance available from the Central Information Commission or State Information Commission, as the case may be;

(f) all remedies in law available regarding an act or failure to act in respect of a right or duty conferred or imposed by this Act including the manner of filing an appeal to the Commission;

(g) the provisions providing for the voluntary disclosure of categories of records in accordance with section 4;

(h) the notices regarding fees to be paid in relation to requests for access to an information; and

(i) any additional regulations or circulars made or issued in relation to obtaining access to an information in accordance with this Act.

(4) The appropriate Government must, if necessary, update and publish the guidelines at regular intervals.

**Power to make rules by Appropriate Government**

27. (1) The appropriate Government may, by notification in the Official Gazette, make rules to carry out the provisions of this Act.

(2) In particular, and without prejudice to the generality of the foregoing power, such rules may provide for all or any of the following matters, namely :

(a) the cost of the medium or print cost price of the materials to be disseminated under sub-section (4) of section 4;

(b) the fee payable under sub-section (1) of section 6;

(c) the fee payable under sub-sections (1) and (5) of section 7;

(d) the salaries and allowances payable to and the terms and conditions of service of the officers and other employees under sub-section (6) of section 13 and sub-section (6) of section 16;

(e) the procedure to be adopted" by the Central Information Commission or State Information Commission, as the case may be, in deciding the appeals under sub-section (10) of section 19; and

(f) any other matter which is required to be, or may be, prescribed.

**Power to make rules by Competent Authority**

**28.** (1) The competent authority may, by notification in the Official Gazette, make rules to carry out the provisions of this Act.

(2) In particular, and without prejudice to the generality of the foregoing power, such rules may provide for all or any of the following matters, namely :

(*i*) the cost of the medium or print cost price of the materials to be disseminated under sub-section (4) of section 4;

(*ii*) the fee payable under sub-section (1) of section 6;

(*iii*) the fee payable under sub-section (1) of section 7; and

(*iv*) any other matter which is required to be, or may be, prescribed Laying of rules.

### Laying of Rules

**29.** (1) Every rule made by the Central Government under this Act shall be laid, as , soon as may be after it is made, before each House of Parliament, while it is in session, for a total period of thirty days which may be comprised in one session or in two or more successive sessions, and if, before the expiry of the session immediately following the session or the successive sessions aforesaid, both Houses agree in making any modification in the rule or both Houses agree that the rule should not be made, the rule shall thereafter have effect only in such modified form or be of no effect, as the case may be; so, however, that any such modification or annulment shall be without prejudice to the validity of anything previously done under that rule.

(2) Every rule made under this Act by a State Government shall be laid, as soon as may be after it is notified, before the State Legislature.

### Power to Remove Difficulties

**30.** (1) If any difficulty arises in giving effect to the provisions of this Act, the Central Government may, by order published in the Official Gazette, make such provisions not inconsistent with the provisions of this Act as appear to it to be necessary or expedient for removal of the difficulty.

Provided that no such order shall be made after the expiry of a period of two years from the date of the commencement of this Act.

(2) Every order made under this section shall, as soon as may be after it is made, be laid before each House of Parliament.

### Repeal

**31. The Freedom of Information Act, 2002 is hereby repealed (5 of 2003)**

**Intelligence and security organisation established by the Central Government:**

1. Intelligence Bureau.
2. Research and Analysis Wing of the Cabinet Secretariat.
3. Directorate of Revenue Intelligence.
4. Central Economic Intelligence Bureau.
5. Directorate of Enforcement.
6. Narcotics Control Bureau.
7. Aviation Research Centre.
8. Special Frontier Force.
9. Border Security Force.

10. Central Reserve Police Force;
11. Indo-Tibetan Border Police.
12. Central Industrial Security Farce.
13. National Security Guards.
14. Assam Rifles.
15. Special Service Bureau.
16. Special Branch (CID), Andaman and Nicobar.
17. The Crime Branch-C.I.D., CB, Dadra and Nagar Haveli, Special Branch, Lakshwadeep Police.
19. T. K. Vishwanathan Secretary to the Government of India.

# 17

# Web Laws-Cyber Laws

New communication systems and digital technology have made dramatic changes in the dissemination of information. Communicators and consumers are increasingly using computers; networks and Internet to communicate information. Computers have replaced paper works. Computers are being used to create, transmit and store information in the electronic form.

Internet is the fourth medium of communication. It is an electronic version of newspapers, magazines, books, catalogue, news bulletins, etc. Internet is a combination of several media technologies and is a world–wide system of inter connected computer networks.

The content of the internet is more relevant to the users. The governance of the content is a matter of critical importance for users. The use of internet on a large scale, simultaneously gave birth to a number of related problems. One of them is cyber crime.

Cyber Crime is closely linked to the issue of illegal and harmful content, which spreads virus, pornography, etc. Hate contents are easily available on the internet and need to be regulated. To control this sort of cyber crimes and other related crimes, the Government of India enacted the Information Technology Act, 2000 on 17th October 2000. The Act gives legal recognition to electronic records, electronic transfer of information and digital signatures.

In India cyber laws are governed by the provisions contrived in the Information Technology Act, 2000. The object of the Act are;

— To provide legal recognition for transactions carried out by means of electronic data interchange and other means of electronic communication which involves the use of alternatives to paper–based methods of communications and storage of information.
— The facilitate electronic filing of documents with the Government agencies and news stories in the quickest time.

The IT Act, 2000 enlists the types of crimes and provides for their punishment and fine.

**Pornography:** Section 67 of the Act makes the publishing and transmitting of obscene material over the internet an offence for which an offender could be punished with an imprisonment of upto 5 years and a fine of Rs. 100,000.

Under Section 66 of the IT Act, 2000, hacking is an offence punishable with imprisonment upto 3 years and fine of Rs. 200,000. The Act also provides for the adjudication and investigation of cyber crimes.

The Act also provides legal recognition to electronic records and gives it legal status at par with the traditional paper record so that it can be considered as evidence in the Court of Law.

Section 3 of the Act provides for the authentication of Electronic Records using the technology of Digital signatures. Section 5 of the Act defines Digital signatures.

Section 4 of the Act provides the required legal validity to the Electronic Records and Digital signatures.

Pointing out the vices of internet, some people argue that the ease of duplicating and disseminating information has led to a situation wherein the internet in under cutting the incentive to innovate in our society others argue that, on the contrary, new laws designed to tighten Intellectual Property Right protections of "fair use" which upholds the rights to use materials protected under copyright for non–commercial purposes.

Section 5(1) of the Act defines Electronic Records to mean data, record, or data generated, image or sound stored, received or sent in an electronic form of or microfilm or computer generated n microfiche.

Section 6 of the Act enables the government departments to accept the filing of any form, application or any other document in electronic form.

Section 7 of the Act allows creation and retention of documents in the form of electronic record. The government departments would be free to specify the format under which these documents would be stored.

Section 8 of the Act provides for an electronic gazette laying down that the requirement of publication in the official gazette will be deemed to have been satisfied if the information is published in Electronic gazette.

**Contraventions and offences–Punishment therefor**

The IT Act defines contraventions and offences and provides penalty and punishment for them. The contraventions, which are civil in nature and carry monetary damages which may go upto Rs. 1 crore. These contraventions will be adjudicated by Adjudicating Officers appointed under the Act.

The offences, which are criminal in nature, carry criminal imprisonment and monetary penalties and shall be tried by the criminal courts.

The governance of "Internet" which is called the fourth medium of Communication, still remains a concept in reach of definition and clarity. Apart from the governments, Internet comes under the umbrella of various other Internet Stake holders. These are private sector International Government and non–Government bodies and civil society. According to the Working Group on Internet Governance (WAIG) of United Nations; "Internet governance is the development and application by Governments, the private sector and civil society in their respective roles of shared principles, norms, rules decision making procedures, and programmes that shake the evolution and use of the Internet".

In a report WAIG said that Internet governance includes some public policy issues, such as critical Internet.

The rapid technological development of the various protocols on the internet has made it very easy to host graphics, images, sounds, movies and other multimedia capabilities on the internet. Multimedia advertisement, including graphics, sound, video, movies can be published and made available to the browsing public.

The advantage of global presence at a very meager expenses saw virtual business boom on the internet The Business Community have been scrambling to take advantage of the tremendous advantage, of the multimedia capabilities and global presence. Many business houses are now creating a presence on the internet by establishing an "internet site" or "web–site". The internet placed the role proprietor, small business firm and a multinational company on the same booting. The global presence is the main advantage. The business company, by the same booting his own "web–site" could advertise his services or products to gain a global presence.

Internet governance is a complexities and complexity of Internet Governance is related to its multi–disciplinary nature, encompassing a variety of objects. Some of these aspects are technology, socio–cultural, economics, development, law and politics. This has brought the question of Internet Governance into focus. But the process of addressing the legal issues and the social consequences of technological developments lags behind the technological innovation in internet resources, the security and safety of the internet and development aspects and issues pertaining to the use of the Internet, the issues are dealt with by the Internet Corporation for Assigned Names and Numbers (ICANN).

# 18

# Concept and Importance of Media Ethics

Right behavior and conduct of its constituents is a sine–quanon of a peaceful, orderly and a living society. Greek philosopher Aristotle believed that happiness of the individual and society, is the ultimate human goal, Aristotle said that the way to behave ethically was that every individual must understand fully what he was doing and he has to select the act for his own sake.

This is all the more important for those who feed the columns of a newspaper or prepare the scripts for broadcasts from reporter's to editors and publishers. Media playing a crucial role in informing, educating and entertaining the people, casts a tremendous responsibility on every person working for any mass media and playing a role in shaping its contents'

The Code of Ethics became necessary, inspite of the laws of the land being fully applicable to all journalists as there were areas in their functioning which were not covered by the laws of the land.

The legal obligations of journalists are also embodied in the Indian Penal Code and other Press Laws. Still Press Commission had to formulate Code of Ethics and were duly endorsed by representative organizations of journalists.

In the interest of participative democracy it is necessary that journalists should disseminate truthful news and views. They function as a two–way channel of communication between the readers and public authorities. They have not only to keep the ruling elite informed of what the people think of the Government, but also to keep the people informed of government decisions and actions. For playing the role of a two–way communication, journalists must avoid manipulative, motivated and biased reports.

An international commission appointed, for the study of communication related problems, by the UNESCO found that ethical norms were being codified in all regions of the world. UNESCO noted that some countries have different codes governing the Press, broadcasting and cinema and they have not been objected to by their professional organizations. It could be objectionable only when they are enforced by law.

The Press (Objectionable Matter) Act, 1951 was the effort in India to evolve a code of Ethics. The All India Newspaper Editors Conference (AINEC) formally extended its support and the Indian Federation of Working Journalists (IFWJ) suggested some amendments which were included.

The Act defines the "Objectionable Matter" as any word, sign or visible presentation which was likely to

(*i*) Incite or encourage any person to resort to violence or sabotage for the purpose of over throwing or undermining the government established by law in India or in any state or its authority in any area.

(*ii*) Incite or encourage any person to commit murder, sabotage or offence involving violence.

(*iii*) Incite or encourage any person to interfere with the supply and distribution of food or other essential commodities or with essential services.

(*iv*) Seduce any member of the Armed Forces form his allegiance or his duty, or prejudice the recruiting of persons to serve in any such forces.

(*v*) Promote feelings of enmity or hatred between different sections of the people of India or

(*vi*) Publish any materials that are grossly indecent, or are scurrilous or obscene or intended for blackmail.

The Act replaced four Acts then in force–The Press (Emergency Powers) Act, the Foreign Relations Act and two States (Protection) Acts.

# 19

# Press Codes

## AINEC Code of Ethics, 1968

The AINEC adopted its own Code of Conduct in 1968, though it applied more to editors than other categories of journalists, its provisions still hold good. These are:

(*a*) A free press can function only in a free society. Communalism is a threat to the fabric of our society and to the nation's solidarity.

(*b*) The press has a vital role to play in the consummation of the fundamental objectives enshrined in the Constitution, namely, democracy, secularism, national unity and integrity and the rule of law. It is the duty of the press to help promote unity and cohesion in the hearts and minds of the people and refrain from publishing material tending to excite communal passions or influence communal hatred.

(*c*) To this end the Press should adhere to the following guidelines, in reporting on communal incidents in the country.

(*i*) All editorial comments and other expressions or opinions, whether through articles, letters to the Editor, or any other form should be restrained and free from scurrilous attacks against leaders or communities and there should be no incitement to violence;

(*ii*) Generalized allegations casting doubts and aspersions on the patriotism and loyalty of any community should be eschewed;

(*iii*) Likewise, generalized charges and allegations against any community of unfair discriminations, amounting to inciting communal hatred and distrust, must be eschewed;

(*iv*) Whereas, truth should not be suppressed, a deliberate slanting of news of communal incidents should be avoided.

(*v*) News of incidents involving loss of life, lawlessness, arson, etc. should be described, reported and headlined with restraint in strictly objective terms and should not be prominently displayed;

(*vi*) Items of news calculated to make for peace and harmony and help in the restoration and maintenance of law and order should be given prominence and precedence over other news;

(*vii*) The greatest caution should be exercised in the selection and publication of pictures, cartoons, poems, etc. so as not to arouse communal passions or hatred;

(*viii*) Names of communities should not be mentioned and terms "majority" and "minority" communities be ordinarily used in the course of reports;

(*ix*) The source from casualty figures are obtained should always be indicated;

(*x*) No facts or figures should be published without the fullest possible verification. However, if the publication of the facts or figures is likely to have the effect of arousing communal passions, those facts and figures may not be given.

## PRESS COUNCIL CODE, 1954

The Press council of India had formulated a code of Ethics to help the media perform their respective roles harmoniously in difficult situations:

(*i*) Provocative and sensational headlines should be avoided.

(*ii*) Headings must reflect and justify the matter printed under them.

(*iii*) Figures of casualties gives in headlines should preferably be on the lower side, incase of doubt about their exactness and where the numbers reported by various sources differ widely.

(*iv*) Headlines containing allegations made in statements should either identify the person/boy making the allegation or at least should carry question marks.

(*v*) Comments and value judgments in presentation of news should be avoided.

(*vi*) Presentation of news should not be motivated or guided by partisan feelings, nor should it appear to be so.

(*vii*) Language employed in writing the news should be temperate and such as may fester the feelings to amity among communities and groups and

(*viii*) Corrections should be promptly published with due prominence and regrets expressed in various cases.

## PRESS COUNCIL CODE ON COMMUNAL MATTERS

The Press Council also formulated its Code of Ethics on the writing about communal events. These are; distortion or exaggeration of facts or incidents in relation to communal vents, or giving currency to rumour, or inferences, use of intemperate language in news or views, encouraging or condoning violence, to invent grievances or to exaggerate real grievances, scurrilous or untrue attack on communities, casts or individuals, falsely, giving a communal colour to an incident fostering feeling of ill will or distrust between communities to embitter relations between different communities or regional or linguistic groups, making disrespectful, derogatory or insulting remarks on different religious faiths or their founder.

## CODE FOR MEDIA PERSONS ADOPTED BY EDITORS GUILD OF INDIA

Based on the code prepared by Britain's Society of Editors, the Editors Guild of India adopted a code of practice for Journalists on August 20, 2002. But the Members of the Guild modified the British Code to suit Indian experience. The Code is mainly addressed to the media persons both in field and at the desk. But it is also addressed to the editors who have a prime role inculcating these codes. Faithful observance of code certainly helps to promote a healthy functioning of the Fourth Estate and a body like Editors Guild can help a lot in the observance of the code by formulating and monitoring the same.

Self regulated code strengthens the demands of media persons for protection of their right to receive and disseminate information in public interest.

There is a constant clash of interest between the media and public authorities. Media take the coverage of "Public Interest" and public authorities in the garb of "public order". The main criteria in deciding the ethics by the journalist should whether, what he or she is disseminating, is in public interest. But publication of rumours and unconfirmed reports can never be justified. This is ethically and morally wrong.

Media persons are accused of invading the privacy of public figures. A number of journalists have been accused of invading the privacy of government officials and other public figures. But it is the right of journalists to expose the misdoings of public authorities and public figures. The public has a right to know the acts of omission and commission by public authorities. The right of the public to know out weights the right to privacy of public authorities

Besides the written code of ethics, there comes several occasions when the media person has himself to take a decision. There are also a number of guiding factors for journalists, like personal ethics, performance code, self–assessment, organizational policies and professional self–regulation.

Some precautions to be taken by media persons should be, the media should set an example through self regulations, it should give priority to public audience than accepting facilities provided by public authorities, and freedom to editors to depute as suitable person for the coverage of an event.

The role of an editor is of vital importance in maintaining the credibility of the publication, accuracy of the facts and figures and publication of correction of incorrect reports But the above all obligation of the editor is to inculcate a sense of respect for all such obligations in the minds of the staff of the publication. The considerations, most important, are to harmonize various conflicting interests and competing ideas about the right of the society and the individual and rights relating to gender, class, caste, religion and community.

Not only the desk persons but all members of the staff must take varied thing. These are verifying facts, segregating facts from direct or implied comments, weeding out rumours/unsubstantiated allegations or innuendos, measuring right to publish and public interest, giving reasonable opportunity to aggrieved person to clarify or contradict, avoiding undue publicity to individual, avoiding exaggeration in the story for the sake of sensationa-lizing it, using anonymity as a matter of exception and not of rule, giving importance to "Human Rights" and privacy of personal feelings in comparison to "Human Interests", to give equal fair treatment to all creeds communities, caste and religion mentioned in the report, not to mention the names of juvenile delinquents, etc.

## PRESS COUNCIL'S GUIDE TO JOURNALISTIC ETHICS

The Press Council published a compendium of broad principles evolved by it through its adjudications principles first in 1983–84 and updated in 1992 published as compilation of the principles of journalistic ethics and guidelines. The following are excerts from the guidelines of 1992 :

The Press Council of India has been established to preserve the freedom of the press and to maintain and improve the standards of newspapers and news agencies. The Council is enjoined to 'build up' a code of conduct for newspapers, news agencies and journalists in accordance with high professional standards. A compendium of broad principles evolved by the Press Council through its adjudications principles was first published in 1983-84. In October 1992, the Council published an updated but succinct compilation of the principles of journalistic ethics sorted out from the adjudications of the Council and the guidelines issued by it in their wake. (The Guide to Journalistic Ethics was further revised and updated in 1995 by the then Chairman, Mr. Justice P. B. Sawant.) Below are excerpts from the 1992 guidelines:

**1. Accuracy and Fairness:** The fundamental objective of journalism, declares the Guide, is to serve the people with news, views, comments and information matters of public interest, in a fair, accurate, unbiased, sober and decent manner. Publication of inaccurate, baseless, graceless, misleading or distorted material should be avoided. All sides of the core issue or subject should be reported.

(a) Verification and checkmg of news before publication is necessary where its publication and the comments based thereon can create complications, such as:

(*i*) where it is likely to incite communal passions.

(*ii*) where it is of a slanderous nature.

(b) However, failure to observe strictly this rule as to pre-publication verification would not necessarily amount to a breach of journalistic ethics on the part of the editor.

(*i*) where the impugned news item was merely a statement made by a responsible political leader of the ruling party at a press conference or a public statement of a recognised leader, or

(*ii*) where the impugned news item was based on the report of an accredited correspondent.

Provided in either case it was in respect to a matter of public concern.

(*c*) Unjustified rumours and surmises should not be set forth as facts.

**2. Journalists should judge no one unheard.**

**3. Cautions against Defamatory Writings:** Newspapers should not publish anything which is *per se* defamatory or libellous against any individual or organisation unless after due care and checking they have sufficient reason to believe that it is true and its publication will be for public good.

**4. Pre-publication Verification of Reports Necessary:**

(*a*) Whenever a newspaper receives a report or article containing defamatory or derogatory imputations or comments against a public figure, public servant or public organisation, touching his/her or its public conduct or character in so far as it appears in that conduct, the editor should, before publishing it, check with due care and attention, its factual accuracy—apart from other authentic sources, with the person on the organisation concerned to elicit his/her or its version, comments or reaction and publish the same. If the person or the organisation, likely to be affected by that report/article, refuses to give his/her counter-version or reaction, despite sincere efforts made by the editor a footnote to that effect should be published along with the report or the article. If from the counter-version given by the person or organisation; concerned, the editors mind is left rocking with doubt in regard to the veracity of any part of the report/article, he should omit from publication that part and publish the rest with consequential amendment, provided the editor is satisfied that the remainder is substantially accurate and its publication will be for public benefit. If such doubt permeates the whole of the report/article, the prudent course for him is not to publish it at all.

(*b*) This salutary rule of journalistic ethics and fairness follow as a necessary corollary from two basic principles: the first is a fundamental canon of natural justice, that no one should be condemned unheard. The second is that freedom of the press is not merely a right of the publishers and editors but also of the readers'/people's right to know all sides of an issue of public interest. The editor, therefore, cannot refuse to publish the reply or rejoinder merely on the ground that in his opinion the story published in the newspaper was true. That is an issue to be left to the judgement of the readers.

**5. Privacy:** Instruction or invasion on the privacy of individuals is not permissible unless outweighed by genuine overriding public interest, not being a prurient or morbid curiosity.

**Explanation:** Things concerning a person's home, family, religion, health, sexuality, personal life and private affairs are covered by the concept of privacy excepting where any of these impinge upon the public or public interest.

Victims of Sex Crimes : Caution against Publication of Names or Pictures.

**6.** While reporting crimes involving rape or molestation of Women, of sexual assault on children, or raising doubts and questions touching the chastity, personal character and privacy of women, the names, photographs of the victims or other particulars leading to their identity should not be published. While such publication serves no legitimate public purpose, it may bring social opprobrium to the victims and social embarrassment to their relations, family, friends, Community, religious order or the institution to which they belong.

7. Newspapers to eschew suggestive guilt by association. They should not name or identify the family or relatives or associates of a person convicted or accused of a crime, when they are totally innocent and a reference to them is not relevant to the matter reported.

**8. Corrections:** When any factual error or mistake is detected or confirmed, the newspaper should publish the correction promptly with due prominence and with apology or expression of regret in a case of serious lapse.

**9. Right of Reply:**

(*a*) The newspaper should promptly publish at the instance of the person feeling aggrieved/or concerned by the impugned publication, a contradiction/reply/rejoiner sent to the editor in the form of a letter or, note the editor has a discretion either to publish it in full or publish its abridged and edited version, particularly when it is inordinately long. But the remainder should be an effective reply to the allegations. However, the editor is not entitled to alter, omit or refuse to publish important portions of the reply/rejoinder which effectively deal with the material allegations in the news item. If the editor doubts the truth or factual accuracy of the contradiction/reply/ rejoinder, even then, it is his/her duty to publish it, with liberty to add separately at the end, an editorial comment doubting its veracity, but only when this doubt is reasonably founded on unimpeachable documentary or other evidential material in his/her possession. The editor should not, in a cavalier fashion, without the application of mind, append such note, as: "we stand by our story". It must be remembered that the liberty to append an editorial comment to a rejoinder or reply is not absolute right. It is a concession which has to be availed of sparingly with due discretion and caution in appropriate cases.

(*b*) However, where the reply/contradiction or rejoinder is being published in compliance with the direction of the Press Council, it is permissible to append a brief editorial note to that effect.

**10. Letters to the Editor:** An editor who decides to open his columns for letters on a controversial subject is not obliged to publish all the letters received in regard to that subject. He is entitled to select and publish only some of them either in entirety or the gist thereof. However, in exercising this discretion he must make an honest endeavour to ensure that what is published is not one sided but represents a fair balance between the views for and against with respect to the principal issue in controversy. In the event of rejoinder upon rejoinder being sent by two parties on a controversial subject, the editor has the discretion to decide at which stage to close the continuing column.

**11. Conjecture, Comment and Fact:** Newspapers should not pass on or elevate conjecture, speculation or comment as a statement of fact. All these categories should be distinctly stated.

Paramount Interests of State, Society and Rights of Individuals not to be jeopardised.

**12.** Newspapers should, as a matter of self-regulation, exercise due restraint and caution in presenting any news, comment or information which is likely to jeopardise, endanger or harm the paramount interests of the state and society, or the rights of individuals, for the protection of which reasonable restriction? may be imposed by law on the right to freedom of speech and expression under Clause (2) of Article 19 of the Constitution of India.

**13. Newspapers may Expose Misuse of Diplomatic Immunity:** The media should make every possible effort to build bridges of cooperation, friendly relations and in developing better understanding between India and foreign states. At the same time, it is the duty of a newspaper to expose if any diplomat is trying to misuse or take undue advantage of the diplomatic immunities.

**14. Covering Communal Disputes/Claslies:** News, views or comments relating to communal or religious disputes/clashes should be published after proper verification of facts, and presented with due caution and restraint in a manner which is conducive to the reaction of an atmosphere congenial to communal harmony, amity and peace. Sensational, provocative and alarming headlines are to be avoided. Acts of communal violence or vandalism should be reported in a manner as may not undermine the people's confidence in the law and order machinery of the state. Giving community-wise figures of the victims of communal riot, or writing to inflame passions, aggravate the tensions, or accentuate the strained relations between the communities/religious groups concerned, or which has a potential to exacerbate the trouble, should be avoided.

Headings should not be sensational/provocative and must justify the matter printed under them.

15. In general, and particularly, in the context of communal disputes or clashes between them.

(*a*) Provocative and sensational headlines should he avoided.

(*b*) Headings must reflect and justify the matter printed under.

(*c*) Headings containing allegations made in statements should either identify the body or the source making it or at least carry quotation marks.

**16. Plagiarism:** Using or passing off the writings or ideas of another as ones own, without crediting the source is an offence against the ethics of journalism.

**17. Recording Interviews and Phone Conversations:** Journalists should not tape-record anyone's conversation without that person's knowledge or consent, except where the recording is necessary to protect the journalist in a legal action, or for other compelling good reasons.

**18. Obscenity and Vulgarity to be Eschewed:**

(*a*) Newspapers/journalists should not publish anything which is obscene, vulgar or offensive to public good taste.

(*b*) Newspapers should not publish an advertisement containing that which is unlawful or illegal, or is contrary to good taste or to journalistic ethics or proprieties.

(*c*) Newspapers should not display advertisements which are vulgar or which, through a picture of a woman in nude of bad posture, provoke the lecherous attention of males as if she herself was a commercial commodity for sale.

(*d*) While publishing the tape-recorded statement of another, the editor should delete obscene or filthy epithets offensive to good public taste, with which the person stating might have punctuated the tenor or tone or his/her answers.

**19. Glorifying Violence to be Eschewed:** Newspapers/journalists should avoid presenting acts of violence, armed robberies and terrorist activities in a manner that glorifies their acts or death in the eyes of the public.

**20. Glorification/Encouragement of Social Evils to be Eschewed:** Newspapers should not allow their columns to be misused for writings which have a tendency to encourage or glorify social evils like Sati Pratha.

**21. Caution in Criticising Judicial Acts:**

(*a*) Excepting where the court sits *in camera* or directs otherwise, it is open to a newspaper to report pending judicial proceedings, in a fair accurate and reasonable manner. But. it should not publish anything.

(*i*) which, in its direct and immediate effect, creates a substantial risk of obstructing, impeding or prejudicing seriously the due administration of justice. or

(*ii*) is in the nature of a running commentary or debate, or records the papers own findings, conjectures, reflections or comments on issues, sub-judice, and which may amount to arrogation to the newspaper the functions of the court or

(*iii*) regarding the personal character of the accused standing trial on a charge of committing a crime.

(*b*) Newspapers should not as a matter of caution, publish or comment on evidence collected as a result of investigative journalism, when, after the accused is arrested and charged, the court become seized of the case; nor should they reveal, comment on confession allegedly made by the accused.

(*c*) While newspapers may, in the public interest, make reasonable criticism of a judicial act of the judgment of a court for public good; they should not cast scurrilous aspersions on, or impute improper motives or personal bias to the judge; nor should they scandalise the court or the judiciary as a whole; or make personal allegations of lack of ability or integrity against a judge.

(*d*) Newspapers should, as a matter of caution, avoid unfair and unwarranted criticism which, attributes to a judge extraneous consideration for performing an act in due course of his/her judicial functions, even if such criticism does not strictly amount to culpable contempt of court.

**22. Newspapers should avoid Cross Commercialism:** While newspapers are entitled to ensure, improve or strengthen their financial viability by all legitimate means, they should not engage themselves through the print media. in mass commercialism or unseemly, cut-throat competition with their rivals, for earning ever more profits for their proprietors, in a manner which is repugnant to high professional standards and good taste, and tends to pull downwards the primary role of the free press as an essential institution of democracy to a secondary subservient place.

**23. Photographs of Dead Bodies of Victims of Crimes/Accidents:** Photojournalism is an important part of the print media. While intrusion through photography into personal grief, likely to hurt sentiments or arouse communal passions, should be avoided, publication of photographs serving the larger public interest cannot be "termed unethical or in bad taste.

In the Indian environment, publication of the photographs of the dead bodies of the victims of accidents or riatural calamity may not be per use wrong unless objected to be near relations of the deceased.

**24. Caste, Religion or Community Disclosures to be Generally Avoided:**

(*a*) In general, the identification of a person belonging to a scheduled caste or depressed class, with reference to his caste or by use of the word 'harijan' should be avoided, particularly when in the context it conveys a sense or attributes a conduct or practice derogatory to that caste.

(*b*) It is not desirable for a journalist to describe a person accused of an offence by mentioning his caste when the caste does not have anything to do with the offence or the crime and plays no part either in the identification of any accused or proceeding, if there be any.

(*c*) Except when it becomes relevant and material, it is not proper and desirable to mention the caste, religion or 'community of an assailant or victim in a news item. 'Mention of caste, creed, religion, or community usually serves no useful purpose, but may at times have the unfortunate effect of creating ill-feeling among communities and individuals.

**25. Editor's Responsibility for all matter published in the Newspaper:**

(*a*) The editor shall assume responsibility for all matter, including advertisements, published in the newspaper. If responsibility is disclaimed, this shall be explicitly stated beforehand.

(*b*) Unconfirmed news shall be identified and treated as such.

**26. Confidence to be Respected:** If information is received from a confidential source, the confidence should be respected. The journalists cannot be compelled by the Press Council to disclose such source; but it shall not be regarded as a breach of journalistic ethics if the source is voluntarily disclosed in proceedings before the Council by the journalist who considers it necessary to repel effectively 'a charge against him/her. This rule, requiring a newspaper not to publish matters disclosed to it in confidence, is not applicable where:

(*a*) consent of the source is subsequently obtained.

(*b*) the editor clarifies by way of an appropriate' footnote that since the publication of certain matters were in the public interest, the information in question was being published although it had been made 'off the record'.

**27. Dummy Advertisements:** Publication of dummy advertisements that have neither been paid for, nor authorised by advertisers, constitute breach of journalistic ethics.

## SOCIETY OF PROFESSIONAL JOURNALISTS CODE OF ETHICS

Accepting its responsibility in maintaining the ethical behaviour and professional integrity of journalists for their credibility, the Members of the society of professional journalists adopted a code of ethics. These are;

(*i*) Journalists should be honest, fair and courageous in gathering, reporting and interpreting information.

(*ii*) Journalists should treat source and subjects as human being deserving respect and compassion. They should be cautions about identifying juvenile suspects or victims of sex crimes and avoid naming them.

(*iii*) Journalist should be free of obligation to any interest other than right to the public to know.

(*iv*) Journalists should be accountable to their readers, listeners and viewers The present version of the code of Society of Professional Journalists was adopted in September 1996.

## TRENDS IN INDIAN JOURNALISM

Journalists, by and large, conform to ethical standards and are better educated and socially responsible.

Objectivity in reporting, writing or interpretating a story is of paramount importance for reporters, by no means can afford to give a one–sided story. It is also in the interest of the publication, if the reporter avoids writing on topics.

Reporters do not generally identify juvenile delinquents by name, nor do they report the name of the victim of rape. A report by name of children below 18 years would prejudice their future life and make them victims of hatred and scorn of society for the rest of their life. But there have been some instances of naming such children.

Journalists have a right to protect their source of information, it is unethical for a journalist to quote some one who divulged the information on the conditions of anonymity.

The concept of trial by media is not acceptable to the public nor any media person should declare a person criminal before he is convicted by a court of law.

But in recent past the role of the media in Jesica Lal murder case has been acclaimed by the people.

Journalists have the responsibility to report any agitation, but they should not write anything which further inflames the community rivalary or passion. In the recent agitation by Gujjar Community when Information and Broadcasting Minister, PR Das Munshi called a meeting of the Editors of TV News channels and advised them to promote community harmony, many eyebrows were raised. The Ministry had sent them advisories not to show old footages of the agitation by Gujjars. The Journalists were of the opinion that any guidelines should come from inside the profession and not from the government.

Several Journalists have been accused of invading the privacy of government officials and other public figures. But it is the responsibility of Journalists to expose the misdoings of Government or public figures. It is in public interest to know how corrupt a Municipal Corporator, a Member of the Legislative Assembly or a Member of Parliament is.

It is morally and ethically wrong to publish any rumour without confirmation of facts.

Jack Anderson, investigative Journalist, once revealed how he had used manipulative tactics to make an errant Senator confess that he was on the payroll of a right wing millionaire. Anderson justified his acts saying, "I have seen the powerful (public figures), become so god–like in their insulation that they forget they're supposed to live by the same laws and rules as the rest of us..."

## PRESSURE GROUPS AND WATCHDOG ORGANIZATION

Besides the Codes of Conduct and Ethics, there are a number of pressure groups and watchdog organizations in various countries that keep a track of media report to correct imbalances.

These are Fair and Accurate Reporting (FAIR) and Centre for Media Education (CME) in United States. FAIR said it stood for exposure and challenge to media bias and the pattern of media exclusion. If identifies the villains responsible for bias and exclusion in the media to "the increasing concentration of the American media in fewer and fewer corporate hands."

In India also the ownership of media is, by and large, concentrated in the hands of big business houses, no such watch dog could so far be developed to keep a watch on media bias.

## ADVISORIES FOR IMPROVING MEDIA CREDIBILITY

Some of the advisories have found a place of prominence in almost all the Code of Ethics adopted by professional organizations and others. The American Society of Newspaper Editors also came up with sex such advisories after a study based on interviews of 3,000 Americans and employing 16 focus groups to find the views of public to improve public interest in journalism and media. These are:

(*i*) Inaccuracies
(*ii*) Sensationalisation
(*iii*) Objectivity
(*iv*) Freedom from manipulation of the press
(*v*) Name sources and avoid anonymous sources
(*vi*) Corrections of errors

The sum and substance of all the codes of Ethics is that Journalists should be solely guided by the "right of the people to know" in their news and views.

## PARLIAMENTARY CODE

The Rajya Sabha in 1976 adopted a Code of Ethics, for journalists and newspapers regarding their social and moral responsibility. The Code said.

1. In the discharge of their duties, journalists shall attach full value to fundamental human social rights, shall hold good faith and fair play in news reports and comments as essential professional obligations.
2. Journalists and newspapers shall highlight activities of the state and public, promote national unity, solidarity, integrity and economic and social progress.
3. Journalists and newspapers shall avoid reports and comments which tend to promote tensions or are likely to lead to civil disorder, mutiny or rebellion. Violence must be condemned unequivocally.
4. Journalists and newspapers shall ensure that information if disseminated is factual. No fact shall be distorted, and information known to be false, or not believed to be true, shall not be published.
5. No sensational report or tendentious report of a speculative nature shall be published. Any report or comments found to be inaccurate shall be rectified for publication.

6. Confidence shall always be respected. Professional secrecy shall be preserved.
7. Journalists' shall not exploit their status for non-journalistic purposes or inquiries and shall not allow personal interests to influence professional conduct.
8. There is nothing so unworthy as the acceptance or demand for a bribe or inducement for the exercise by a journalist of his power to give or deny publicity to news or comment.
9. Journalists and newspapers shall not indulge in personal controversies in which no public interest is involved.
10. Journalists and newspapers shall not give currency to public rumours or gossip or even verifiable news affecting the private life of individuals.
11. Newspapers shall refrain from publishing matter (including advertisements) which are obscene or is likely to encourage vice, crime and unlawful activities.
12. Journalists and newspapers shall promote and project the national objectives of democracy, socialism and secularism.
13. Journalists and newspapers shall refrain from giving tendentious treatment to news and disturbances involving caste, community, class, religion, region or language groupings, and shall not publish details of the number or identity of groups involved in such disturbances except as officially authorised.
14. Journalists and newspapers shall not publish information and comments detrimental to the interest of the sovereignty and integrity of India, the security of the state and friendly relations with foreign countries (newspapers include journals, magazines and periodicals.)

# 20

# Broadcast Codes

All India Radio's Code for commercial Advertising originally covered advertising on television also. It lays down standard of conduct for advertisers.

**The code of commercial Advertising:** Doordarshan published in 1956, lays down standard for conduct for advertisers on Indian television. Both All India Radio and Doordarshan had the monopoly in advertising till the advent of satellite channels and FM radios in early 1990s. As Prasar Bharti, which has Doordarshan and AIR under it, is a public broadcaster run with tax payers' money, it had obviously, its own code of conduct. Some rules of conduct are as follows:

1. Advertising shall be designed as to conform to the laws of the country and should not offend the morality, decency, and religious susceptibilities of the people.
2. No advertisement shall be permitted which :
   (a) derides any race, caste, colour, creed and nationality.
   (b) is against any of the directive principles, or any other provision of the Constitution of India
   (c) tends incite people to crime, cause disorder or violence or breach of law, or glorified violence or obscenity in any way;
   (d) presents criminality as desirable;
   (e) adversely affects friendly relations with foreign States.
   (f) exploits the national emblem, or any part of the constitution, or the person or personality of national leader or state dignity; or
   (g) relates to or promotes cigarettes and tobacco products, liquor, wines and other intoxicants.
3. No advertisement message shall in any way be presented as news.
4. No advertisement shall be permitted, the objects where of are wholly or mainly of a religious or political nature; advertisements must not be directed towards any religious or political end or have relation to any industrial dispute.

5. Advertisements for services concerned with the following shall not be accepted;
   (a) Money lenders
   (b) Chit funds
   (c) Saving Schemes and lotteries other than those conducted by central or state government organizations, nationalized or recognized banks, and public sector undertakings,
   (d) Matrimonial agencies
   (e) Unlicensed employment services
   (f) Fortune tellers or sooth sayers, etc, and those with claims of hypnotism.
   (g) Foreign goods and foreign banks.

The AIR Code exhorts the advertisers to be familiar with various laws and enactments and codes concerning mass media and advertising. Some of these include the following :

1. Drugs and Cosmetic Act, 1940.
2. Drugs Control Act, 1950
3. Drugs and Magic Remedies (Objectionable Advertisement) Act, 1957
4. Copyright Act, 1957
5. Trade and Merchandise Marks Act, 1958.
6. Prevention of Food Adulteration Act, 1954.
7. Pharmacy Act, 1948
8. Prize Competition Act, 1955
9. Emblems and Names (Prevention of Importer Use) Act, 1950
10. Consumer Protection Act, 1950
11. Indecent Representation of Women (Prohibition) Act, 1986.
12. AIR/Doordarshan Code
13. Code of Ethics issued by ASCI.

# 21

# Advertisement Ethics

Advertisement are defined by the Advertising Standards Council of India (ASCI) as a 'paid communication addressed to the public ... to influence (their) opinion or behaviour, Ethics of advertising are stipulated in the regulatory codes on advertising. But there are some aspects of advertising which cannot be regulated.

Like other professions, the profession of advertising also has a code of ethics which is elaborate and provides practical guidelines to practitioners.

The first code of ethics for advertising was devised by the American Association of Advertising Agencies in 1924. Member agencies pledged not to knowingly produce advertising that contained.

- false or misleading statements or exaggeration, visual or verbal
- testimonials that do not reflect the real choice of competent witness
- price claims that are misleading
- comparisons that unfairly disparaged a competing product or servia
- unsupported claim/claims that distorted the true meaning of statements made by professional and scientific authorities.
- statements, suggestion or pictures offensive to public decency

While notions of 'public decency' vary from country to country and also change overtime, the substance of ethical code outlined continues to remain still relevant. A multinational brand will advertise the same product through different campaigns in different countries.

# 22

# Advertisement Ethics in India

Advertisement contents are regulated by self-regulatory bodies. In India it is regulated by the ASCI code. The ASCI was formulated to 'achieve the acceptance of fair advertising practice in the best interests of the ultimate consumers. The ASCI has a motto 'Regulate your self or some body else will, The ASCI is a representative body of people from the world of advertising.

Some of the main points of the of the ASCI's code include the following

(a) Advertising should be so designed as to conform not only to the low but also to the moral aesthetic, and religious sentiments of the country in which it is published

(b) Advertisement likely to bring contempt or disrepute to the professional should not be permitted.

(c) Advertising should be truthful, avoid distorting facts and misleading the public by means of implications and omissions.

(d) Advertising should not be permitted to contain exaggerated claims that inevitably disappoint the public.

(e) Direct comparison with competing brands or firms and disparaging references are in no circumstances permitted.

(f) In decent, vulgar, suggestive, repulsive, or offensive themes or treatments should be avoided.

(g) No advertisement should offer to refund money paid.

(h) Advertisements must not carry claim of drugs to prevent or cure any diseases or ailments.

The Code, according to ASCI, is not in competition with law. Its rules, and the machinery through which they are enforced, are designed to complement legal controls, not to usurp or replace them. Although the decisions of the council in dealing with cases do not have a legal bearing, experience has shown that the concerned advertising agencies have followed the council's advise by and large.

**Advertising and children:** The ASCI's code of advertising practice has the following guidelines on the use of children in advertising :

Advertisement addressed to children shall not contain anything whether in illustration or otherwise, which might result in their physical, mental, or moral harm, or which exploits their vulnerability. No advertisement, therefore,

(a) Shall encourage children to enter strange places, or to converse with strangers in an effort to collect coupons, wrappers, labels or the like.
(b) Should depict children learning dangerously outside windows and over bridges or climbing dangerous cliffs and the like.
(c) Should show children climbing or reaching dangerously to reach products for any other purpose, or show children using or playing with matches or any inflammable or explosive substance; or playing with or using sharp knives, guns, or mechanical or electrical appliances, the careless use of which could lead to their suffering cuts, burns, shocks or other injury or
(d) Feature minors for tobacco or alcohol based products.

Thought the conditions laid down by the ASCI may not generally be violated per se by the advertisers, the same acts (which, according to the ASCI, are harmful and dangerous for children), enacted by elders are at times aped and emulated by children, if past experience is any indication. Many studies suggest-that children below a certain age can not differentiate between dreams and reality. They copy and imbibe things they see in their lives. According to one of the reports of Federal Trade Commission (FTC) in the USA 'many young children including an apparent majority of those under the age of eight–are so naive that they cannot perceive the selling purposes of television advertising or otherwise comprehend or evaluate it and tend ... to view a commercial simply as a form of information programming'. The FTC took up the issue with certain companies and the advertisements which were deemed to have a harmful impact on children were withdrawn. More over, research has shown that when as young as three years old children recognize the difference between programmes and ads and as they are aware of the intention of ads they will reject ads that do not fit in with their own or friends's experience.

However, cross cultural media like internet can reach advertisement all over the world. This poses a potential problem for regulation, as regulations are country specific.

# 23

# The Indian Penal Code, 1860

**(Relevant Provisions)**

**124 A. Sedition:** Whoever, by words, either spoken or written, or by signs, or by visible representation, or otherwise, brings or attempts to bring into hatred or contempt, or excites or attempts to excite disaffection towards, the Government established by law in India. shall be punished with imprisonment for life, to which fine may be added, or with imprisonment which may extend to three years, to which fine may be added, or with fine.

**153A. Promoting enmity between different groups on grounds of religion, race, place of birth, residence, language, *etc.*, and doing acts prejudicial to maintenance of harmony :** (1) Whoever:

(a) by words, either spoken or written, or by signs or by visible representations or otherwise, promotes or atternpts to promote, on grounds of religion, race, place of birth, residence, language, caste or community or any other ground whatsoever. disharmony or feelings of enmity, hatred or ill-will between different religious, racial, language or regional groups or castes or communities, or

(b) commits any act which is prejudicial to the maintenance of harmony between different religious, racial, language or regional groups or castes or communities, and which disturbs or is likely to disturb the public tranquillity, or

(c) organizes any exercise, movement, drill or other similar activity intending that the participants in such activity shall use or be trained to use criminal force or violence or knowing it to be likely that the participants in such activity will use or be trained to use criminal force or violence, or participates in such activity intending to use or be trained to use criminal force or violence or knowing it to be likely that the participants in such activity will use or be trained to use criminal force or violence, against any religious, racial, language or regional group or caste or community and such activity for any reason whatsoever causes or is likely to cause fear or alarm or a feeling of insecurity amongst members of such religious, racial, language or regional group or caste or community, shall be punished with imprisonment which may extend to three years, or with both.

**Offence committed in place of worship, *etc.*:** (2) Whoever commits an offence specified in sub-section (1) in any place of worship or in any assembly engaged in the performance of religious worship or religious ceremonies, shall be punished with imprisonment which may extend to five years and shall also be liable to fine.

(*i*) Under this section, the promotion of ill–feeling has to be between different classes or sections of people. Hence, in Bennett Coleman and Co. v. Stale of J&K. (1975 Cr LJ 211 - paras 9–10). no offence was made out under this section when a journal made disparaging comments on all the residents of a particular Stale regarding their social and cultural development.

**153B. Imputations, assertions prejudicial to national-integration:** (1) Whoever. by words either spoken or written or by signs or by visible representations or otherwise:

(a) makes or publishes any imputation that any class of persons cannot, by reason of their being members of any religious, racial, language or regional group or caste or community, bear true faith and allegiance to the Constitution of India as by law established or uphold the sovereignty and integrity of India, or

(b) asserts-counsels advises, propagates or publishes that any class of persons shall, by reason of their being members of any religious, racial, language or regional group or caste or-community, be denied or deprived of their rights as citizens of India, or

(c) makes or publishes any assertion, counsel, plea or appeal concerning the obligation of any class of persons, by reason of their being members of any religious, racial, language or regional group or caste or community, and such assertion, counsel, plea or appeal causes or is likely to cause disharmony or feelings of enmity or hatred or ill-will between such members and other persons, shall be punished with imprisonment which may extend to three years, or with fine, or with both.

(2) Whoever commits an offence specified in sub-section (1), in any place of worship or in any assembly engaged in the performance of religious worship or religious ceremonies, shall be punished with imprisonment which may extend to five years and shall also be liable to fine.

**171G. False statement in connection with an election:** Whoever with intent to affect the result of an election makes or publishes any statement purporting to be a statement of fact which is false and which he either knows or believes to be false or does not believe to be true, in relation to the personal character or conduct of any candidate shall be punished with fine.

(*i*) **In Narayanaswamy v. Devaraju,** AIR 1926 Mad 316, the court held that section 17 IG does not relate 10 any person other than a candidate at a election.

(*ii*) **In Anthony v. Nedachezion,** the court differentiated between sections 171 G and 499. While truth is a complete defence under section 171G, it is no defence under section 499, unless the accused can come under any of the exceptions to section 499.

**292. Sale. etc. of obscene books, etc :** (1) For the purposes of sub-section (2), a book. pamphlet, paper, writing, drawing, painting, representation, figure or any other object, shall be deemed to be obscene if it is lascivious or appeals to the purient interest or if its effect or (where it comprises two or more distinct items) the effect of any one of its items, is, if taken as a whole, such as to tend to deprave and corrupt person, who are likely, having regard to all relevant circumstances, to read, see or hear the matter contained or embodied in it.

(2) Whoever:

(a) sells, lets to hire, distributes, publicly exhibits or in any manner puts into circulation, or for purposes of sale. hire, distribution, public exhibition or circulation, makes. produces or has in his possession any obscene book, pamphlet, paper, drawing, painting, representation or figure or any other obscene object whatsoever, or

(b) imports, exports or conveys any obscene object for any of the purposes aforesaid, or knowing or having reason to believe that such object will be sold, let to hire, distributed or publicly exhibited or in any manner put into circulation, or

(c) takes part in or receives profits from any business in the course of which he knows or has reason to believe that any such obscene objects are for any of the purposes aforesaid, made, produced, purchased, kept, imported, exported, conveyed, publicly exhibited or in any manner put into circulation, or

(d) advertises or makes known by any means whatsoever that any person is engaged or is ready to engage in any act which is an offence under this section, or that any such obscene object can be procured from or through any person, or

(e) offers or attempts to do any act which is an offence under this section, shall be punished on first conviction with imprisonment of either description for a term which may extend to two years, and with fine which may extend to two thousand rupees, and, in the event of a second or subsequent conviction, with imprisonment of either description for a term which may extend to five years, and also with fine which may extend to five thousand rupees.

**Exception:** This section does not extend to:

(a) any book, pamphlet, paper, writing, drawing, painting, representation or figure:

(*i*) the publication of which is proved to be justified as being for the public good on the ground that such book, pamphlet, paper, writing, drawing, painting, representation or figure is in the interest of science, literature, art of learning or other objects of general concern, or

(*ii*) which is kept or used bonafide for religious purposes;

(*b*) any representation sculptured, engraved, painted or otherwise represented on or in :

(*i*) any ancient monument within the meaning of the Ancient Monuments and Archaeological Sites and Remains Act, 1958 (24 of 1958), or

(*ii*) any temple, or on any car used-tor the conveyance of idols, or kept or used for any religious purpose.

**293. Sale, etc., of obscene objects to young person:** Whoever sells, lets to hire, distributes, exhibits or circulates to any person under the age of twenty years any such obscene object as is referred to in the last preceding section, or offers or attempts so to do, shall be punished on first conviction with imprisonment of either description for a term which may extend to three years, and with fine which may extend to two thousand rupees and, in the event of a second or subsequent conviction, with imprisonment of either description fora term which may extend to seven years, and also with fine which may extend to five thousand rupees.

**294 A. Keeping lottery office:** Whoever keeps any office or place for the purpose of drawing any lottery not being a State lottery or a lottery authorised by the State Government, shall be punished with imprisonment of either description for a term which may extend to six months, or with fine, or with both.

And whoever publishes any proposal to pay any sum, or to deliver any goods, or to do or forbear doing anything for the benefit of any person, on any event or contingency relative or applicable to the drawing of any ticket, lot, number or figure in any such lottery, shall be punished with fine which may extend to one thousand rupees.

**295A. Deliberate and malicious acts, intended to outrage religious feelings of any class by insulting its religion or religious beliefs:** Whoever, with deliberate and malicious intention of outraging the religious feelings of any class of citizens of India, by words, either spoken or written, or by signs or by visible representations or otherwise, insults or attempts to insult the religion or the religious beliefs of that class, shall be punished with imprisonment of either description for a term which may extend to three years, or with fine, or with both.

**499. Defamation:** Whoever, by words either spoken or intended to be read, or by signs or by visible representations, makes or publishes any imputation concerning any person intending to harm, or knowing or having reason to beliefs that such imputation will harm, the reputation of such person, is said, except in the cases hereinafter expected, to defame that person.

character of that person, or lowers the character of that person in respect of his caste or of his calling, or lowers the credit of that person, or causes it to be believed that the body of that person is in a loathsome state, or in a state generally considered as disgraceful.

**First Exception:** *Imputation of truth which public good requires to be made or published*—It is not defamation to impute anything which is true concerning any person, if it be for the public good that the imputation should be made or published. Whether or not it is for the public good is a question of fact.

**Second Exception:** *Public conduct of public servants*—It is not defamation to express in a good faith any opinion whatever respecting the conduct of a public servant in the discharge of his public functions, or respecting his character, so far as his character appears in that conduct, and no further.

**Third Exception:** *Conduct of any person touching any public question*—It is not defamation to express in good faith any opinion whatever respecting the conduct of any person touching any public question, and respecting his character, so far as his character appears in that conduct, and no further.

**Fourth Exception:** *Publication of reports of proceedings of Courts*—It is not defamation to publish substantially true report of the proceedings of a Court of Justice, or of the result of any such proceedings.

**Explanation:** A Justice of the Peace or other officer holding an inquiry in open Court preliminary to a trial in a Court of Justice, is a Court within the meaning of the above section.

**Fifth Exception:** *Merits of case decided in Court or conduct of witnesses and others concerned*—It is not defamation to express in good faith any opinion whatever respecting the merits of any case, civil or criminal, which has been decided by a Court of Justice, or respecting the conduct of any person as a party, witness or agent, in any such case, or respecting the character of such person, as far as his character appears in that conduct, and no further.

**Sixth Exception:** *Merits of public performance*—It is not defamation to express in good faith any opinion respecting the merits of any performance which its author has submitted to the judgment of the public, or respecting the character of the author so far as his character appears in such performance, and no further.

**Seventh Exception:** *Censure passed in good faith by person having lawful authority over another*—It is not defamation in a person having over another any authority, either conferred by law or arising out of a lawful contract made with that other, to pass in good faith any censure on the conduct of that other in matters to which such lawful authority relates.

**Eight Exception:** *Accusation preferred in good faith to authorised persoa*—It is not defamation to prefer in good faith an accusation against any person to any of those who have lawful authority over that person with respect to the subject-matter of accusation.

**Ninth Exception:** *Imputation made in good faith by person for protection of his or other's interests*—It is not defamation to make an imputation on the character of another provided that the imputation be made in good faith for the protection of the interests of the person making it. or of any other person, or for the public good.

**Tenth Exception:** *Caution intended for good of person to whom conveyed or for public good*—It is not defamation to convey a caution, in good faith, to one person against another, provided that such caution be intended for the good of the person to whom it is conveyed, or of some person in whom that person is interested, or for the public good.

**500. Punishment for defamation:** Whoever defames another shall be punished with simple imprisonment for a term which may extend to two years, or with fine, or with both.

**501. Printing or engraving matter known to be defamatory:** Whoever prints or engraves any matter, knowing or having good reason to believe that such matter is defamatory of any person, shall be punished with simple imprisonment for a term which may extend to two years, or with fine, or with both.

**502. Sale of printed or engraved substance containing defamatory matter:** Whoever sells or offers for sale any printed or engraved substance containing defamatory matter, knowing that it contains such matter, shall be punished with simple imprisonment for a term which may extend to two years, or with fine, or with both.

**505. Statements conducing to public mischief:** (1) Whoever makes, publishes or circulates any statement, rumour or report :

(a) with intent to cause, or which is likely to cause, any officer, soldier, sailor or airman in the Army, Navy or Air Force of India to mutiny or otherwise disregard or fail in his duty as such; or

(b) with intent to cause, or which is likely to cause, fear or alarm to the public, or to any section of the public whereby any person may be induced to commit an offence against the State or against the public tranquility; or

(c) with intent to incite, or which is likely to incite, any class or community of persons to commit any offence against any other class or community; shall be punished with imprisonment which may extend to three years, or with fine or with both.

(2) **Statements creating or promoting enmity, hatred or ill-will between classes:** Whoever makes, publishes or circulates any statement or report containing rumour or alarming news with intent to create or promote, or which is likely to create or promote on grounds of religion, race, place of birth, residence, language, caste or community or any other ground whatsoever, feelings of enmity, hatred or ill-will between different religious racial, language or regional groups or castes or communities, shall be punished with imprisonment which may extend to three years, or with fine, or with both.

(3) **Offence under sub-section (2) committed in place of worship, etc.:** Whoever commits an offence specified in sub-section (2) in any place of worship or in an assembly engaged in the performance-of religious worship or religious ceremonies, shall be punished with imprisonment which may extend to five years and shall also be liable to fine.

**Exception:** It does not amount to an offence, within the meaning of this section when the person making, publishing or circulating any such statement, rumour or report, has reasonable grounds for believing that such statement, rumour or report is true and makes, publishes or circulates it in good faith and without any such intent as aforesaid.

## THE CODE OF CRIMINAL PROCEDURE, 1973

### (Relevant Provisions)

**91.** Summons to produce document or other thing: (1) Whenever any court or any officer in charge of a police station considers that the production of any document or other thing is necessary or desirable for the purposes of any investigation, inquiry, trial or other proceeding under this Code hy or before such court or officer, such court me issue a summons, or such officer a written order, to the person in whose possession or power such document or thing is believed to be, requiring him to attend and produce it. or to produce it. at the time and place stated in the summons or order.

(2) Any person required under this section merely to produce a document or other thing shall be deemed 10 have complied with the requisition if he causes such document or thing to be produced instead of attending personally to produce the same.

(3) Nothing in this section shall be deemed:

(a) to affect, sections 123 and 124 of the Indian Evidence Act, 1872 (1 of 1872), or the Bankers. Books Evidence Act, 1891 (13 of 1891), or

(b) to apply to a letter, postcard, telegram or other document or any parcel or thing in the custody of the postal or telegraph authority.

**93. When search-warrant may be issued :** (1)

(a) Where any court has reason to believe that a person to whom a summons or order under section 91 or a requisition under sub-section (1) of section 92 has been, or might be, addressed, will not or would not produce the document or thing as required by such summons or requisition, or

(b) where such document or thing is not known to the Court to be in the possession of any person, or

(c) where the court considers that the purposes of any inquiry, trial or other proceeding under this Code will be served by a general search or inspection,

it may issue a search-warrant; and the person to whom such warrant is directed, may search or inspect in accordance therewith and the provisions hereinafter contained.

(2) The court may, if it thinks fit, specify in the warrant the particular place or part thereof to which only the search or inspection shall extend; and the person charged with the execution of such warrant shall then search or inspect only the place or part so specified.

(3) Nothing contained in this section shall authorise any Magistrate other than a District Magistrate or Chief Judicial Magistrate to grant a warrant to search for a document, parcel or other thing in the custody of the postal or telegraph authority.

**95. Power to declare certain publications forfeited and to issue search-warrants for the same :** (1) **Where :**

(a) any newspaper, or book, or

(b) any document, wherever printed appears to the State Government to contain any matter the publication of which is punishable under section

124A or section 153A or section 153B or section 292 or section 293 or section 295A of the Indian Penal Code (45 of 1860), the State Government may, by notification, stating the grounds of its opinion, declare every copy of the issue of the newspaper containing such matter, and every copy of such book or other document to be forfeited to Govemment, and thereupon any police officer may seize the same wherever found in India and any Magistrate may by warrant authorise any police officer not below the rank of sub-inspector to enter upon and search for the same in any premises where any copy of such issue or any such book or other document may be or may be reasonably suspected to be.

(2) In this section and in section 96 :

(a) "newspaper" and "book" have the same meaning as in the Press and Registration of Books Act, 1867 (.25 of 867);

(b) "document" includes any painting, drawing or photograph, or other visible representation

(3) No order passed or action taken under this section shall be called in question in any court otherwise than in accordance with the provision? of section 96.

**96. Application to High Court to set aside declaration of forefeiture:** (1) **Any** person having any interest in any newspaper, book or other document, in respect of which a declaration of forefeiture has been made under section 95. may, within two months from the date or publication in the Official Gazette of such declaration, apply to the High Court to set aside such declaration on the ground that the issue of the newspaper or the book or other document, in respect of which the declaration was made. did not contain any such matter as is referred to in sub-section (1) of section 95.

(2) Even-such application shall where the High Court consists of three or more Judges, be heard and determined by a Special Bench of the High Court composed of three Judges and where the High Court consists of less than three Judges, such Special Bench shall be composed of all the Judges of that High Court.

(3) On the hearing of any such application with reference to any newspaper, any copy of such newspaper may be given in evidence in aid of the proof of the nature or tendency of the words, signs or visible representations contained in such newspaper, in respect of which the declaration of forfeiture was made.

(4) The High Court shall, if it is not satisfied that the issue of the newspaper, or the book or other document, in respect of which the application has been made, contained any such matter as is referred to in sub-section (1) of section 95, set aside the declaration of forfeiture.

(5) Where there is a difference of opinion among the Judges forming the Special Bench, the decision shall be in accordance with the opinion of the majority of those Judges.

**108. Security for good behaviour from persons disseminating seditious matters:** (1) When an Executive Magistrate receives information that there is within his local, jurisdiction any person who, within or without such jurisdiction:

(*i*) either orally or in writing or in any other manner, intentionally disseminates or attempts to disseminate or abets the dissemination of:

 (*a*) any matter the publication of which is punishable under section 124A or section 153A or section 153B or section 295A of the Indian Penal Code (45 of 1860), or

 (*b*) any matter concerning a Judge acting or purporting to act in the discharge of his official duties which amounts to criminal intimidation or defamation under the Indian Penal Code,

(*ii*) makes, produces, publishes or keeps for sale, imports, exports, conveys, sells, lets to hire, distributes, publicly exhibits or in any other manner puts into circulation any obscene matter such as is referred to in section 292 of the Indian Penal Code (45 of 1860),

and the Magistrate is of opinion that there is sufficient ground for proceeding, the magistrate may, in the manner hereinafter provided, require such person to show cause why he should not be ordered to execute a bond, with or without sureties, for his good behaviour for such period, not exceeding one year, as the Magistrate thinks fit.

(2) No proceeding shall be taken under this section against the editor, proprietor, printer or publisher of any publication registered under, and edited, printed and published in conformity with. the rules laid down in the Press and Registration of Books Act. 1867 (25 of 1867) with reference to any matter contained in such publication except by the order or under the authority of the State Government or some officer empowered by the State Government in this behalf.

**144. Power to issue order in urgent cases of nuisance or apprehended danger :** (l) In cases where, in the opinion of a District Magistrate, a Sub-divisional Megistrate or any other Executive Magistrate specially empowered by the State Government in this behalf, there is sufficient ground for proceeding under this section and immediate prevention or speedy remedy is desirable, such Magistrate may, by a written order stating the material facts of the case and served in the manner provided by section 134, direct any person to abstain from a certain act or to take certain order with respect to certain property in his possession or under his management, if such Magistrate considers that such direction is likely to prevent, or tends to prevent, obstruction, annoyance or injury to any person lawfully employed, or danger to human life, health or safety, or a disturbance of the public tranquillity, or a riot, or an affray.

(2) An order under this section may, in cases of emergency or in cases where the circumstances do not admit of the serving in due time of a notice upon the person against whom the order is directed, be passed ex pane.

(3) An order under this section may be directed to a particular individual, or to persons residing in a particular place or area, or to the public generally when frequenting or visiting a particular place or area.

(4) No order under this section shall remain in force for more than two months from the making thereof:

Provided that, if the State Government considers it necessary so to do for preventing danger to human life, health or safety or for preventing a riot or any affray, it may, by notification, direct that an order made by a Magistrate under this section shall remain in force for such further period not exceeding six months from the date on which the order made by the Magistrate would have, but for such order, expired, as it may specify in the said notification.

(5) Any Magistrate may, either on his own motion or on the application of any person aggrieved, rescind or alter any order made under this section, by himself or any Magistrate subordinate to him or by his predecessor-in office.

(6) The State Government may, either on its own motion or on the application of any person aggrieved, rescind or alter any order made by it under the proviso to sub-section (4).

(7) Where an application under sub-section (5), or sub-section (6) is received, the Magistrate, or the State Government, as the case may be, shall afford to the applicant an early opportunity of appearing before him or it, either in person or by pleader and showing cause against the order, and if the Magistrate or the State Government, as the case may be, rejects the application wholly or in part, he or it shall record in writing the reasons for so doing.

**196. Prosecution for offences against the State and for criminal conspiracy to commit such offence:** (1) No court shall take cognizance of:

(a) any offence punishable under Chapter VI or under section 153A, section 295A or sub-section (1) of section 505 of the Indian Penal Code (45 of 1860), or

(b) a criminal conspiracy to commit such offence, or

(c) any such abetment, as is described in section 108A of the Indian Penal Code (15 of 1860).

Except with the previous sanction of the Central Government or of the State Government. (1 A) No court shall take cognizance of: (1)

(a) any offence punishable under section 153B or sub-section (2) or sub-section (3) of section 505 of the Indian Penal Code (45 of 1860), or

(b) a criminal conspiracy to commit such offence, except with the previous sanction of the Central Government or of the State Government or of the District Magistrate.

(2) No court shall take cognizance of the offence of any criminal conspiracy punishable under section 120B of the Indian Penal Code (45 of 1860), other than a criminal conspiracy to commit an offence punishable with death, imprisonment for life or rigorous imprisonment for a term of two years or upwards, un less the State Government or the District Magistrate has consented in writing to the initiation of the proceeding:

Provided that where the criminal conspiracy is one to which the provisions of section 195 apply, no such consent shall be necessary.

(3) The Centra] Government or the State Govenment may, before according sanction under sub-section (1) or sub-section (1 A) and the District Magistrate may, before according sanction under sub-section (1A) and the State Government or the District Magistrate may, before giving consent under sub-section (2), order a preliminary investigation by a police officer not being below the rank of Inspector, in which case such police officer shall have the powers referred to in sub-section (3) of section 155.

**199. Prosecution for defamation:** (1) No court shall take cognizance of an offence punishable under Chapter XXI of the Indian Penal Code (45 of 1860) except upon a complaint made by some person aggrieved by the offence:

Provided that where such person is under the age of eighteen years, or is an idiot or a lunatic, or is from sickness or infirmity unable to make a complaint, or is a woman who, according to the local customs and manners, ought not to be compelled to appear in public, some other person may, with the leave of the court, make a complaint on his or her behalf.

(2) Notwithstanding anything contained in this Code, when any offence falling under Chapter XXI of the Indian Penal Code (45 of 1860) is alleged to have been committed against a person who, at the time of such commission, is the President of India, the Vice-President of India, the Government of a State, the Administrator of a Union territory or a Minister of the Union or of a State or of a Union territory, or any other public servant employed in connection with the affairs of the Union or of a State in respect of his conduct in the discharge of his public functions a court of Session may take cognizance of such offence, without the case being committed to it, upon a complaint in writing made by the Public Prosecutor.

(3) Every complaint referred to in sub-section (2) shall set forth the facts which constitute the offence alleged, (the nature of such offence and such other particulars as are reasonably sufficient to give notice to the accused of the offence alleged to have been committed by him.

(4) No complaint under sub-section (2) shall be made by the Public Prosecutor except with the previous sanction :

(a) of the State Government, in the case of a person who is or has been the Governor of the Stale or a Minister of that Government;

(b) of the State Government, in the case of any other public servant employed in connection with the affairs of the State;

*(c)* of the Central Government, in any other case.

(5) No Court of Session shall take cognizance of an offence under sub-section (2) unless the complaint is made within six months from the date on which the offence is alleged to have been committed.

(6) Nothing in this section shall affect the right of the person against whom the offence is alleged to have been committed, to make a complaint in respect of that offence before a Magistrate having jurisdiction or the power of such Magistrate to take cognizance of the offence upon such complaint.

**327. Court to be open:** (1) The place in which any Criminal Court is held for the purpose of inquiring into or trying any offence shall be deemed to be an open court to which the public generally may have access, so far as the same can conveniently contain them:

Provided that the presiding Judge or Magistrate may, if he thinks fit, order at any stage of any inquiry into, or trial of, any particular case, that the public generally, or any particular person, shall not have access to, or be or remain in, the room building used by the court.

(2) Notwithstanding anything contained in sub-section (1), the inquiry into and trial of rape or an offence under section 376, section 376A, section 376B, section 376C or section 376D of the Indian Penal Code (45 of1860) shall be conducted in camera :

Provided that the presiding Judge may, if he thinks fit, or on an application made by either of the parties, allow any particular person to have access to, or be or remain in, the room or building used by the court.

(3) Where any proceedings are held under sub-section (2), it shall not be lawful for any person to print or publish any matter in relation to any such proceedings, except with the previous permission of the court.

**345. Procedure in certain cases of contempt:** (1) When any such offence as is described in section 175, section 178, section 179, section 180 or section 228 of the Indian. Penal Code (45 of 1860) is committed in the view or presence of any Civil, Criminal or Revenue Court, the court may cause the offender to be detained in custody and may at any time before-the rising of the court on the same day, take cognizance of the offence and, after giving the offender a reasonable opportunity of showing cause why he should not be punished under this section; sentence the offender to fine not exceeding two hundred rupees, and, in default ot payment of fine, to simple imprisonment for a term which may extend to, one month, unless such fine be sooner paid.

(2) In every such case the court shall record the facts constituting the offence, with the statement (if any) made by the offender as well as the finding and sentence.

(3) If the offence is under section 228 of the Indian Penal Code (45 of 1860), the record shall show the nature and stage of the judicial proceeding in which the court interrupted or insulted was sitting, and the nature of the interruption or insult.

**349. Imprisonment or committal of person refusing to answer or producer document:** If any witness or person called to produce a document or thing before a Criminal Court refuses to answer such question as are put to him or to produce any document or thing in his possession or power which the court requires him to produce, and does not, after a reasonable opportunity has been given to him so to do, offer any reasonable excuse for such refusal such court may. for reasons to be recorded in writing, sentence him to simple; imprisonment or by warrant under the hand of the Presiding Magistrate or Judge commit him to the custody of an officer of the court for any term not exceeding seven days, unless in the meantime, such person consents to be examined and to answer, or to produce the document or thins and in the event of his persisting in his refusal he may be dealt with according to the provisions of section 345 or section 346.

**350. Summary procedure for punishment for non-attendance by a witness in obedience to summons:** (1) If any witness being summoned to appear before a Criminal Court legally bound to appear at a certain place and time in obedience to the summons and without just excuse neglects or refuses to attend at that place or time or departs from the place, where he has to attend before the time at which it is lawful for him to depart, and the court before which the witness is to appear is satisfied that it is expedient in the interests of justice that such a witness should be tried summarily, the court may take cognizance of the offence and after giving the offender an opportunity of showing cause why he should not be punished under this section, sentence him to fine not exceeding one hundred rupees.

(2) In every such case the court shall follow, as nearly as may be practicable, the procedure prescribed for summary trials.

# Index